ASSASSINATION

ASSASSINATION

Twenty Assassinations That Changed History

By Lee Davis

Special Editions

Produced by Transedition Books, 11-15 The Vineyard, Abingdon OX14 3PX, England

Picture research manager Jo Rapley. Designed by Richard Johnson.
Typesetting and further design by Gecko Ltd. Printed in Slovenia by Mladinska Knjiga

BDD Special Editions
An imprint of BDD Promotional Book Company, Inc.
1540 Broadway
New York, N. Y. 10036

First published in the United States of America in1993 by BDD Special Editions

ISBN 0-7924-5854-0

Table Of Contents

INTRODUCTION

Assassination is murder. But murder isn't always assassination. It has to do with time, and place: Murder may occur in an intimate setting, under secret circumstances. Assassination almost never does. On the contrary, it seeks—nay, demands—the forum of a public place, the presence of an audience, the receptive eyesight of worldwide scrutiny. Only the assassinations of Rasputin and Nicholas II were done in the dark and in secret. But they were special cases. Most assassinations are public spectacles, and for a very good reason: Assassination has, at its heart and by necessity, the motivation of a belief.

That belief may be as simple as a fancied slight or as complex as a philosophy; as closely held as a catechism or as widely embraced as a form of government, a system of laws, or an ordering of ideas.

The point is that although one person is the object of an assassin's bullet or knife or bomb, that person is never the sole target. The victim is usually a symbol, as the act of assassination is symbolic, even though its effects may be as emotionally devastating to each of us as the passing of a close relative.

Consider the recollections of the great poet, Walt Whitman, after the assassination of President Abraham Lincoln. Stunned, he recalled, he and his mother sat drinking endless cups of coffee, waiting for each edition of the newspaper, hoping against reality that the next paper would bring news of a recovery.

Or, consider an afternoon 98 years later, in an electronic age, when millions, grief-stricken and silent, sat before television sets for hours, while the Greek tragedy of the assassination of President John F. Kennedy played out its tale of heroic vulnerability, intrigue, multiple murder, and ultimate, ritual catharsis. A generation of Americans would always remember exactly where they were at the precise moment the awful news of the President's death reached them.

Profound and terrible. But the bringing about of these personal experiences was not the primary reason for the assassination. Nor is assassination usually a purely personal matter. As personally close as the killer might be to the victim, the figure caught in the sniper's site or trembling at the point of the killer's knife is overridingly symbolic. Brutus, as noble an individual as he may have been, stabbed his friend Caesar not as a man, but as a symbol of power gone awry.

John Wilkes Booth apparently had enough problems of the ego to keep a clinic full of psychiatrists busy. But he ultimately killed Lincoln, not as a man, but as a symbol of tyranny and of humiliation for the South. Lee Harvey Oswald (or whoever killed Kennedy) committed this assassination not to sadden millions, but to change the course of history, to sidetrack, reroute, and reverse the policies of the President's administration.

Martin Luther King, Malcolm X, Mohandas Gandhi, Indira Gandhi, Pancho Villa, Huey Long, Robert Kennedy, and Benigno Aquino were charismatic leaders whose deaths were designed to deprive their followers of the figureheads they needed to accomplish their goals. Marat, Rasputin, Nicholas II, Somoza, Sadat, McKinley, Leon Trotsky, and Lord Mountbatten were murdered by representatives of opposing political views who wished to make a statement. Only Carl Weiss, who killed Huey Long, and Charles Guiteau, who assassinated President James Garfield, seem to have been acting from purely personal motives. And in the sustained view of history, they form a distinct minority. The assassination of Huey Long will probably always be shrouded in mystery, and Charles Guiteau was a man who, by any interpretation of the word, was unique.

All of this becomes logical when you consider the very origin of the name assassin. It begins with the actions of an 11th-century Shiite convert named Hasan ibn-al-Sabbah. For 50 years, Hasan conducted a struggle against Sunni orthodoxy and Turkish rule in Islamic Persia by establishing a mountain fortress, where he trained an army of fanatical politico-religious killers. For years, these butchers fanned out from the fortress to murder military, political, and religious leaders who challenged Hasan. They were so suicidally, irrationally, dedicated to their tasks, it was widely believed that they were stimulated by hashish, and so were called "hashish-eaters", which was shortened in Arabic to "assassins".

From the 11th century until today, the motivation for an act of assassination has overwhelmingly been either political or religious, and has been carried out either by a fanatic who is willing to die for a cause, or by a person who is set up as a patsy by others who are unwilling to pay the price of their lives for their beliefs. The distaste for assassination by professional killers is understandable. Rarely—very rarely—does the assassin escape alive. He or she is either killed on the spot, or captured and then either executed or incarcerated for life.

There is very little future for an assassin, and therefore, dedicated murderers of the great are always eager to martyr themselves, in contrast to the patsies. Think, for instance, of the gallows pronouncements of Guiteau and the Czologsz, and the pre-guillotine defiance of Charlotte Corday. And then, contrast that with the repeated protestations of innocence of Lee Harvey Oswald, James Earl Ray, and Sirhan Sirhan. Their classic patsy behavior gives credence to the theories that the supposedly one-man-one-gun assassinations of John F. Kennedy, Dr. Martin Luther King, and Robert Kennedy were really conspiracies for whom others took the blame and the punishment.

Whatever the set-up, the motives or the accused, there is no denying the power of assassination. It changes history, brings about wars, affects the destiny of millions of lives. The death of an extraordinary leader is a kind of collective death, but it's also a great leveller, proof positive that the powerful and the great are as vulnerable as the very least of us. And perhaps this, in the end, is why we continue to reread with fascination the stories of their public deaths.

L.D.

Marie anne Charlotte
Corday au citoyen
Marat.
pour avoir Droit

JEAN-PAUL MARAT

POSITION:	*Member of the French National Convention*
DATE:	*July 13, 1793*
PLACE:	*Paris, France*
HOW:	*Dagger*
WHO:	*Charlotte Corday*
CONVICTED:	*Yes. Guillotined on July 17, 1793*
MOTIVE:	*To rid France of a monster*
DIRECT CONSEQUENCE:	*The savagery of the Reign of Terror*

ACCORDING to the best evidence, Jean-Paul Marat was a detestable creature. Bloodthirsty, ambitious, impatient, hysterical, bombastic, and probably insane, he nonetheless had a profound effect on the French Revolution and its aftermath. For a time, he held the center of the stage in the revolution, his words ringing in the ears of the populace. And when, as his power was waning, he was assassinated, this populace made a martyr of him. More he could not have wished, in all of his tormented lifetime.

BORN IN Boudry, Neuchatel, Switzerland, on May 24, 1743, to a lower middle-class family, Marat was the oldest of six children. The family name was Mara, but Jean-Paul, to appear more French, changed it to Marat. One of his brothers, under the name of Monsieur de Boudry, became a tutor in the court of Catherine the Great of Russia, and his sister Albertine is chiefly remembered for her tireless work in sanctifying the name of Jean-Paul Marat after he was killed.

At the age of 16, he left home to become a tutor in Bordeaux, where he studied medicine for two years, and then completed his studies in Paris. In 1765, at the age of 22, he went to England, and there he began to write the many essays and books, on both medicine and politics, that would occupy a large portion of his life.

To those who remembered him, he bore a striking physical resemblance to Napoleon Bonaparte. Scarcely five feet tall, he had an oversized trunk, bowed legs, and strong arms. His face seemed overly large for his body; his forehead was high and prominent, as was his nose. His yellowish gray eyes were piercing and searching, and sometimes extraordinarily gentle, at war with expression on his lips, which were customarily curled. And when he spoke, it was usually in a thin, sonorous, slightly hoarse voice that had an ability to ring to the rafters of the assembly. He deliberately dressed like the lower classes, shirt open at the neck, a bandage around his always disarrayed brown hair, and pistols in his belt. Small wonder he was able to intimidate taller men.

But it was his brilliant mind that rushed him forward to public notice and historical notoriety, and that mind was first put to paper when he was in England. There, he wrote *The Chains of Slavery*, a book that virulently attacked despots, but doled out its milder phrases for good monarchs. They were rare, but existed, he concluded.

Back in France, he continued to publish tracts, each of them more radical than the preceding one, each leading naturally to the French Revolution. On September 12, 1789, he published the first edition of his famous journal. The first five editions he called *Le Publiciste parisien*. But Marat's ambitions were grander than merely being a Parisian. He wanted to be the Friend of the People, and the journal became *L'Ami du peuple*.

Before that time, his thinking was fairly conventional. He was a liberal monarchist who believed in restricting the power of the monarchy, but certainly not eliminating it. He idolized Louis XVI. But as the king dragged his royal feet in sanctioning some of the decrees of the constituent assembly and failed to endorse the assembly's declaration of the rights of man, disillusion set in. Marat began to feel that the king was about to abdicate, after fomenting a counter-revolution, and that he was secretly forging alliances with foreign powers.

SUCCESSIVE issues of the journal, as well as a flood of pamphlets written by Marat, continued to support the idea of a limited monarchy, yet he supported the declaration of the rights of man, which stated that the rights of the people should be established before the privileges of the king. Gradually, Marat began to drift away from his more moderate views.

Camille Desmoulins described his activities as early as the October beginnings of the revolution: "Marat flies to Versailles, returns like a flash, makes alone as much noise as four trumpets on the last day of judgment, and cries to us: O Dead! Awaken!" This high-profile behavior was bound to attract the attention of the authorities, and Marat was constantly charged with treason and forced into hiding, only to emerge, to be charged again, and disappear again. It would be a pattern that described his life.

By 1792, he resembled a political pendulum, swinging back and forth between hatred of the monarchy and distrust of the new constitution. He was strongly in favor of the establishment of a dictatorship in France, particularly after the king tried to flee the country on June 21, 1791. But the people would have none of it.

Marat went to England in the early part of 1792, and for four months was safe but removed from the events that were tending toward the establishment of a French republic. He returned in the summer and again trumpeted his support of a dictatorship, again to deaf ears.

AND THEN, on September 2, 1792, Marat was invited to become a member of the *Comité de Surveillance* of the Paris Commune. That very day, the September massacres began, and Marat would be forever linked to them. In the eyes of some historians, he would be responsible for them.

On that day, rumors spread like fire through Paris that royalist prisoners in the jails were about to break out, and go on a rampage of bloody vengeance against those who put them there. Immediately, a systematic slaughter of prisoners began. Only a few did the butchering, but the entire city was aware of it, and did nothing either to prevent or stop it. Three days later, between 900 and 1,600 prisoners—estimates vary—had been killed in their cells or on the public execution blocks. And all without trial.

If Marat was responsible for this wholesale and barbaric bloodshed, it was by indiscretion. He was given to hyperbolic posturing, both on paper and in person. In the May 27, 1791 issue of *L'Ami du peuple*, he had fulminated,

> ". . . eleven months ago five hundred heads would have sufficed; perhaps five hundred thousand will fall before the end of the year. France will have been flooded with blood, but it will not be more free because of it . . ."

And as recently as August 19, 1792, he had exhorted the people to "rise and let the blood of traitors flow again. It is the only means of saving the Fatherland."

But that is the only documented evidence that he was responsible for the September massacres. True, writing such things was very much like pouring oil on a fire, and his irresponsibility, at least, condemns him. The charges by his later enemies that he had asked for 273,000 heads is unprovable, but he did little to condemn the bloodletting.

MARAT became a member of the National Convention, which, on September 22, 1792, made France a republic. Three days later, *L'Ami du peuple* became *Le Journal de la République Française*.

By early 1793, he had repudiated his dictatorship theory and had called for the death of Louis XVI. After the king was executed, he cried out in the Convention, "I believe in the Republic at last!"

By now, the National Convention, like Gaul, was divided into three distinct parts: The vast majority of its members were centrists. On the right were the Girondins (so called because they represented departments in the Gironde and neighboring regions). On the left were the deputies from Paris, known as the Mountain, because they sat higher up in the assembly's rows of seats than the others. The Mountain was headed by Robespierre and Marat.

From the National Convention's beginning, a pitched battle raged between Marat and the Girondins. He accused them of being the largest obstacle to the success of the republic. They accused Danton, Robespierre, and him of trying to establish a dictatorship. Marat rose to the defense of all three of them, concluding his impassioned speech by drawing a pistol from his belt, pointing it at his forehead and shouting that if the decrees of accusation were carried out against him, he would blow his brains out. He didn't and they weren't, but these sorts of theatrics did nothing to heal the breach with the Girondins.

The crossfire continued. On February 25, 1793,

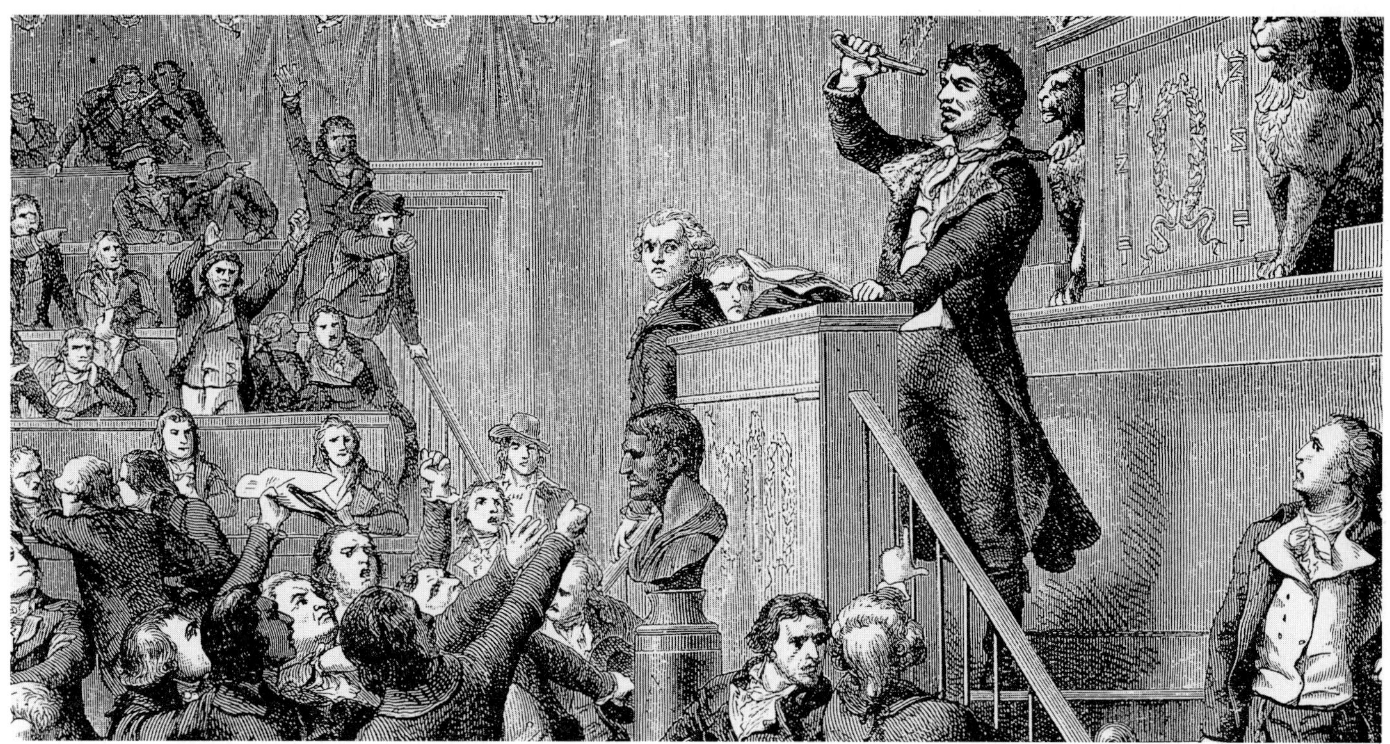

Marat threatens to shoot himself if the Convention votes against him (September 25, 1792).

there was a food riot in Paris, and Marat was accused of fomenting it. (There is some proof that he did; his issue of the *Journal* of that day noted that starving people in other countries had appropriated food from shops.) He countered by reminding the Convention that the Girondins had argued for moderation in the trial of Louis XVI, and he intimated that they were not only fomenting anti-Parisian feeling among the masses, but planning to carve up France into a group of small republics.

By the spring of 1793, the Girondins had assembled enough supporters to introduce the articles of accusation that were needed in order to put Marat in prison. He had, they said, preached pillage and murder, proposed a dictatorship, and urged the dismantling of the Convention. They were two thirds correct, but the revolutionary tribunal, after deliberating for 45 minutes, acquitted Marat.

He was hoisted on the shoulders of some of his admirers, and transported from the court to the Convention, where it soon became apparent that the Girondins' attempt to topple the Mountain had boomeranged. Marat's revenge was swift and sweet. Within months, accused and convicted of counter-revolutionary activity, the Girondin leaders were either chased from the country, or beheaded. By the end of October, 1793, they were no longer a force or a presence in France.

IT WAS Marat's last act of public incitement. He had been ill since 1788 with a festering skin disease which was first diagnosed as acute pruritus, aggravated by the times he had been forced to hide from authorities in the sewers of Paris. Long-range diagnosis from the perspective of modern medicine speculates that it was an advanced form of herpes. By 1793, it had been complicated by a lung complaint, and the only way Marat could find relief from the intense pain and discomfort was by remaining immersed in water, in a copper bathtub that was specially built for him. The tub was constructed like a shoe, with a writing board at the position of the topmost laces. Thus, he could conduct business from it and still be largely concealed from view.

Meanwhile, 24-year-old Marie-Anne-Charlotte Corday d'Armans, a tall, strong-willed, mystical, and romantic young woman who lived in Caen, in Normandy, was planning to rid her country of its chief scourge, Jean-Paul Marat. A descendant of the great French dramatist Corneille, she was devoted to the work of Voltaire and Plutarch, which she read at the home of her aunt after her convent education.

At the convent, her biblical studies had drawn her to the story of Judith, with whom she identified.

After their expulsion from the Convention, several Girondin leaders escaped to Normandy, where they held meetings in which they vowed revenge upon those who had expelled them. Charlotte Corday attended some of these meetings, and the ringing words of Jeanne Pierre Brissot fired her to action. "This monster [Marat] is unfeeling, violent, and cruel," Brissot intoned. "Three hundred thousand heads must be struck off before liberty is established. That will be until this man Marat, whose soul is kneaded in blood and dirt, and is a disgrace to humanity and the revolution, is dead."

CHARLOTTE Corday, on the pretext of having to procure some family papers, obtained a note of introduction to the Convention from, one of the exiled Girondins, Deputy Barbaroux. She wrote a hasty note to her father stating that she was off to England, and asking him to pardon her, and to forget her.

On Tuesday, July 9, she boarded a train for Paris. She planned to assassinate Marat on the floor of the Convention. Two days later, she arrived in Paris, purchased, for two francs, a sharp dinner knife at the Palais Royal, then took a room in the Hotel de la Providence in the Rue des Vieux Augustins.

The next morning, she presented her letter of introduction at the Tuileries. But Marat was nowhere to be seen. His mission was accomplished; at the age of 50, he had reached the inevitable conclusion that revolutions are best conducted by young men. Besides, his skin disease had debilitated him enough to confine him to the bathtub in his apartment at 30 Rue des Cordeliers.

Charlotte Corday returned to the hotel and wrote a letter to Marat: "Citizen, I have just arrived from Caen. Your love for your native place doubtless makes you desirous of learning the events which have occurred in that part of the republic. I shall call at your house in about an hour. Have the goodness to receive me and give me a brief interview. I will put you in a condition to render great service to France."

She sent the letter off, and was refused an audience. Undaunted, she appeared herself the second time, with a stronger letter, representing her as a victim of Girondin counter-revolutionary plots. There were secrets and names she could reveal to Marat, the letter said. Again, she was refused admittance.

But on July 13, she determined that, no matter what, she was going to enter Marat's apartment and kill him. Late that afternoon, she dressed herself in a spotted negligee costume, under which she concealed the knife, her birth certificate, and a paper she had written entitled *Adresse aux Français*, which contained the political reasons for her actions. She braided her long black hair, donned a hat with a black cockade, and ordered a hackney cab.

In the apartment at 30 Rue des Cordeliers, Marat sat in his high copper tub, writing. His body was swathed in wet towels, which were dampened and changed by his mistress, Simonne Evrard. His sister and an editor, Laurent Bas, worked in a separate room, preparing the next edition of the *Journal*.

Shortly after 7 p.m., Charlotte Corday left her hotel. At a little before eight, she arrived at Marat's apartment. According to the later testimony of Bas, ". . . she got out of a hackney cab and asked to speak to citizen Marat. She was carrying a fan in her hand. The concierge replied that he was not available at the moment. She said that this was the third time she had called and that it was most tiresome not to be admitted to him . . . citizeness Marat then went to ask her brother if the person was to be admitted and citizen Marat said she was."

Marat greeted her perfunctorily, but soon became interested in what she had to say. There were plotters in Caen, she said, threats to the republic. Who were they? he demanded.

"Eighteen deputies from the Convention rule there in collusion with the Department.

"What are their names?" he asked, his interest and enthusiasm rising.

She began to reel off their names: Barbaroux, Petion, Louvet—

He seized a pen and began to write. "They will soon be guillotined," he said.

And at that moment, Charlotte Corday stood, ripped the knife from her blouse and plunged it deeply into Marat's chest, piercing his left lung and aorta. He fell back, shrieked for Simonne. "A moi, ma chère amie! (Help me, my dear!)" he cried. Simonne then dashed into the room, and ran to Marat, whose wound was pouring blood into the bath-water. She pressed her hand over the wound,

As an artist records the scene, Charlotte Corday is prepared for the guillotine.

trying to close it, but it was too late. He was already dead.

Charlotte Corday calmly collected her fan and began to walk from the room, but Laurent Bas seized a chair and knocked her to the floor. She attempted to get up, and he seized her by the breasts and threw her down again. While he was pummeling her, she cried, "Je m'en fous! (I don't care!) The deed is done; the monster is dead!"

AND HE was, physically. But only physically. "I am the anger, the just anger, of the people and that is why they listen to me and believe in me," he had once said to Robespierre. And now that anger erupted. Charlotte Corday was tried and guillotined within four days of the assassination.

Marat became an instant, forceful martyr. His elaborate state funeral was attended by thousands. His body lay in state for two days, until early putrefaction set in. Busts of him were struck, and one was placed in the Convention. Jacques Louis David painted his immortal rendering of the assassination. Montmartre became Montmarat. Streets, buildings and 37 towns changed their names to Marat. Poems and hymns were written to him. He was compared to Jesus. His heart was embalmed and enshrined at the old Eglise des Cordeliers, which had become the revolutionary Club des Cordeliers. His mistress was awarded a pension. His sister embarked on a lifelong mission to immortalize his name. His ashes were awarded a place of honor in the Pantheon.

And the rumors that this was the first in a series of assassinations planned by counter-revolutionaries fired the populace. The Reign of Terror gained bloody force. The martyred and now mythical Marat had more power in death than the living Marat could have possibly dreamed of.

ABRAHAM LINCOLN

POSITION:	*President of the U.S.A.*
DATE:	*April 15, 1865*
PLACE:	*Washington, D.C.*
HOW:	*Gunshot*
WHO:	*John Wilkes Booth*
CONVICTED:	*No. Killed at his hiding place*
MOTIVE:	*Avenging South's defeat in the Civil War*
DIRECT CONSEQUENCE:	*Repressive measures enacted against the South*

ON December 2, 1859, John Brown, the half-mad religious fanatic, who, with a band of men, tried to take over various warehouses in Harpers Ferry, Virginia, in protest of slavery and in the hope of arousing the blacks of the South to set themselves free, was hanged. Present at the execution was the popular actor, John Wilkes Booth. He was, as was practically everyone else in the crowd of spectators that day, glad to see Brown dead, happy to note that his attempt at rebellion had failed.

Five and a half years later, after having experienced both personal diminishment and the bitter failure of a much wider attempt at rebellion, John Wilkes Booth would, in a self-styled attempt to revenge the besmirched honor of the South, assassinate President Abraham Lincoln. It is not beyond belief that the genesis of that awful night in April 1865 owed much to what Wilkes witnessed on a December evening in 1859 in Harpers Ferry. It was, after all, the motto of the State of Virginia that Booth repeated, as he leaped to the stage of Ford's Theater after shooting the President. "*Sic semper tyrannis!* (thus ever to tyrants)" he intoned, melodramatically, using his best actorly projection.

AND, to many in the vanquished Confederacy, Abraham Lincoln was a tyrant who had murdered more than he had healed. The victor, after all, is never loved by the vanquished, and the South had been vanquished just five days before, when General Robert E. Lee surrendered the Army of northern Virginia to General Ulysses S. Grant at Appomattox Court House, Virginia.

The war would stutter on for another month, but for all intents and purposes, it ended on April 9, 1865, with Lee's surrender. Abraham Lincoln could then breathe a well-earned sigh of relief. His life had been a long journey, full of frustrations and disappointments and compromises. A tall, gangly, self-taught and self-contained man, born in a log cabin in Kentucky, but claiming New Salem, a small town near Springfield, Illinois as his home, Lincoln entered Congress in 1847 as a Whig, but in 1856 joined the antislavery Republican Party.

His famous debates with Stephen A. Douglas for the Senate seat from Illinois lost him the Senate, but gained him the nomination for the Presidency in 1860. He won it by a slim margin and almost immediately became embroiled in the sad business of the sundering of the Union. By the time he was inaugurated, in March of 1861, seven Southern states had seceded from the Union. Although he attempted to placate the South by fostering the preservation of the Union over the abolition of slavery, Lincoln could not hold the country together, and on April 12, 1861, the Civil War began. It would encompass four of the bloodiest, most violent years in the nation's history. About 600,000 men would die. One-quarter of all of the white men in the South would lose their lives. In 1866, a year after the war ended, one-fifth of the budget of the State of Mississippi would be spent on artificial limbs.

As Southern victory piled on Southern victory, as the schism deepened between North and South, as one incompetent Northern general after another lost tens of thousands of men, Lincoln had much time to arrange his moral priorities. Perhaps they had always been in place. Those who were near him and gazed into those infinitely sad and gentle eyes felt an essential, peaceful goodness and greatness in the man. And so, it seems that there might have been moral as well as political reasons for his issuance of the Emancipation Proclamation on September 22, 1862. It would set the slaves free by edict, gain him the support of the Abolitionists, and bring down the full fury of the South and its sympathizers upon him.

ONE OF these sympathizers was John Wilkes Booth. Five feet ten inches tall, slight, possessed of long, flowing, black hair and a chalky white complexion, he was a fiercely egomaniacal man who labored, from the beginning to the end of his professional career, in the shadow of both his father, Junius Brutus Booth, and his brother, Edwin Booth.

He professed his support for the Southern cause, but could never bring himself to fight for it on a battlefield. Instead, as the fortunes of war turned more and more toward the North, and Lincoln was elected to a second term in office, he hatched a plan to kidnap the President and transport him to Richmond, where he could be used as a bargaining chip to end the war in the South's favor. By late 1864, Booth had gathered a group of five conspirators around him. They met in Mrs. Mary Surratt's boarding house in Washington, D.C. to plan their strategies, none of which was destined to succeed.

The group was composed of two of Booth's boyhood friends, Michael O'Laughlin and Sam Arnold, who had fought as Confederate soldiers in the war, but were considerably less than enthusiastic about the kidnap plot; George A. Atzerodt, a small, sly, and unlikeable carriage maker from Port Tobacco; David Herold, a drug clerk; and John Surratt, who was a Confederate courier, and whose mother managed the boardinghouse in whose attic they met.

On January 18, 1865, they plotted to seize the President at Ford's Theater, where, it was reported, he, Mrs. Lincoln, and two friends would be attending a performance of *Jack Cade*, starring the great American Shakespearian actor Edwin Forrest. At the last minute, the President canceled his plans to attend the theatre. They barely had time to cancel their own appearances.

On March 18, they planned to kidnap Lincoln as he rode his carriage to the Soldier's Home on Seventh Street. Once again, the President changed his plans, and once again, the conspirators scattered.

And then, the war ended, and kidnapping became an exercise in futility. Frustrated, angry at the cowardice that had kept him from killing Yankees, Booth determined to have his revenge upon the North, the President, the fates, his family, and himself. He would assassinate Lincoln personally; he had acquired another dedicated conspirator, Lewis Powell (who had lately changed his name to Lewis Paine), and he would simultaneously murder Secretary of State William Seward. George Andrew Atzerodt would kill Vice President Andrew Johnson. That way, the South and John Wilkes Booth would both be avenged.

HIS opportunity presented itself immediately. It was announced publicly that President and Mrs. Lincoln and General and Mrs. Grant would attend a performance at Ford's Theater of *Our American Cousin*, starring Laura Keane, on Friday night, April 14. Booth had recently appeared at Ford's. He knew the theatre and he knew its stage hands, and he gained access to both during the day of the performance.

He chatted with a stage hand; at 6 p.m., he wandered into the theatre, and discovered that the lock to the Presidential box was broken. Four and a half weeks earlier, Thomas Raybold, a ticket seller, had led a party of disgruntled and late playgoers to the Presidential box because their seats had been forfeited to on-time theatregoers. He had decided that the expediency of kicking the door in was quicker than a trip downstairs for the key. He smashed the lock with his foot, let the party into the box and decided not to report his misdeed.

And so, for a change, the fates seemed to be siding with John Wilkes Booth. He drilled a hole in the door of the unlocked box that would give him a clear view of the rocking chair that Lincoln would occupy that night. He hid a plank that would be used to jam the door to the box area, cleaned up his wood shavings, and departed.

Meanwhile, at the White House, all was anything but cheerful. General Grant and his wife would not be attending the theatre. A weary President tried to induce Secretary of State Stanton and his wife to take their places, but Stanton detested the theatre, and refused. Lincoln's instinct told him to cancel the reservation. For several nights, he had been haunted by a nightmare in which he wandered through the corridors of the White House and eventually came upon his own body. But his sense of responsibility to the people on this, his first public appearance since the winning of the war, overrode both his instinct and his premonitions. He invited a young army major,

T E NEW YORK ERALD.

WHOLE NO. 10459. NEW YORK, SATURDAY, APRIL 15, 1865. PRICE, FOUR CENTS.

IMPORTANT.

ASSASSINATION OF PRESIDENT LINCOLN

The President Shot at the Theatre Last Evening.

SECRETARY SEWARD

DAGGERED IN HIS BED BUT NOT MORTALLY WOUNDED.

Clarence and Frederick Seward Badly Hurt.

ESCAPE OF THE ASSASSINS.

Intense Excitement in Washington.

SCENE AT THE DEATHBED OF MR. LINCOLN.

J. Wilkes Booth, the Actor, the Alleged Assassin of the President,

&c., &c., &c.

THE OFFICIAL DISPATCH.

WAR DEPARTMENT,
WASHINGTON, APRIL 15—1:30 A. M.

Major General Dix, New York:

This evening at about 9:30 P. M., at Ford's Theatre, the President, while sitting in his private box with Mrs. Lincoln, Mrs. Harris and Major Rathburn, was shot by an assassin, who suddenly entered the box and approached behind the President.

The assassin then leaped upon the stage, brandishing a large dagger or knife, and made his escape in the rear of the theatre.

The pistol ball entered the back of the President's head and penetrated nearly through the head. The wound is mortal.

The President has been insensible ever since it was inflicted, and is now dying.

About the same hour an assassin, whether the same or not, entered Mr. Seward's apartments, and under pretense of having a prescription was shown to the Secretary's sick chamber. The assassin immediately rushed to the bed and inflicted two or three stabs on the throat and two on the face.

It is hoped the wounds may not be mortal. My apprehension is that they will prove fatal.

The nurse alarmed Mr. Frederick Seward, who was in an adjoining room, and he hastened to the door of his father's room, when he met the assassin, who inflicted upon him one or more dangerous wounds. The recovery of Frederick Seward is doubtful.

It is not probable that the President will live through the night.

General Grant and his wife were advertised to be at the theatre this evening, but he started to Burlington at six o'clock this evening.

At a cabinet meeting, at which General Grant was present, the subject of the state of the country and the prospect of a speedy peace was discussed. The President was very cheerful and hopeful, and spoke very kindly of General Lee and others of the confederacy, and of the establishment of government in Virginia.

All the members of the Cabinet except Mr. Seward are now in attendance upon the President.

I have seen Mr. Seward, but he and Frederick were both unconscious.

EDWIN M. STANTON,
Secretary of War.

THE HERALD DISPATCHES.

WASHINGTON, April 14, 1865.

Assassination has been inaugurated in Washington. The bowie knife and pistol have been applied to President Lincoln and Secretary Seward. The former was shot in the throat, while at Ford's Theatre to-night. Mr. Seward was badly cut about the throat, while in bed at his residence.

SECOND DISPATCH.

WASHINGTON, April 14, 1865.

An attempt was made about ten o'clock this evening to assassinate the President and Secretary Seward. The President was shot at Ford's Theatre. Result not yet known. Mr. Seward's throat was cut, and his son badly injured.

There is intense excitement here.

Details of the Assassination.

WASHINGTON, April 14, 1865.

Washington was thrown into an intense excitement a few minutes before eleven o'clock this evening, by the announcement that the President and Secretary Seward had been assassinated and were dead.

The wildest excitement prevailed in all parts of the city. Men, women and children, old and young, rushed to and fro, and the rumors were magnified until we had nearly every member of the Cabinet killed. Some time elapsed before authentic data could be ascertained in regard to the affair.

The president and Mrs. Lincoln were at Ford's Theatre, listening to the performance of the American Cousin, occupying a box in the second tier. At the close of the third act a person entered the box occupied by the President and shot Mr. Lincoln in the head. The shot entered the back of his head and came out above the temple.

The assassin then jumped from the box upon the stage and ran across to the other side, exhibiting a dagger in his hand, flourishing it in a tragical manner, shouting the same words repeated by the desperado at Mr. Seward's house, adding to it, "The South is avenged," and then escaped from the back entrance to the stage, but in his passage dropped his pistol and his hat.

Mr. Lincoln fell forward in his seat and Mrs. Lincoln fainted.

The moment the astonished audience could realize what had happened the President was taken and carried to Mr. Peterson's house in Tenth Street, opposite to the theatre. Medical aid was immediately sent for, and the wound was at first supposed to be fatal, and it was announced that he could not live; but at half-past twelve he is still alive, though in a precarious condition.

As the assassin ran across the stage Col. J. B. Stewart, of this city, who was occupying one of the front seats in the orchestra, on the same side of the house as the box occupied by Mr. Lincoln, sprang to the stage and followed him; but he was obstructed in his passage across the stage by the fright of the actors, and reached the back door about three seconds after the assassin had passed out. Col. Stewart got to the street just in time to see him mount his horse and ride away.

The operation shows that the whole thing was a preconcerted plan. The person who fired the pistol was a man about thirty years of age, about five feet nine, spare built, fair skin, dark hair, apparently bushy, with a large moustache. Laura Keene and the leader of the orchestra recognized him as J. Wilkes Booth the actor, and a rabid secessionist. Whoever he was, it is plainly evident that he thoroughly understood the theatre, and all the approaches and modes of escape to the stage. A person not familiar with the theatre could not have possibly made his escape so well and quickly.

The alarm was sounded in every quarter. Mr. Stanton was notified and immediately left his house.

All the other members of the cabinet escaped attack.

Cavalrymen were sent out in all directions, and dispatches were sent to all the fortifications and it is thought they will be captured.

About half-past ten o'clock this evening, a tall, well-dressed man made his appearance at Secretary Seward's residence, and applied for admission. He was refused admission by the servant, when the desperado stated that he had a prescription from the Surgeon General and that he was ordered to deliver it in person. He was still refused, except upon the written order of the physician. This he pretended to show and pushed by the servant and rushed up stairs to Mr. Seward's room. He was met at the door by Mr. Fred Seward, who notified him that he was master of the house, and would take charge of the medicine. After a few words had passed between them he dodged by Fred Seward and rushed to the Secretary's bed and struck him in the neck with a dagger, and also in the breast.

It was supposed at first that Mr. Seward was killed instantly, but it was found afterwards that the wound was not mortal.

Major William H. Seward, Jr., paymaster, was in the room and rushed to the defense of his father and was badly cut in the side by the assassin, but not fatally.

The desperado managed to escape from the house, and was prepared for escape by having a horse at the door. He immediately mounted his horse and sang out the motto of the State of Virginia, "Sic Semper Tyrannis," and rode off.

Surgeon General Barnes was immediately sent for, and he examined Mr. Seward and pronounced him safe. His wounds were not fatal. The jugular vein was not cut, nor the wound in the breast deep enough to be fatal.

WASHINGTON, April 15—1 A. M.

The streets in the vicinity of Ford's Theatre are densely crowded by an anxious and excited crowd. A guard has been placed across Tenth street and F and E streets, and only official persons and particular friends of the President are allowed to pass.

The popular heart is deeply stirred, and the deepest indignation against leading rebels is freely expressed.

The scene at the house where the President lies in extremis is very affecting. Even Secretary Stanton is affected to tears. When the news spread through the city that the President had been shot, the people, with pale faces and compressed lips, crowded every place where there was the slightest chance of obtaining information in regard to the affair.

After the President was shot, Lieutenant Rathburn caught the assassin by the arm, who immediately struck him with a knife, and jumped from the box, as before stated.

The popular affection for Mr. Lincoln has been shown by this diabolical assassination, which will bring eternal infamy, not only upon its authors, but upon the hellish cause which they desire to avenge.

Vice-President Johnson arrived at the White House, where the President lies, about one o'clock and will remain with him to the last.

The President's family are in attendance upon him also.

As soon as intelligence could be got to the War Department, the electric telegraph and the Signal Corps were put in requisition to endeavor to prevent the escape of the assassins, and all the troops around Washington are under arms.

Popular report points to a somewhat celebrated actor of known secession proclivities as the assassin; but it would be unjust to name him until some further evidence of his guilt is obtained. It is rumored that the person alluded to is in custody.

The latest advices from Secretary Seward reveal more desperate work there than at first supposed. Seward's wounds are not in themselves fatal; but in connection with his recent injuries, and the great loss of blood he has sustained, his recovery is questionable.

It was Clarence A. Seward, instead of Wm. H. Seward, Jr., who was wounded. Fred. Seward was also badly cut as were also three nurses, who were in attendance upon the Secretary, showing that a desperate struggle took place there. The wounds of the whole party were dressed.

ONE O'CLOCK A. M.

The President is perfectly senseless, and there is not the slightest hope of his surviving. Physicians believe he will die before morning. All of his Cabinet except Secretary Seward are with him. Speaker Colfax, Senator Farwell, of Maine, and many other gentlemen are also at the house awaiting the termination.

The scene at the President's bedside is described by one who witnessed it as most affecting. It was surrounded by his Cabinet ministers, all of whom were bathed in tears, not even excepting Mr. Stanton, who, when informed by Surgeon General Barnes, that the President could not live until morning, exclaimed, "Oh, no, General; no, no," and with an impulse natural as it was unaffected, immediately sat down on a chair near his bedside and wept like a child.

Senator Sumner was seated on the right of the President's couch, near the head, holding the right hand of the President in his own. He was sobbing like a woman, with his head bowed down almost on the pillow of the bed on which the President was lying.

TWO O'CLOCK A. M.

The President is still alive, but there is no improvement in his condition.

THE PRESS DISPATCHES.

WASHINGTON, April 15—12:30 A. M.

The President was shot in a theatre to-night, and is perhaps mortally wounded.

SECOND DISPATCH.

WASHINGTON, April 15—1 A. M.

The President is not expected to live through the night. He was shot at a theatre.

Secretary Seward was also assassinated. No arteries were cut.

Additional Details of the Assassination.

WASHINGTON, April 15—1:30 A. M.

President Lincoln and wife, with other friends, this evening visited Ford's Theatre, for the purpose of witnessing the performance of the American Cousin.

It was announced in the papers that General Grant would also be present, but that gentleman took the late train of cars for New Jersey.

The theatre was densely crowded, and all seemed delighted with the scene before them. During the third act, and while there was a temporary pause for one of the actors to enter, a sharp report of a pistol was heard, which merely attracted attention, but suggested nothing serious, until a man rushed to the front of the President's box, waving a long dagger in his right hand, and exclaiming "Sic Semper Tyrannis!" and immediately leaped from the box, which was in the second tier, to the stage beneath, and ran across to the opposite side, making his escape, amid the bewilderment of the audience, from the rear of the theatre, and mounting a horse, fled.

The screams of Mrs. Lincoln first disclosed the fact to the audience that the President had been shot, when all present rose to their feet, rushing towards the stage, many exclaiming "Hang him! Hang him!"

The excitement was of the wildest possible description, and of course there was an abrupt termination of the theatrical performance.

There was a rush towards the President's box, when cries were heard: "Stand back and give him air." "Has any one stimulants?"

On a hasty examination it was found that the President had been shot through the head, above the back of the temporal bone, and that some of the brain was oozing out.

He was removed to a private house opposite to the theatre, and the Surgeon General of the Army was sent for to attend to his condition.

On an examination of the private box blood was discovered on the back of the cushioned rocking chair on which the President had been sitting, also on the partition and on the floor. A common single barreled pocket pistol was found on the carpet.

A military guard was placed in front of the private residence to which the President had been conveyed. An immense crowd was in front of it, and deeply anxious to learn the condition of the President. It had been previously announced that the wound was mortal, but all hoped otherwise. The shock to the community was terrible.

At midnight, the Cabinet, with Messrs. Sumner, Colfax and Farnsworth, Judge Curtis, Governor Oglesby, General Meigs, Colonel Hay, and a few personal friends, with Surgeon General Barnes and his immediate assistants, were around his bedside.

The President was in a state of syncope, totally insensible, and breathing slowly. The blood oozed from the wound in the back of his head.

The surgeons exhausted every possible effort of medical skill, but all hope was gone.

The parting of his family with the dying President is too sad for description.

The President and Mrs. Lincoln did not start for the theatre until fifteen minutes after eight o'clock. Speaker Colfax was at the White House at the time and the President stated to him that he was going. Mrs. Lincoln had not been well, but because the papers had announced that General Grant and they were to be present, and, as General Grant had gone North, he did not wish the audience to be disappointed. He went with apparent reluctance, and urged Mr. Colfax to go with him, but that gentleman had made other engagements, and with Mr. Ashman, of Massachusetts, bid him good by.

When the excitement at the theatre was at its wildest height reports were circulated that Secretary Seward had also been assassinated.

On reaching the gentleman's residence a crowd and a military guard were found at the door and on entering it was ascertained that the reports were based on facts.

Everybody there was so excited that scarcely an intelligent word could be gathered. But the facts are substantially as follows:

About ten o'clock a man rang the bell, and the call having been answered by a colored servant, he said he had come from Dr. Verdi, Secretary Seward's family physician, with a prescription, at the same time holding in his hand a small piece of paper folded, and saying, in answer to a refusal, that he must see the Secretary, as he was entrusted with particular instructions regarding the medicine.

He still insisted on going up, although repeatedly informed that no one could enter the chamber. The man pushed the servant aside, and walked hastily towards the Secretary's room, and was then met by Mr. Frederick Seward, of whom he demanded to see the Secretary, making the same representation which he did to the servant.

What further passed in the way of colloquy is not known; but the man struck him on the head with a billy, severely injuring the skull and felling him almost senseless.

The assassin then rushed into the chamber and attacked Major Seward Paymaster United States Army, and Mr. Hansell, a messenger of the State Department, and two male nurses, disabling them all.

He then rushed upon the Secretary, who was lying in bed, in the same room, and inflicted three stabs in the neck, but severing, it is thought and hoped, no arteries, though he bled profusely.

The assassin then rushed down stairs, mounted his horse at the door and rode off before an alarm could be sounded, and in the same manner as the assassin of the President.

It is believed that the injuries of the Secretary are not fatal nor those of either of the others, although both the Secretary and the Assistant Secretary are very seriously injured.

Secretaries Stanton and Wells, and other prominent officers of the Government, called at Secretary Seward's to inquire into his condition, and there heard of the assassination of the President.

They then proceeded to the house where he was lying, exhibiting of course intense anxiety and solicitude.

An immense crowd was gathered in front of the President's house, and a strong guard was also stationed there. Many persons evidently supposing he would be brought to his home.

The entire city to-night presents a scene of wild excitement, accompanied by violent expression of indignation and the profoundest sorrow; many shed tears.

The military authorities have despatched mounted patrols in every direction, in order, if possible, to arrest the assassins. The whole metropolitan police are likewise vigilant for the same purpose.

The attacks, both at the theatre and at Secretary Seward's house took place about the same hour—ten o'clock—thus showing a preconcerted plan to assassinate those gentlemen. Some evidence of the guilt of the party who attacked the President are in possession of the police.

Vice-President Johnson is in the city, and his headquarters are guarded by troops.

EXTRA.

8:10 A. M.

New York, Saturday, April 15, 1865.

DEATH OF THE PRESIDENT.

Further Details of the Great Crime.

ADDITIONAL DISPATCHES FROM THE SECRETARY OF WAR.

What is Known of the Assassins.

THE OFFICIAL DISPATCHES.

WAR DEPARTMENT,
WASHINGTON, April 15—9:10 A. M.

Major General Dix, New York:

The President continues insensible and sinking. Secretary Seward remains without change; Frederick Seward's skull is fractured in two places, besides a severe cut upon the head. The attendant is still alive but hopeless. Major Seward's wounds are not dangerous.

It is now ascertained with reasonable certainty, that two assassins were engaged in the horrible crime, Wilkes Booth being the one that shot the President, and the other an accomplice, whose name is not known, but whose description is so clear that he can hardly escape.

It appears from papers found in Booth's trunk that the murder was planned before the 4th of March, but fell through then, because the accomplice backed out until "Richmond could be heard from."

Booth and his accomplice were at the livery stable at 6 o'clock last evening, and left here with their horses at 10 o'clock, or shortly before that hour.

It would appear that they had, for several days been seeking their chance, but for some unknown reason it was not carried into effect until last night.

One of the assassins has evidently made his way to Baltimore; the other has not yet been traced.

EDWIN M. STANTON,
Secretary of War.

THE PRESIDENT DEAD.

WAR DEPARTMENT,
WASHINGTON, April 15—7:30 A. M.

Major General Dix, New York:—

Abraham Lincoln died this morning at twenty-two minutes past 7 o'clock.

EDWIN M. STANTON
Secretary of War.

IMPORTANT FROM SOUTH AMERICA.

Surrender of Montevideo to Gen. Flores—Brazil in Possession of the City, &c.

The Brazilian mail arrived at Lisbon April 2, bringing the following advices:

Montevideo has surrendered to General Flores. The Brazilians now (March 11) occupy the city.

RIO JANEIRO, March 11, 1865.

Exchange 25 5-8 a 26 1-4.

Coffee—Sales of good first at 65.66. Shipments, 100,000 bags. Stock, 100,000 bags. Freight, 50.321-8.

BAHIA, March 11, 1865.

Exchange 26 1-4. Cotton nominal.

PERNAMBUCO, March 11, 1865.

Exchange 26 1-2 a 27.

News From San Francisco.

SAN FRANCISCO, April 12, 1865.

The exports of treasure for the quarter just ended, show a falling off of about six and a half million as compared with the same period last year.

SAN FRANCISCO, April 14, 1865.

The Pacific mail steamship, Sacramento sailed to-day, with a large number of passengers for New York, and $1,153,000 in treasure, of which nearly $700,000 go to New York.

The steamship Moses Taylor sailed for San Juan Del Sur, with numerous passengers.

The market continues variable and unsettled, and traders pursue a continuous policy. Prices of Eastern goods are slowly falling.

Sailed, ship Flying Eagle, for Boston.

New Orleans Markets.

NEW ORLEANS, April 8,
VIA CAIRO, April 14, 1865.

The New Orleans markets are at a stand still. Low middling cotton is quoted at 42c. per pound, and good superfine flour at $9 per barrel.

THE REBELS.

JEFF. DAVIS AT DANVILLE.

His Latest Appeal to his Deluded Followers.

He Thinks the Fall of Richmond a Blessing in Disguise as it Leaves the Rebel Armies Free to Move From Point to Point.

HE VAINLY PROMISES TO HOLD VIRGINIA AT ALL HAZARDS.

Lee and His Army Supposed to Be Safe.

BRECKINRIDGE AND THE REST OF DAVIS' CABINET REACH DANVILLE SAFELY.

The Organ of Gov. Vance, of North Carolina, Advises the Submission of the Rebels to President Lincoln's Terms.

&c., &c., &c.

JEFF. DAVIS' LAST PROCLAMATION.

VIRGINIA TO BE HELD BY THE REBELS AT ALL HAZARDS.

DANVILLE, VA., April 5, 1865.

The General-in-Chief found it necessary to make such movements of his troops as to uncover the Capital. It would be unwise to conceal the moral and material injury to our cause resulting from the occupation of our capital by the enemy. It is equally unwise and unworthy of us to allow our own energies to falter and our efforts to become relaxed under reverses, however calamitous they may be. For many months the largest and finest army of the confederacy, under command of a leader whose presence inspires equal confidence in the troops and the people, has been greatly trammelled by the necessity of keeping constant watch over the approaches to the capital, and has thus been forced to forego more than one opportunity for promising enterprise. It is for us, my countrymen, to show by our bearing under reverses, how wretched has been the self-deception of those who have believed us less able to endure misfortune than to encounter dangers with courage.

We have now entered upon a new phase of the struggle. Relieved from the necessity of guarding particular points, our army will be free to move from point to point to strike the enemy in detail far from his base. Let us but will it and we are free.

Animated by that confidence in spirit and fortitude which never yet failed me, I announce to you, fellow-countrymen, that it is my purpose to maintain your cause with my whole heart and soul; that I will never consent to abandon to the enemy one foot of the soil of any one of the States of the Confederacy, and that Virginia—noble State—whose ancient renown has been eclipsed by the still more glorious recent history, whose bosom has been bared to receive the main shock of this war; whose sons and daughters have exhibited heroism so sublime as to render her illustrious in all time to come—that Virginia, with the help of the people and by the blessing of Providence, shall be held and defended, and no peace ever be made with the infamous invaders of her territory.

If by the stress of numbers we shall ever be compelled to a temporary withdrawal from her limits or those of any other border State, again and again will we return, until the baffled and exhausted enemy shall abandon in despair his endless and impossible task of making slaves of people resolved to be free.

Let us then, not despond, my countrymen; but relying on God, meet the foe with fresh defiance and with unconquered and unconquerable hearts.

JEFFERSON DAVIS.

The Evacuation of the Rebel Capital.

THE FIRST REBEL ACCOUNT OF HOW THE CITY WAS ABANDONED.

[From the Danville, (Va.,) Register, April 5.]

Persons who left the capital Sunday night and Monday morning represent that the scene which followed the evacuation of the city by our troops beggars description. To preserve order and protect the property of the citizens who unavoidably remained there, as far as could be done, the Nineteenth Virginia militia under Colonel Evans, was placed on police duty in the city to await the coming of the enemy; but accounts state that they failed to render any aid or protection to the people whatever. On Sunday night a mob of the lower classes of the city, composed, it is said, mostly of the foreign element, visited a number of the largest store houses of the city and robbed them of their contents. It is affirmed that Main street was pillaged, and then burned, and that some of the milling establishments were also committed to the flames. We have no doubt that a considerable portion of the brave city has been laid in ashes and a number of the people insulted, outraged, robbed and massacred. How painful the thought that the place should be given over to rapine and plunder, even before the public enemy entered its limits. But the fact only proves that the people of Richmond have had secret enemies in their own midst, scarcely less savage and even more treacherous and vindictive than the open foe.

We are told that the people banded together during the violent proceedings of the mob and resisted them with force, a street fight ensuing, in which several persons were killed.

No intelligence has reached us of the enemy's troops occupying the city. The last trains on the Danville railroad which came out of the place on Monday morning and passengers upon them had heard nothing from the enemy. The greater portion of Grant's Army was transferred to the south side of the James River some days ago, only the command of General Ord, which is composed mostly, if not entirely, of negro troops, being left on the north side. This command will enter and occupy the city. Some of our people who are acquainted with the character of General Ord think they have reason to hope that his treatment of the unfortunate people of Richmond will not be so hard, and cruel and inhuman as that which has fallen upon the heads of our fellow townsmen in other captured cities.

The newspapers of Richmond, we suppose, will fall into the hands of the enemy. The evacuation of the city was so sudden and unexpected, scarcely anyone being prepared for it—that no time was left for the removal of so cumbersome an establishment as a city newspaper office. In a few days we may expect to hear that the Enquirer, or the Whig, or the Examiner is issued as a Yankee paper.

All the rolling stock on the Richmond and Danville Railroad in running order was saved on the retreat from Richmond. A few old cars not in a movable condition, were left at Manchester. No train was captured by the enemy near the Junction as was at one time reported, and indeed, we do not believe that any body of Yankees had struck the road at any point up to yesterday evening.

The Secretary of War, the Quartermaster General, Commissary General and a number of other officers of our government, left Richmond on horseback and will probably arrive at this place to-morrow.

Should General Lee establish his lines east of the Junction, we suppose the State Legislature will be convened at Lynchburg.

All the specie and other valuables belonging to the banks at Richmond were removed from the city on Saturday, and have been carried to places of safety.

A considerable amount of goods purchased by the State for distribution to the people, we regret to learn, had to be left behind. Also the state archives remained in the city, but we perceive no motive the enemy can have in destroying them, as they will no doubt endeavor to occupy the city permanently and establish a State government at Richmond under the federal Union.

Lee's Army Supposed to be in a Safe Position.

(From the Raleigh Confederate, April 7.)

This is the time for rumor manufacturers who are engaged in a wholesale business. Sometimes they have it that whole brigades deserted in the last great battle, among others, Cook's brigade is selected as the bearer of this stigma. We are assured that such a statement has no foundation whatever; that no treachery induced the disaster at Petersburg; that our forces fought splendidly, and the enemy only succeeded by overwhelming numbers. We are convinced, too, from facts we cannot mention, that Lee's army is in a safe position, and that his future movements will be directed with the skill and energy which distinguished our great captain.

Having anticipated the probable loss of Richmond, and fully recognizing the importance of the disaster, we are, nevertheless, not of the number of those who give up the cause. In the Southern confederacy, this day, there is military strength of men, material and supplies to make independence certain. It is the people themselves whether they secure or lose their liberties.

Rebel Particulars of the Battle of Petersburg.

(From the Raleigh Confederate, April 7.)

An officer who left Richmond at nine o'clock on Monday morning last, informs us that the time he left, the city was in flames from Clay to Canal streets. The Shockoe warehouse and other entree ports of supplies were burned. The bridges had also been fired.

No mob or violence of any kind had occurred up to the period when he left, so that the reports of a destructive mob on Sunday night are untrue. The enemy's cavalry entered the city as the train moved off that he came out in. The story of the mob, therefore, we hope is entirely erroneous.

This officer describes the fighting on Saturday as terrible beyond description. The enemy forced column after column of our works, tapping our lines on the extreme right. They came nine columns deep. Eight columns faltered and were broken by the obstinacy of our defence; but the ninth broke over our forces like a whirlwind. He says the destruction of the enemy was immense. Our loss, we think, consists mainly in prisoners taken by the enemy. All the prisoners whom we captured were drunk, having been prepared, according to the Yankee tactics, for the terrible ordeal. Lieutenant General A. P. Hill was certainly killed. General Fitz Lee was not killed as reported, or General W. H. F. Lee. No general officer from North Carolina was killed as far as he heard. On Monday, Sheridan attacked Fitz Lee and was handsomely repulsed.

The Organ of Gov. Vance, of North Carolina, Advising General Lee to Submit to Mr. Lincoln's Terms.

(From the Raleigh Confederate, April 7.)

The Conservative occasionally seems to fall into very mysterious hands, and to come under the control of an incomprehensible influence. On the day before yesterday the paper availed itself of a period of extreme reverses and disaster to renew the attempt to cast odium on our own citizens, which has been a favorite policy with its politics leaders ever since the reverses began, and after it was no longer politic to claim that they "made the revolution." Yesterday it sends to the public a leader of still more extraordinary import. From what we comprehend of it, it seems to be a distinct proposition to submit and surrender upon the terms proposed by Lincoln. This has never yet, as we can recollect of, been more distinctively proposed even by journals whose loyalty has been called in question. The Conservative says: "It is nonsense to propose to treat with the North with any expectation of concession that the confederacy is a government," and hence says the Conservative, "If our authorities are determined to force this condition upon the North as a basis of negotiation, then the North will never negotiate." What is this but surrender? Not only surrender, but an assertion to the world that the defense of the past four years has been of a position which is one of sheer nonsense—one which the North never could admit. We have not seen in this controversy as bold and unconditional a justification of the northern invasion, for, if we sought to force a claim inconsistent with reason, and to demand an "admission" which "is an absurdity in anything like government," and the North only resisted such claim and refused such admission, then we are in the wrong and the Yankee government is right, and the writer of the article to which we are replying does well when he advises General Lee not to "block up his way at the threshold, by presenting a basis to which he knows the enemy will not yield, but to meet him on his own ground," as "the only way to open the negotiation." When we remember what "his own ground" is upon which the Conservative proposes to meet the enemy, we may readily understand how much it is prepared to concede. "His own ground" measured the length of three propositions: submission to the laws and constitution of the United States, the laying down of our arms and acquiescence to Lincoln's proclamations. This is the ground on which the author of the editorial desires General Lee to meet Lincoln and "secure a talk about peace." We have no idea that Gov. Vance will support this idea; but it is very unfortunate that now, in the very moment when everything should be said to uphold the hope and confidence of the army and people, such sentiment should obtain publication in the organ of the governor.

High Prices in an Overstocked Market.

[From the Raleigh Confederate, April 7.]

Our market on the arrival of the Weldon train on yesterday, became overstocked with shad. They went off slowly at $50 per pair.

Exchange of Rebel General Vance.

[From the Ashville, (N. C.) News.]

The exchange of prisoners seems to go steadily on. We have seen a large number of our mountain boys, who have reached home after a protracted imprisonment. Among others we were gratified to meet Brigadier General R. B. Vance, who reached home some days since. He looks rather worsted by his long confinement, but as is usual with him, is full of life, cheerful and buoyant. The General is a great favorite of the people in this section, and everybody was glad to see him.

City Intelligence.

EASTER SUNDAY AT ST. ANN'S CHURCH. The admirers of sacred music made truly effective by a well trained choir, have an opportunity of indulging their taste by repairing to St. Ann's Church on Easter Sunday evening, the doors opening at seven, the concert beginning at eight. Three of the pieces are from Gordigiani, three from Rossini and one from each of the composers, Verdi, Donizetti, Vonrimst, Dachauer and Gounod. We need only mention the names of Signor Reinne and Messrs. Schmitz, Schubert and Dachauer to insure confidence in the vocal results. The ladies are quite distinguished for soprano and contralto execution, and no exertion will be spared to make the musical feast worthy of the day.

A NEW CHURCH.—An advertisement among our religious notices announces the opening of the new Church of the Holy Trinity, Madison Avenue, corner of Forty-second street, on Sunday. Sermons will be preached at the three sessions by the Rev. Dr. Tyng, of St. George's; Rev. Dr. Dyer and the Rev. Stephen H. Tyng, Jr., the pastor of the church. It promises to be an occasion of great interest to residents on Murray Hill.

CROTON AQUEDUCT CONTRACTS.—The following contracts have been issued by the department. Laying crosswalks from south-west corner of Fifty-ninth street and Broadway, to the junction of Broadway and Eighth avenue, to Matthew Murray, $625. Cobble stone pavement in Hammond street, west of Thirteenth avenue, Christy Dowd, $1,918.35. Sewer in Forty-third street, from Lexington avenue to Fourth avenue, John Duffy, Jr., $1,918.50. Sewer in Forty-sixth street from Eleventh avenue to seventy-five feet west of Tenth avenue, John Rourke, $5,226.30. Fifty-second street sewer from Sixth to Seventh avenues, Joseph Moore, $4,830. Sewer in Twenty-fifth street to Fifth avenue, Jas. Cunningham, $22,941.56.

MRS. EMMA HARDING delivers her able lecture on "Politics in the Pulpit" this evening, at Dotworth Hall. To test the lady's ability any questions the audience desire to ask will be answered.

MAN DROWNED.—On the morning of the 13th inst. a journeyman housepainter whose name is believed to be Barnard Burns, was accidentally drowned at Guntherville, Long Island. His body had not yet been claimed by his friends. Mr. J. R. Acker, of No. 9 McDonald street, will give facilities to anyone who can identify the corpse.

Major Henry Rathbone, and his fiancée Clara Harris to accompany Mrs. Lincoln and himself to the theatre that night. The two accepted.

IT WAS Good Friday, and, after the fact, the timing of this tragedy was not lost upon those who felt that, as surely as Christ, Lincoln was a martyr to a just and good cause whose enemies would stop at nothing. The Presidential party arrived late, and the performance was stopped for the playing of "Hail to the Chief" by the small theatre orchestra. Ford's Theater was a small place, and the Presidential box was close to the stage. The exhausted President could be near to the action, but, in his rocking chair, could be hidden enough to nod off now and then.

Meanwhile, Booth was downing two brandies at a nearby bar. They were invigorating enough to raise his courage to the threshold of action. Shortly before 10 p.m., he entered Ford's Theater. No sentries were posted outside, despite the fact that Lincoln had received 80 letters in the last week threatening him with mortal harm. He had asked for, but had been denied, a special guard that night. Partway through the performance, his personal guard, John Parker, had become bored with his assignment outside the Presidential box and had wandered off to a nearby saloon.

Lincoln's First Lady, Mary Todd Lincoln

ALL WAS going inordinately, almost eerily, well for John Wilkes Booth. He knew the play well. He was aware that the Brother Jonathan character, the American cousin who could outwit, with his native intelligence, any foreign nobleman in a trice, and whose chin-whiskered countenance would one day become the model for Uncle Sam, would garner the most applause and the greatest abundance of laughs. That would be the moment to fire on the President. The audience reaction would cover the report of his revolver when he fired it.

Booth bided his time until Brother Jonathan entered the scene. Then, as the laughter of the audience rose in a comforting wave, he entered the Presidential box. In his left hand, he held a dagger. In his right was a derringer pistol. He aimed it at the President, and squeezed the trigger.

His aim was accurate. The ball entered Lincoln's head from the back, traversed the brain, and lodged behind his right eye. He slumped forward without a sound. Henry Rathbone, hearing the shot, rose from his seat, and the wild-eyed Booth charged the Major with his dagger, slashing his arm to the bone. Booth now leaped to the edge of the Presidential box and vaulted from it, but his right spur caught on the red, white and blue bunting draped over the front of the box, and he landed with a thud on the stage, breaking his left leg. Rousing himself, he shouted his epithet and limped into the wing and through the stage door to escape into the street.

The bleeding and dying President was carried across Tenth Street to a boarding house, where he was laid diagonally across a bed—he was too tall to lie normally in it—and where his not altogether stable wife Mary Todd Lincoln implored him to speak to her.

MEANWHILE, across Washington, Booth's accomplice, Lewis Powell/Paine talked his way into Secretary Seward's house, by claiming to be delivering medicine to the Secretary who was recovering from a carriage accident. Encountering Seward's son on the staircase, he bludgeoned him with the butt of his gun, fracturing his skull. Then, he forced his way into the Secretary's bedroom, and stabbed him repeatedly. The Secretary's daughter Fanny and a male nurse dragged him away from the bed, but he smashed them against the wall, and staggered out into the upstairs hallway, where he came upon a State Department messenger named Hansell. He plunged his knife into the startled man, who fell to the carpet, then he dashed into the street, crying, "I'm mad! I'm mad!"

Both Seward and his son would recover from their wounds; Hansell would die.

In another part of Washington, George Atzerodt, given the task of killing Vice President Johnson, lost his nerve and failed to act.

IN THE boarding house on Tenth Street, the President's life slowly ebbed, as the members of the cabinet gathered, first unofficially, then officially around the deathbed. At 7:22 a.m., April 15, 1865, he quietly died. He simply stopped breathing, and to those who were there, it seemed that his face settled into its first peaceful expression in four years.

"Now he belongs to the ages," said Secretary Stanton, as silver dollars were placed on the President's eyes. In his pocket, Lincoln had been carrying nine newspaper clippings and a five-dollar Confederate bill.

It was a cold, wet day, and Lincoln's covered body was taken first to the East Room of the White House, then placed on display in the Capital Rotunda. It would take his funeral train 12 days to make the 1,622 mile trip from Washington to Springfield, Illinois, where, on May 4th, he would arrive home. For a while, his body would lie in state in the St. Louis state house, where, four years earlier, Lincoln had proclaimed, "A house divided against itself cannot stand." Finally, he was laid to rest in Oakridge cemetery.

Mary Todd Lincoln did not accompany the President's body to Illinois. She never recovered from the assassination; ultimately, her son Robert would commit her to a mental institution, where she would spend the rest of her life.

On April 26th, John Wilkes Booth was cornered in a Virginia tobacco barn by army regulars, who set fire to the barn while he was in it. Shot in the neck as he was flushed out of the barn, he raised both hands, muttered, "Useless, useless," and died.

On July 7th, all of the accomplices, including Mary Suratt, who was probably only guilty of owning the house in which the conspirators met, were executed in the courtyard of the old penitentiary building in Washington.

ANDREW JOHNSON would assume the Presidency, and become embroiled in horrendous political battles with radical Republicans, led by Secretary Stanton. An effort to impeach him failed by one vote, but his power was sapped, and repressive measures were instituted against the South.

All of this lent credence to the often-uttered but never proved theory that John Wilkes Booth's conspiracy was more far-reaching than his band of ten. Secretary of War Stanton, it was speculated, backed by Northern big-business interests, masterminded the plot to kill Lincoln before he could put into practice his gentle ideas of Reconstruction. The objectives of this supposed plot were carried out as Northern businessmen ruthlessly exploited the South, once Johnson had been silenced. But, as with the conspiracy theories put forth 98 years later, after the assassination of President John F. Kennedy (see page 84) nothing was officially proven.

IT WAS the first Presidential assassination in the United States. It would not be the last, but it would be one of the most tragic. Under Lincoln's guidance, a large portion of the people of America had ceased saying "The United States are. . ." and begun saying "The United States is. . ." Under his future guidance, the nation might have healed itself. When his moral leadership was no longer available, corruption prevented this. True Civil Rights for all would have to wait another hundred years for realization, and even then, they would come with qualifications.

TICKET OFFICE
LADIES ONLY

JAMES A. GARFIELD

POSITION:	*President of the United States*
DATE:	*July 2, 1881*
PLACE:	*Washington, D.C.*
HOW:	*Gunshot*
WHO:	*Charles J. Guiteau*
CONVICTED:	*Yes. Hanged on June 30, 1882*
MOTIVES:	*Divine inspiration; refusal of appointment*
DIRECT CONSEQUENCE:	*Creation of a federal appointments system*

THE summer of 1881 was a usual Washington summer: hot, fetid, humid, and impossible; the sort of summer that convinced those who could that Washington was a place to vacate between June and September. And that was just what James A. Garfield was about to do when he entered the ladies' waiting room of the Baltimore & Peconic Railroad Depot at Constitution Avenue and Sixth Street on the afternoon of Saturday, June 18, 1881. He would never make his train. Before he and his company could clear the waiting room, he would be felled by a bullet in the back, fired by Charles J. Guiteau, a probably insane writer-editor-lawyer-evangelist-swindler, who fancied that he had been unjustly denied both an ambassadorship to Austria and a consularship to Paris.

No assassin in U.S. history left a paper trail as specific and extensive as Guiteau; no one was more peculiar, preposterous, or paranoid than he. And yet, he shared the conviction with Lincoln's assassin, John Wilkes Booth, that he was God's hired killer, and with McKinley's murderer, Joseph Czolgosz, that the country would be infinitely better off as a result of his actions.

"His [Garfield's] removal is an act of God . . . it was the Deity's act, not mine," testified Guiteau before the jury that eventually convicted him.

DARK complected, bearded and short, possessing gray-blue eyes, dirty blonde hair and a piercing expression, Guiteau carried his five foot five, 125-pound girth lightly and softly, as if he were born to dance, rob, or sneak up on someone. He was born in Freeport, Illinois, the third of three children, on September 8, 1841, to a family that was steeped, thanks to the father, in the teachings of the Reverend John H. Noyes, the leader of the Oneida Community.

This collective farm, located outside of Oneida, New York, preached that Jesus Christ had already been reborn in the year 70 A.D., and that all believers, especially those who dwelled in the Community, could join Christ now. Oneida was the beginning of the heavenly kingdom, a place of prayer and what he termed "complex marriages"—in other words, free love.

Luther Guiteau, Charles' father, was considered by his Illinois colleagues merely eccentric, particularly when he went on about his immortality, but he may have been more—or less—than that. A brother, a niece, and a nephew ended up in insane asylums, and there was some official discussion about the sanity of two of his sisters.

Charles, the inheritor of some of this, enrolled in college after high school, but soon abandoned it and went to live in the Oneida Community. There he became convinced, as he wrote to his father, ". . . that I am in the employ of *Jesus Christ & Co.*, the very ablest and strongest firm in the universe, and that what I can do is limited only by their power and purpose."

He moved to New York, tried, unsuccessfully, to start a chain of religious newspapers, retreated again to Oneida, and swindled those in charge out of enough money to send him back to New York and then to Chicago, where he became a debt-collection lawyer. There he met and married 16-year-old Annie Bunn, with whom he embarked on a five-year binge of renting apartments and then leaving just before the rent came due. In 1874, Annie divorced him, charging adultery. He confessed that he had used her money to entertain prostitutes, one of whom had given him syphilis.

Guiteau now became interested in politics. His first plan was to support Horace Greeley for President, after which he would apply for and

THE DAILY DISPATCH.
MYERS & BRICKELL, Publishers and Proprietors.

Largest Daily Circulation in Columbus.

Office, No. 26 North High Street.

TERMS:—15 cents a week; 65 cents a month, and $7.00 a year.

Columbus Evening Dispatch.

VOL. XI.---NO. 70. COLUMBUS, O., TUESDAY, SEPTEMBER 20, 1881. PRICE THREE CENTS.

THIRD EDITION.

MOURNING

The Death of Our Heroic President.

The Nation Clothes Itself in Sackcloth and Ashes

AND CRIES TO HEAVEN FOR THE MEANING

Of This Saddest of Sad Dispensations

Which Have Been Visited Upon Our Country;

THEN BOWS ITS HEAD IN SAD SUBMISSION

To the Will of Him Who Rules the Universe

And Who Doeth All Things Wisely and Well.

Tearful Preparations for Performing the Last Rites

Over the Body of Our Second Martyr Chief,

Whose Name Will Be Handed Down to Posterity

With Those of Washington and the Murdered Lincoln.

THE RECEIPT OF THE SAD NEWS AT VARIOUS POINTS.

Spirit of the Press and People at the National Bereavement.

The Closing Moments of the President's Life.

NEW YORK, Sept. 20.—The *Times'* Long [illegible]

FOURTH EDITION.

THE NATION'S DEAD.

PREPARATIONS FOR THE RECEPTION AT THE CAPITAL.

Putting the Capitol and the White House in Readiness—Orders to Army and Navy—Guiteau Informed of the President's Death—Talk About the Incoming Administration—Will the Senate be Convened?—Opinions of Certain Senators.

WASHINGTON, Sept 20.—At the Executive Mansion, this morning, Assistant Private Secretary Pruden was found arranging in convenient shape all the private papers of the deceased President. A dispatch from Private Secretary Brown stated that the party composing the President's household would leave Long Branch to-morrow morning. It is not definitely known whether the remains will be brought to the Executive Mansion or taken directly from the depot to the Capitol. The annual summer house cleaning has been in progress for some time at the Mansion, and furniture, carpets, chandeliers, etc., have nearly all been removed for renovation. Strenuous efforts are now being made to restore the apartments to receive members of the household to-morrow.

The news of President Garfield's death reached the city about 11 o'clock last evening, through the simple announcement by the Associated Press, "The President is dead." In an incredibly short time the sad tidings were borne [illegible]

THE FOREST CITY.

Preparations for the Burial—The City in Mourning.

CLEVELAND, Sept. 20.—An impromptu meeting of citizens was held this forenoon in the Mayor's office, at which preliminary steps were taken toward arrangements for the expected reception of the President's remains. Committees were appointed, and a general meeting will be held this afternoon. Hon. Amos Townsend, member of Congress for this district, was delegated to go immediately to Long Branch, to place himself in communication with the Government authorities and correspond with the committees here. Mr. Townsend left by the first train after the meeting.

The City Council met this forenoon and adopted memorial resolutions and appointed committees to co-operate with the Mayor in whatever may be necessary for paying the final respects to the country's honored dead. Column rules of all the newspapers are reversed and broad black lines stripe every page. J K Emmett, starring at the Euclid Opera House, terminated his engagement immediately on learning of the President's death.

The following telegram was sent, to-day, for the Trustees of Lakeview Cemetery as foreshadowed in last night's report:

Mrs. J. A. Garfield, Elberon, Long Branch:

In behalf of the Trustees, we tender you ground in Lakeview Cemetery for the burial of our lamented President, such as you or your friends may select.

JOSEPH PERKINS,
J. H. WADE,
H. B HAYNE,
SELAH CHAMBERLAIN,
P. A. BABCOCK,
WM. BINGHAM, Ex. Com.

This was supplemented by the following, sent by the Mayor of Cleveland to-day:

To Mrs James A. Garfield, Long Branch, New Jersey:

The people of this city who have borne such love and honor to your husband most sincerely and earnestly desire that his grave may be made here among us. Allow me, dear madam, to add to this publicly expressed desire of our citizens my own personal and official concurrence.

R. R. HERRICK, Mayor.

All the military and Masonic organizations of the city and adjacent county have tendered to Mayor Herrick their [illegible]

[illegible]

...evening, were fatally shot by George Pease, the alleged husband of the former. The cause was jealousy. The murderer was arrested.

The Mrs Garfield Fund.

NEW YORK, Sept. 20.—Brown Brothers, this morning, sent a contribution of $5,000 to the fund for Mrs Garfield.

Maritime.

NEW YORK, Sept. 20.—Arrived—Arabia, from Liverpool.

receive the post of Minister to Chile. The plan was aborted when Greeley died.

He then embarked on a career of evangelism, selling insurance, and writing, producing a book entitled *The Truth: A Companion to the Bible*. It was partially to promote this book, he would tell a courtroom three years later, that he killed James A. Garfield, the President of the United States.

GARFIELD, born on November 19, 1831, in Cuyahoga County, Ohio, pursued a career in politics and public life that began immediately after his graduation from college. In 1859, after working dedicatedly for the Republican Party, he was elected to the Ohio state legislature. Young enough to fight in the Civil War, he served as a General in the Union Army, and in 1863 was elected to the United States House of Representatives as a Republican congressman from Ohio.

In August of 1880, both he and Guiteau found themselves in New York, at the old Fifth Avenue Hotel, at a Republican rally designed to patch up differences between the Stalwarts and the Half-Breeds, the two warring factions within the party.

Garfield had been nominated by the Republicans that summer during a bruising convention. He had gone to it as campaign manager for John Sherman, but the wars between the Stalwarts, who were against civil-service reform and the acceptance of the South as part of the Union, and the Half-Breeds, who favored civil-service reform and the treatment of the South as a part of the Union, resulted in a marathon of speeches and 36 ballots. On the 36th ballot, Garfield received the nomination. He was a compromise candidate who leaned, almost imperceptibly, toward the Half-Breeds. It was to patch up the differences between these two groups that the August rally in New York was scheduled.

Guiteau had written a speech for General Grant, whom the Stalwarts had originally nominated for a third term, but he managed to change its title to "Garfield Against Hancock" (W.S. Hancock was the Democratic candidate) in time to distribute it in the lobby of the Fifth Avenue Hotel in August. The speech was largely a diatribe against the South which proclaimed *Uncle Tom's Cabin* a "matchless work of fiction."

Even before Garfield was elected President, Guiteau lobbied on the strength of the speech for an ambassadorship to Austria. Failing at that, he managed to insinuate himself in March of 1881 into a crowd of jobseekers at the White House (in those times, the President dispensed jobs much like royalty had before him), and managed to press a copy of the oration, signed and with two words, "Paris consulship" added to it, into President Garfield's hand.

Nothing, of course, happened. Guiteau nevertheless persisted, bombarding the White House and State Department with visits and letters. He sent off a copy of the speech to Secretary of State Blaine, with a note that stated unequivocally and inaccurately, ". . . this speech . . . was about the first shot in the rebel war claim idea, and it was the idea that elected General Garfield."

By May, Guiteau had become enough of an annoyance to be barred from the White House. It did not keep him from haunting Blaine in the corridors of the State Department until the Secretary finally shouted at him, "Never speak to me again about the Paris consulship as long as you live!"

Meanwhile, Garfield was having troubles within the Republican Party. Two New York senators, both strong Stalwarts, resigned in protest over his handling of a customs nomination. Wounded by constant rejection and out of funds, Guiteau seized upon this news as proof positive that Garfield was leading the country toward destruction, and should be destroyed himself.

HE RETREATED to room 222 of the Rigg House, an inexpensive hotel in Washington, to pray, and on May 18, at about 8 o'clock in the evening, according to his later trial testimony, he was visited by God, who urged him both to save the Republic and to publicize his book *The Truth*.

On June 6, he entered John U. O'Meara's gunshop at the corner of Fifteenth and F Streets, and inquired about a handsome revolver on display in the window. It was a self-cocking, .44 caliber British bulldog with a white bone handle.

On June 8, he returned to the shop with $15 he had borrowed from his cousin, Washington electrician George Maynard. He purchased, for $10, the revolver, a box of cartridges, and, for some reason known only to him, a woman's penknife.

He was totally unschooled in firearms; this was the first revolver he had ever held, much less owned. The shopowner showed him how to load it, and suggested he try it out in a wood bordering the Potomac. Guiteau followed his advice.

The following Sunday, President Garfield attended the National City Christian Church, on Vermont Avenue, and Guiteau, carrying the loaded revolver, stood at the rear of the church. "I could not think of a more sacred place for removing him than while he was at his devotions," he would testify later, but for some reason, he failed to translate the thought into action.

On June 16, Guiteau sat down at his desk in the Rigg House and wrote an imaginary speech to be given to the American people. It concluded, "In the President's madness he has wrecked the once grand old Republican party, and for this he dies."

The following day, Washington newspapers noted that the President and his wife would be traveling to Long Branch, New Jersey that afternoon. Guiteau determined that he would shoot the President before he boarded the train. But, again according to his testimony, "Mrs. Garfield looked so thin, and she clung so tenderly to the President's arm that I did not have the heart to fire on him."

Several other opportunities came and went, and Guiteau let them drift by. He decided not to kill the President when he returned to Washington alone from Long Branch because the day was too hot and sultry. He followed Garfield and Secretary Blaine during an evening stroll from the White House to Blaine's house and back, but "I felt tired and wearied by the heat, so nothing was done about it then," he recalled.

But the next morning, Saturday, July 2, 1881, was different. Apparently revived, he rose at 5 a.m., took a leisurely walk, returned to the Rigg House for breakfast, went up to his room, stuffed the revolver into his hip pocket, picked up a package which contained his meticulously prepared autobiography, the speech to the American people, a note which bequeathed the revolver and the package's contents to the State Department Library, a note granting the *New York Herald* permission to serialize his book *The Truth*, and a copy of the book. Guiteau included finally an encapsulating, and highly materialistic, note. It linked the proposed assassination with directions from God, and concluded:

> I am clear in my purpose to remove the President. Two points will be accomplished. It will save the Republic, and it will create a demand for my book, The Truth. See page 10. This book was not written for money. It was written to save souls. In order to attract public attention the book needs the notice the President's removal will give it.
>
> C. G.

Meanwhile, across Washington, the President, weary after his first four months in office, was preparing to leave on a vacation that would take him on a yachting trip up the Hudson and on land to his alma mater, Williams College, where he was to deliver the commencement address. Ironically, the parlor car that would take him out of Washington was number 222—the same number as that on the door of Guiteau's room at the Rigg House.

Garfield left the White House at 9 a.m., in a State Department coupé, accompanied by Secretary Blaine. His sons followed in a White House carriage. At 9:20, the President arrived at the Baltimore & Potomac Depot. He and Blaine chose to enter through the ladies' waiting room.

In a corner of the room, wearing a black coat, black vest, black trousers, and a broad-brimmed black felt hat pulled low over his eyes, stood Charles Guiteau. The President and Blaine strode through the waiting room, and had almost reached its far door, when Guiteau stepped from behind a bench, reached into his pocket for the revolver, crossed the waiting room to within a few feet of the President, and fired.

"My God, what is this?" asked the President, breathlessly, and staggered forward. The bullet had entered his back, fracturing his 11th and 12th ribs, then pierced the backbone, smashing the first lumbar vertebra, and severing a major artery before it came to rest behind his pancreas.

Guiteau rushed closer and fired again. The second bullet went wide, drilling a hole in the President's sleeve. Garfield collapsed on the floor, and Guiteau sprinted for the exit, where a hack he had hired from an unsuspecting cabbie waited for him. But he was wrestled to a bench by Patrick Kearney, a Washington policeman. Guiteau went limp. "It's all right. Keep quiet, my friend," he told the policeman. "I wish to go to jail. Now Arthur is President of the United States. I am a Stalwart of Stalwarts." He reached into his pocket and handed the bewildered policeman a letter to General William Tecumsah Sherman, Commander of the Army, warning him to dispatch troops to the jail to

The White House draped in black, in mourning for President Garfield

prevent civil violence. A shouting crowd menaced the policeman and his prisoner, but did nothing. Guiteau was rushed to the Washington jail and thrown into a cell recently vacated by a grave-robber.

BACK AT the depot, the President, who was saved from bleeding to death by the natural formation of an aneurysm at the severed spot in his artery, was bundled into a hastily summoned, horse-drawn ambulance. The ambulance returned him to the White House, where Robert Todd Lincoln, his Secretary of War, no doubt flooded with horrible memories, exclaimed "My God, how many hours of sorrow I have passed in this town!"

The President had a restless night, but by morning, he seemed to rally. To counteract the continuing Washington heat, an air-cooling machine, in which air was passed through an iron chamber containing 3,000 feet of Turkish toweling saturated with water dripping from granulated ice and salt, was trundled into the White House. A fan drew the cooled air into an ice chamber, where it was dried, then purified with charcoal and finally blown through a flue that carried it to the President's bedroom.

Alexander Graham Bell, the inventor of the telephone, was brought in with his "induction balance," a sort of 19th-century land mine detector, which located the bullet in the President's body. No attempt was made by his doctors—who included Dr. Joseph K. Barnes, who had attended to President Lincoln's wounds—to extract it.

Bulletins cascaded from the White House. Special editions of major newspapers constantly informed the public about the President's condition. He continued to improve, and the country breathed more easily. Then, on July 23, his temperature escalated sharply to 104 degrees. Gloom settled over the White House and the nation. Then, the President rallied again. By August 10, he was strong enough to resume some of his official duties, signing papers from his bed. But the remainder of the summer would be spent in a disturbing series of crises and recoveries, all of which took their toll on the steadily weakening

Garfield. By September, his weight had fallen from over 200 pounds to 130. On September 6, his doctors gave in to the President's pleas and permitted a move to Elberon. In this small settlement on the New Jersey shore near Long Branch, a British citizen, Charles G. Francklyn, would open his 24-room home to Garfield.

Special preparations were made to smooth the journey. Intersections on the horsecar tracks on Pennsylvania Avenue were covered with sawdust. A railroad siding at the depot was extended to the street, in order that the horse-drawn Adams Express Wagon that would carry Garfield in his bed need not rattle him over the cobble-stone street by the depot. In the train, Garfield was loaded onto heavy springs in a special, screened, air-cooled car. Orders were telegraphed along the route to silence all bells and whistles, and a special pilot engine was sent ahead to clear the tracks of all other trains.

Garfield's assassin, Charles J. Guiteau

Seven hours and 250 miles later, the train pulled up, on a temporary spur, to the Francklyn estate. It was cool; water breezes and the onset of autumn made the President's bedroom eminently liveable. He rested comfortably for a little over two weeks. And then, on the morning of September 19, he woke with an ominous chill.

His strength seemed to visibly diminish as the day progressed. He fell asleep at 10 p.m., and then he woke with a horrendous pain just above his heart. The aneurysm had broken, and by 10:35, he was dead.

From the time he arrived in jail until the beginning of his trial, on November 14, 1881, Charles Guiteau busily wrote. His magnum opus during those days was a new but unfinished book: *The Life and Theology of Charles Guiteau. Prepared by Himself.* Life in jail was not without its dangers. One of the men assigned to guard him shot at him through the window of his cell and grazed his head; a drunk fired at him when he was being brought back to his cell from the courtroom. By and large, how-ever, Guiteau seemed to enjoy his notoriety.

He alternately scolded the court and sang to it, while his lawyers mounted an insanity defense. He told the jury, "To hang a man in my mental condition . . . would be a lasting disgrace to the American people. Let your verdict be that it was the Deity's act, not mine." This peroration he followed by singing the first line of "John Brown's Body" and then reciting the rest. The prosecution was scarcely better. It introduced in evidence the bullet-punctured backbone of the assassinated President, and allowed it to be passed from hand to hand through the jury and the rest of the court, including Guiteau.

On January 25, 1882, the jury found the assassin both sane and guilty. Guiteau leaped to his feet, while bedlam overtook the courtroom. "My blood will be on the heads of that jury, don't you forget it!" he caterwauled. "That is my answer! God will avenge this outrage!" Guiteau put together his last will and testament, in which he suggested a monument be raised to him with the inscription, "Here lies the body of Charles Guiteau, Patriot and Christian. His soul is in glory."

Nearly 4,000 people crowded the streets outside the jail on June 30, 1882, the day of his execution. Lemonade and cake were sold at hastily erected stands, and business was brisk.

Two hundred and fifty people were let into the

prison courtyard to witness the hanging. Guiteau, shoes shined and hair freshly combed, was led to the scaffold at 12:27 p.m. Verbal to the end, he recited a prayer which ended, "I therefore predict that this nation will go down in blood and that my murderers from the Executive to the hangman will go to hell."

Then, while the hangman made his preparations, Guiteau recited a poem that he said would have sounded better put to music. It would be, a little over a hundred years later, when Stephen Sondheim added notes to its words in his musical *Assassins*:

I am going to the Lordy;
I am so glad.
I am going to the Lordy;
I am so glad.
I am going to the Lordy,
Glory Hallelujah! Glory Hallelujah!
I am going to the Lordy . . .
I wonder what I will do when I get to the
Lordy?
I guess that I will weep no more when I get to
the Lordy.
Glory Hallelujah!
I wonder what I will see when I get to the
Lordy?
I expect to see most splendid things beyond
all earthly conception
When I am with the Lordy, Glory Hallelujah!

The trap door was sprung at 12:40 p.m. Guiteau's last words, uttered from beneath his black hood, were "Glory, glory, glory . . ."

THERE WAS no glory day for the Stalwarts. President Chester Arthur worked diligently to prod Congress into authorizing the Half-Breed concept of the creation of the Civil Service Commission.

It came into being in 1883, two years too late to prevent men like Guiteau from petitioning a President personally for a government position, and then exacting a bloody revenge, when ambition was disappointed.

WILLIAM MCKINLEY

POSITION:	*President of the USA*
DATE:	*September 5, 1901*
PLACE:	*Buffalo, New York*
HOW:	*Gunshot*
WHO:	*Leon Czolgosz*
CONVICTED:	*Yes. Executed in the electric chair*
MOTIVE:	*Anarchism*
DIRECT CONSEQUENCE:	*Theodore Roosevelt reverses McKinley's programs*

ANARCHISM flourished at the beginning of the 20th century. A theory that freedom can only be achieved through the total abolition of the state and the substitution of free agreements between individuals, it dates back to Zeno of Citum, the founder of Stoic philosophy. It remained mostly the property of philosophers until its practitioners put it to violent use in late 19th-century Russia, in the assassination of King Humbert I on July 29, 1900, in Monza, Italy, and in the eruption of anti-anarchist fever in America in the 1920s, which ultimately, in 1927, led to the twin executions of Sacco and Vanzetti, two Italian anarchists linked by circumstantial evidence to the murder of a bank guard in a holdup in Braintree, Massachusetts.

After Humbert's assassination, there was talk of an anarchist plot to kill world leaders, including President McKinley. No such plot was unearthed, and despite the fact that Leon Czolgosz, McKinley's assassin, was an anarchist, and claimed American anarchist Emma Goldman as his inspiration, there was no evidence that he acted in consort with other anarchists. Till the moment of his execution, Czolgosz would assert that he acted alone.

MCKINLEY was a President who accomplished much, particularly in the field of foreign affairs. A native of Niles, Ohio, he served in the Union Army during the Civil War, and entered Congress as a Republican in 1872. His policies were always staunchly conservative, and thus attracted the attention of the powerful financier and politician Marcus A. Hanna, who controlled the Ohio Republican machine, and whose efforts were considered largely responsible for securing the Republican Presidential nomination for McKinley in 1896.

The Democrats that year went into a radical mode and nominated William Jennings Bryan on a silver-standard platform. McKinley, running on a platform of the gold standard and high tariffs, won handily.

Once in office, he turned his attention to foreign affairs. The Spanish American War was fought in his Presidency, and it was with this that the United States is generally considered to have entered the world arena as a world power. As a result of it, McKinley demanded and received the Philippines for the U.S., and later annexed Hawaii and made Cuba an American protectorate. His Open Door Policy to China further raised the prestige and power of the United States, and he won reelection easily in 1900.

HOWEVER, fate and the determination of one man, fired by Emma Goldman's words, cut short this term and opened the door for the colorful Presidency of Theodore Roosevelt, who was Vice President under McKinley.

Sometime in 1901, 29-year-old Leon Czolgosz (pronounced "Colgosh"), born in Detroit and the son of Russian-Polish parents, attended a lecture by the young, charismatic and feverish anarchist Emma Goldman. "Her doctrine that all rulers should be exterminated was what set me to thinking so my head nearly split with the pressure," confessed Czolgosz in mid-September, after shooting the President. "Miss Goldman's words went right through me, and when I left the lecture I had made up my mind that I would have to do something heroic for the cause I loved."

At the end of August, while in Chicago, the potential assassin read that President McKinley would be attending the Pan American Exposition in Buffalo. Czolgosz went to Buffalo, rented a room in a rooming house over a saloon, and waited. On

Tuesday, September 3, he bought a .32 caliber Iver Johnson pistol with an owl's head stamped on either side of its handle, and went to the exposition grounds with a plan in mind to kill the President as he left his private railroad car. The police moved the crowds back far enough to prevent Czolgosz from getting close enough to shoot.

On Wednesday, September 4, the murderer was able to lose himself in a crowd listening to the President's speech, but again, he was forced to stand too far from McKinley to get off an accurate shot.

Finally, on the afternoon of September 5, it was announced that the President would hold an audience in the Temple of Music, a white stucco palace that stood between the Fountain of Abundance and the Court of Lilies. The building was the apotheosis of World's Fair architecture at its most realized: an ornate octagonal gilded dome trimmed in green was its signature; busts of the great composers resided over the tinted windows of its facade; sculpted groupings of muses adorned the space above its massive doors.

McKinley delivered a short speech in the open air, near the fountain, and then entered the Temple for a 10-minute audience with the public. He was scheduled to leave for Cleveland the next morning to attend a Grand Army of the Republic encampment. The doors to the Temple of Music were flung open at 4 p.m. Czolgosz joined the surge of people who were quickly formed into a double line. As an organ recital ended and the President mounted a palm-appointed, flag-draped dais at one end of the building, the assassin drew out his pistol and wrapped it and his hand in a white handkerchief.

THE PRESIDENT had been warned repeatedly by his aides that there was a risk of assassination. The shooting of King Humbert was, rumors had it, the opening volley in a series of anarchist killings, and McKinley was their next, obvious target. The day before his appearance in Buffalo, his secretary, George B. Cortelyou had pleaded with him merely to speak, and cancel the reception.

"Why should I?" replied the President. "No one would wish to hurt me."

Nevertheless, nearly 50 guards—federal, state, and city—were stationed at various positions around the Temple of Music that afternoon. But it was a hot and humid day, and there was much mopping of brows with handkerchiefs on the line of well-wishers. Not only that. A man several places ahead of Czolgosz had a bandaged right hand. The handkerchief-wrapped revolver faded into a sea of white.

He moved forward. The throng pressed in on the President, who was smiling congenially and shaking hands. On one side of him stood John G. Milburn, the president of the exposition. Surrounding him in a semi-circle were secret service agents.

The double line inched ahead, then funneled into a single line. Czolgosz approached the dais. Secret service agents George Foster and Samuel R. Ireland were closest to the President. They were not the eagle-eyed agents of today; that genre would develop after the events of that afternoon in Buffalo. But still, these two men were watchful, and Ireland, who thought that Czolgosz was suffering from a burned hand, placed his own hand on the assassin's shoulder as he approached the President. His purpose was to steady the man and move him forward, once he had shaken hands with the Chief Executive.

THE PRESIDENT smiled and extended his hand. But Czolgosz never took it. Instead, he flung the President's hand aside, raised the handkerchief-concealed gun, and fired twice, hitting McKinley once in the chest and once in the abdomen. The President started, turned pale, and backed up into a chair. Instantly, eight men dived on top of Czolgosz, bearing him to the ground, and wrestling the gun from him. The handkerchief had been set on fire by the shot, and one of the secret service men burned his hand on it. Now Czolgosz was catapulted to his feet, and Foster floored him with a left to the nose. Soldiers and secret service men pounced on the prostrate assassin, beating him with fists and gun butts. One soldier reversed his rifle and was about to run Czolgosz through with his bayonet. But the white and gasping President cried out, "Be easy with him, boys!"

The crowd began to panic. Guards cleared the hall while the secret service men hustled the assassin to a small room to the side of the dais. There, he was thrown onto a table, and again beaten, repeatedly. "We thumped him and slapped his face," James Parker, a waiter who had helped to collar Czolgosz later testified. "I took a knife out of my pocket and started to cut his throat, but he

SECOND EDITION **The Wichita Daily Eagle.**

VOLUME XXXV. WICHITA, KANSAS: SATURDAY MORNING, SEPTEMBER 7, 1901. NUMBER 96

PRESIDENT M'KINLEY SHOT DOWN BY AN ANARCHIST IN BUFFALO

One Bullet Perforates Both Walls of the Stomach and Disappears---The Other Makes Only Flesh Wound.

HIS CONDITION VERY SERIOUS, BUT THERE IS HOPE

Both Holes in Stomach Are Closed by Stitches, With No Drainage, by the Surgeon.

CZOLGOCZ THE ASSASSIN, APPROACHES TO SHAKE HANDS AND THEN FIRES

Surrounding Crowd at the Reception Pounces Upon Him and Holds Him Down---He Narrowly Escapes Lynching---His Interview ---President Falls and Asks If He Is Shot---Removed to Hospital---Shows Great Calmness and Courage---Mrs. McKinley Not Notified at First but Later Is Told and Shows Courage---Nation Bowed in Grief ---The News at Washington---Expressions From the World---Details of the Awful Crime.

Buffalo, Sept. 7.—The president's physician issued the following bulletin at 5 o'clock:

"The president is free from pain and resting well. Temperature 100.2; pulse 120; respiration 24."

Chicago, Sept. 6.—Five anarchists were arrested here tonight on information from Buffalo. One of the five is Abraham Isekk.

Buffalo, Sept. 6.—President McKinley was shot and seriously wounded by a would-be assassin while holding a reception in the Temple of Music at the Pan-American grounds a few minutes after 4 o'clock this afternoon. One shot took effect in the right breast, the other in the abdomen. The first is not of a serious nature, and the bullet has been extracted. The latter pierced the abdominal wall and has not been located.

:40 p. m., the following bulletin attending physicians was the only on of the condition of the presi- wounds:

president is rallying and is rest- .mfortably. At 10:15 p. m., tem- re 100.1 degres; pulse 124, respira- 24. (Signed.)

"P. M. RIXEY.
"M. B. MANN.
"R. PARKEE.
"H. MYNTER.
'EUGENE WANBIN."

(Countersigned.)
"GEORGE B. CORTELYOU,

The assailant was immediately arrested and was thrown to the ground and quick as a flash twenty men were upon him. When rescued he was covered with blood from a gash in his face.

Lynch Him, Lynch Him" Is the Cry.

Cries of lynching were heard in every direction, but the police managed to get the man out of the grounds and locked him up in a station house a short distance from the grounds. Later he was removed to police headquarters. Detective Geary was near the president and the president fell into his arms.

shot?" asked the president. cer opened the president's vest g blood replied: "Yes, I am u are, Mr. President."

dent Under Doctors' Care.

sident was at once taken to the y hospital where a bullet which ed against the breast bone was Later the president was re- resting easily. clock Dr. Roswell Parkee, the wn surgeon arrived at the hos- after putting the president un- anesthetic began probing for the the abdomen.

risoner declares he is Fred Nie- Detroit. When arrested he was why he had shot the president, "I am an anarchist and have y duty." he denied to a police official that an anarchist.

CKEST DAY IN HISTORY"

lo Is Wild With Surging Multitudes Thronging Streets.

falo, Sept. 6.—Just a brief 24 hours ago the newspapers of the city blazoned forth in all the pomp in headline type: "The Proudest Day in Buffalo's History." Tonight, in sackcloth and ashes, in sombre type, surrounded by gruesome borders in black, the same newspapers are telling in funeral tones a horrified populace the deplorable details of "The Blackest Day in the History of Buffalo."

President McKinley, the idol of the American people, the nation's chief executive and the city's honored guest, lies prostrate, suffering pangs inflicted by the bullet of a cowardly assassin, while his life hangs in the balance.

Mrs. McKinley Shows Fortitude

Out on Delaware avenue, at the home of John G. Milburn, president of the Pan-American exposition, with tearful face and heart torn by conflicting hopes and fears, sits the faithful wife, whose devotion is known to all the nation.

SHORTLY AFTER 4 O'CLOCK

President Attacked by Crowd While Receiving in Temple of Music.

It was a few minutes after 4 p. m., while President McKinley was holding a public reception in the great temple of music on the Pan-American grounds, that the cowardly attack was made—with what success time alone can tell.

Standing in the midst of crowds numbering thousands, surrounded by every evidence of good will, pressed by a motley throng of people, showered with expressions of love and loyalty, besieged by multitudes, all eager to clasp his hands; amid these surroundings, with the ever recurring plaudits of an army of sight seers ringing in his ears, the blow of the assassin fell, and in an instant pleasure gave way to pain, admiration to agony, folly turned to fury and pandemonium followed.

Tonight a surging, swaying, eager multitude throngs the city's main thoroughfares, choking the streets in front of the principal newspapers, scanning the bulletins with anxious eyes and groaning or cheering in turn at each succeeding announcement, as th enature of the message sinks or buoys their hopes.

ASSASSIN COMMON LOOKING

Presses His Lips Together and Assumes an Air of Indifference.

Down at police headquarters, surrounded by stern faced inquisitors of the law, is a medium sized man of commonplace appearance, with his gaze fixed direct upon the floor, who presses his lips firmly together and listens with an air of assumed indifference to the persistent stream of questions, arguments, objurgations and admonitions with which his captors seek to compel or induce him to talk.

It was just after the splendid organ recital in the splendid temple that the dastardly attempt was made.

Diabolical Plan of Horror.

Planned with all the diabolical ingenuity and finesse of which anarchy or nihilism is capable, the would-be assassin carried ou the work without a hitch, and should his designs fail and the president survive, only to Divine Providence can be attributed the beneficent result.

The president, though well guarded by United States secret service detectives, was fully exposed to such an attack as occurred. He stood at the edge of the raised dias upon which stands the great pipe organ at the east side of the magnificent structure. Throngs of people crowded in at the various entrances to gaze upon their executive, perchance to clasp his hand, and then file their way out in the good natured mob that every minute swelled and multiplied at the points of ingress and egress to the building.

The president was in a cheerful mood and was enjoyng to the full the hearty good will which everywhere met his gaze. Upon his right hand stood John G. Milburn of Buffalo, president of the Pan-American exposition, chatting with the president and introducing to him especially persons of note who approached. Upon the president's left stood Mr. Cortelyou.

DASTARDLY DEED DONE

When President Greeted Damnable Villian With Friendly Handshake.

It was shortly after 4 p. m. when one of the throng which surrounded the pdesidential party, a medium sized man of ordinary appearance and plainly dressed in black, approached as if to greet the president. Both Secretary Cortelyon and President Milburn noticed that the man's hand was swathed in a bandage or handkerchef. Reports of by-standers differ as to which hand. He worked his way amid the stream of people up to the edge of the dais until he was within two feet of the president.

President McKinley smiled, bowed and extended his hand in that spirit of congeniality the American people so well know, when suddenly the sharp crack of a revolver rang out loud and clear above the hum of voices, the shuffling of myriad feet and vibrating waves of applause that ever and anon swept here and there over the assemblage.

There was an instance of almost complete silence. The president stood stock still, a look of hesitancy, almost of bewilderment on his face. Then he retreated a step, while a pallor began to steal over his features. The multitude, only partially aware that something serious had happened, paused in surprise, while necks were craned and all eyes turned as one to the rostrum, where a great tragedy was being enacted.

Assassin is Borne to Ground.

Then came a commotion. Three men threw themselves forward, as with one impulse, and sprang toward the would-be assassin. Two of them were United States secret service men who were on the lookout, and whose duty it was to guard against just such a calamity as had here befallen the president and the nation. The third was a by-stander, a negro, who had only an instant previously grasped the hand of the president. In a twinkling the assassin was borne to the ground, his weapon was wrested from his grasp, and strong arms pinioned him down.

Crowd Awakes as From Lethargy.

Then the multitude which thronged the edifice began to come to a realizing sense of the awfulness of the second scene to which they had been unwilling witnesses. A murmur arose, spread and swelled to a hum of confusion, then grew to a babel of sounds and later to a pandemonieum of noise. The crowds that a moment before had stood mute and motionless, as in bewildered ignorance of the enormity of the thing, now with a single impulse surged forward toward the stage of the horrid drama, while a hoarse cry welled up from a thousand throats and a thousand men charged forward to lay hands upon the perpretrator of the crime.

Scene of Wild Confusion.

For a moment the confusion was terrible. The crowd serged forward regardless of consequences. Men shouted and fought, women screamed and children cried. Some of those nearest the doors fled from the edifice in fear of a stampede, while hundreds of others from the outside struggled blindly forward in the effort to penetrate the crowded building and solve the mystery of the excitement and panic which at every moment grew and swelled within the congested interior of the edifice.

Inside on the slightly raised dais was enacted within those few feverish moments a tragedy so dramatic in character, so thrilling in its intensity that few who looked on will ever be able to give a succinct account of what really did transpire. Even those who attended the president came out of it with blanched faces, trembling limbs and beating hearts, while their brains throbbed with a tulmut of conflicting emotions which could not be clarified into a lucid narrative of the events as they really transpired.

PRESIDENT ALONE CALM

With Steady Step Retires to Seat and Bows Head in Hands.

Of the multitude which witnessed or bore a part in the scene of turmoil and turbulence there was but one mind which seemed to retain its eliqubribum, one hand which remained steady, one eye which gazed with unflinching calmness and one voice which retained its even tenor and faltered not at the most critical juncture.

They were the mind and the hand and the eye and the voice of President McKinley.

After the first shock of the assassin's shot, he retreated a step. Then as the detectives leaped upon his assailant he turned, walked steadily to a chair and seated himself, at the same time removing his hat and bowing his head in his hands.

In an instant Secretary Cortelyou and President Milburn were at his side.

President Admonishes All to be Calm

His waistcoat was hurriedly opened, the president meanwhile admonishing those about him to remain calm, and telling them not to be alarmed.

"But you are wounded," cried his secretary, "let me examine."

"No, I think not," answered the president. "I am not badly hurt, I assure you."

Worst Fears are Confirmed.

Nevertheless his outer garments were hastily loosened and when a trickling stream of crimson was seen to wind its way down his breast, spreading its telltale stain over the white surface of the linen, their worst fears were confirmed.

A force of exposition guards were soon on the scene, and an effort was made to clear the building. By this time the crash was terrific. The crowd on the floor surged forward toward the rostrum, while despite the strenous efforts of the police and guards the throng struggled madly to obtain admission.

Exposition Building Is Cleared.

The president's assailant after being seized, was hustled by expositon guards to the rear of the building, where he was held while the building was cdeared, and later he was turned over to Superintendent Bull of the Buffalo police department, who took the prisoner to No. 13 police station and afterward to police headquarters. As soon as the crowd in the temple of music had been dispersed sufficiently the president was removed in the automobile ambulance and taken to the hospital, where an examination was made. The best medical skill was summoned ,and iwihtn a brief period several of Buffalo's best known practitioners were at the patient's side.

ON OPERATING TABLE

One Ball Is Extracted and Wounds of Mr. McKinley Dressed.

The president retained the full exercise of his faculties until placed on the operating table and subjected to anaesthetics. Upon the first examination it was ascertained that one bullet had taken effect in the breast just below the nipple, causing a comparatively harmless wound. The other took effect in the abdomen, about four inches to the left of the navel, and about on a level with it. Upon arrival at the exposition hospital the second bullet was probed for. The walls of the abdomen were opened, but the ball was not located.

President Removed to Milburn Home

The incision was closed, and after a hasty consultation it was decided to remove the patient to the home of President Milburn. This was done, the automobile ambulance being used for the purpose. Arriving at the Milburn residence, all persons save the medical attendants, nurses and officials were excluded, and the task of probing for the bullet which had lodged in the abdomen was begun by Dr. Rosswell Parke. When the news of the crime was telephoned to the home of President Milburn, where Mrs. McKinley was resting, immediate steps were taken to spare her the shock of a premature statement of the occurrence before the true condition of the president should be ascertained. Guards were stationed, and no one was permitted to approach the house . When it was decided to remove the president from the exposition hospital to the Milburn residence the news was broken to Mrs. McKinley as gently as might be. She bore the shock remarkably well ,and displayed the utmost fortitude.

AT MILBURN HOME

Many Distinguished People Call There During Night.

Secretary Cortelyou said that a telegraph office would be established at once in the Milburn residence and bulletins giving the public the fullest information possible would be issued at short intervals.

At the Milburn house were Secretary of Agriculture Wilson, President Milburn, Director General Buchanan of the Pan-American exposition, Dr. Rixey and Secretary Cortelyou. Telegrams poured in by hundreds, and Secretary Cortelyou was kept busy replying to them. Two stenographers with their typewriters were placed in the parlor, which was quickly transformed into a bustling room.

While the wounded president was being borne from the exposition hospital to the Milburn residence between rows of onlookers with bared heads, a far different spectacle was being witnessed along the route of his assailant's journey from the scene of his crime to police headquarters. The trip was made so quickly that the prisoner was landed safely within the wide portals of the police station before anyone was aware of his presence.

How the News Spread.

The news of the attempted assassination having in the meanwhile been spread broadcast by the newspapers, like wildfire it spread from mouth to mouth. Then bulletins began to appear on the boards along Newspaper row, and when the announcement was made that the prisoner had been taken to police headquarters only two blocks distant from the newspaper section, the crowd surged down toward the Terrace, eager for a glimpse of the prisoner. At police headquarters they were met by a strong cordon of police, which was drawn up across the pavement on Pearl street and admittance was denied to any but officials authorized to take part in the examination of the prisoner. In a few minutes the crowd had grown from tens to hundreds, and these in turn quickly swelled to thousands, until the street was completely blocked with a mass of humanity. It was at this juncture that some one raised the croy of "lynch him." Like a flash the cry was taken up and the whole crowd, as if ignited by the single match thus applied, re-echoed the cry, "Lynch him!" Closer the crowd surged forward. Denser the throng became, as new arrivals sweeled each moment the swaying multitude. The situation was becoming critical when suddenly the big doors were flung open and a squad of reserves advanced with solid front, drove the crowd back from the curb, then across the street, and gradually succeeded in dispersing them from about the entrance to the station. Inside the station house were assembled District Attorney Penney, Superintendent of Police Bull, Captain Reagan of the First precinct, and other officials.

Was Communicative at First

The prisoner at first proved quite communicative, so much so, in fact, that little dependence could be placed upon what he said. He first gave his name as Fred Nieman, said his home was in Detroit, and that he had been in Buffalo about a week. He said he had been boarding at a place in Broadway. Later this place was located as John Nowak's saloon, a Raines law hotel, No. 1078 Broadway. Here the prisoner occupied room 8. Nowak, the proprietor, said he knew very little about his guest. He came there, he declared, last Saturday, saying that he had come to see the Pan-American exposition, and that his home was in Toledo. He had been alone at all times about Nowak's place, and had had no visitors. In his room was found a small traveling bag of cheap make. It contained an empty cartridge box and a few clothes. With these facts in hand the police went at the prisoner with renewed vigor in the effort to obtain either a full confession or a straight account of his identity and movements prior to his arrival in Buffalo. He at first admitted that he was an anarchist, in sympathy at least, but denied strenuouesly that the attempt on the life of the president was a result of a preconcerted plot on the part of any anarchist society.

At times he was defiant and again indifferent. But at no time did he betray the remotest sign of remorse. He declared the deed was not premeditated, but in the same breath refused to say why he perpetrated it. When charged by District Attorney Penny with being the instrument of a onrganized band of conspirators, he protested vehemently that he never even thought of perpetrating the crime until this morning. After long and persistent questioning it was announced at the police headquarters that the prisoner had made a partial confession, which he had signed. As near as can be learned tonight, the facts contained in the confession are:

The man's name is Leon Czolgocs. He is of Polish-German extraction. His home is in Cleveland, where he has seven brothers and sisters. He is an avowed anarchist and an ardent disciple of Emma Goldman, whose teachings, he alleges, are responsible for today's attack on the president. He denies steadfastly that he is the instrument of any body of anarchists or the tool of any coterie of plotters. He declares he did not even have a confederate. His only reason for the deed, he declares, is that be believed the present form of government in the United States was unjust, and he concluded that the most effective way to remedy it was to kill the president. These conclusions, he declares, he reached through the teachings of Emma Goldman.

WASHINGTON IS PARALYZED

Streets are Crowded With Anxious Watchers for Latest News.

Washington,, Sept. 6.—The news of the shooting of President McKinley, which reached Washington first through the medium of the Asociated Press late this afternoon, caused a tremendous sensation. So frequent have been the rumors of this sort often put afloat in recent years for stock jobbing purposes, general disposition at first was to withhold full acceptance of the story of the news, but when it was confirmed a feeling of deep gloom and profound sorrow spread over the city for Mr. McKinley's delightful personality had endeared him to the citizens of Washington, apart from the official class, in a degree that rarely has been equalled.

It was some time before the force of the blow was appreciated: the people were stunned, and they could not respond at once and fully comprehend the extent of the great disaster that had fallen upon the country and themselves. Then the newspapers began to appear; the carriers rushed madly through the streets and crowds of people began to gather from all quarters of the city around the newspaper bulletin boards.

The telephone system of the city was paralysed for a time and many were the calls upon the news offices and until the officials who might be supposed to have some knowledge of the details of the shooting that the operators were overwhelmed.

First News Reaches White House

A reporter for the Associated Press carried to the White House the first bulletin announcing the shooting of the president. The executive mansion was reached at never flinched. Gamest man I ever saw in my life." The police pulled him from the table and hustled him into a police van, which sped to police headquarters, where the assassin was tossed into the "sweat box," a euphemism for a tiny room where the third degree was administered.

MEANWHILE, the wounded President was taken to the Exposition hospital. The wound to the chest was superficial, but the shot to the stomach was considerably worse. The bullet would never be found, but it had torn through the stomach wall and was probably lodged in McKinley's back.

The doctors closed up the wound to the stomach and McKinley was transported by ambulance to the home of the Exposition president. At first, the news about the President's condition was good. Senator Hanna, who was in Buffalo with the President, released encouraging bursts of information. Next day, the New York Times trumpeted, "All the official bulletins showed great gains and inspired those near the President to state positively that he would recover rapidly. The strain on the heartstrings of the Nation has been relieved." McKinley was responding well. The President was hungry and thirsty, and was given nourishment. He asked for a cigar and was refused. For the next three days, McKinley seemed to be mending.

McKinley's assassin, Leon Czolgosz

And then, shortly after 2 a.m., after being fed his first food by mouth, the President took a sudden turn for the worse. By 6 o'clock on the evening of September 14, it was clear that he was dying. At 7 o'clock, he woke and asked for Mrs. McKinley, who was in ill health, both physically and emotionally, and they spent some time together. At about 2 a.m., he murmured a passage from the hymn "Nearer my God to Thee," said to his wife and the attending physician, "Good-bye, all. Good-bye. It is God's way. His will be done." And at 2:15, he died.

The autopsy revealed gangrene poisoning as the cause of death. The bullet was never found. Its path, through both walls of the stomach and through the kidney, had become gangrenous.

At least 100,000 people passed by the catafalque containing the President's open coffin in Buffalo City Hall the next day. Brief funeral services had been held earlier at the Milburn house, and a state funeral would be conducted later, once the body had been brought to Washington.

Czolgosz, tried and found guilty, showed no emotion, either at his sentencing or on October 20, in Auburn, New York, when, at 7:12 a.m., he was strapped into the electric chair. "I killed the President because he was the enemy of the good people—the good working people," he said. "I am not sorry for my crime," and 30 seconds later, the switch was thrown.

Later that day, he was placed in his coffin, and, after it was lowered into the grave, a carboy of sulfuric acid was poured onto the body. Doctors estimated that within 12 hours, the corpse of Czolgosz would be thoroughly disintegrated. That night, he was burned in effigy in Hempstead, Long Island.

To the end, he maintained that he acted completely on his own. But certain members of the police, the press, and the public refused to believe this. In Chicago, nine anarchists were thrown in jail on charges of conspiracy to assassinate the President. No evidence was developed and they were set free two and a half weeks later.

In New York City, John Joseph Most, a known anarchist, was arrested in a saloon at 69 Gold Street for publishing an inflammatory article in the German language newspaper he edited. A suspected anarchist was mobbed at 186th Street and 11th Avenue.

A young orator gathered a goodly crowd on West 125th Street. Led by him, they gathered together to cross the Hudson and burn down Paterson, New Jersey, reportedly a stronghold of anarchy, where the assassination of King Humbert had been planned. More level-headed police talked them out of their journey.

In New Mexico, which was then a territory, U.S. marshals arrested an anarchist who played violin in a saloon. Vigilantes in Kansas, routed a meeting of anarchists. In Casper, Wyoming, a man insanely professed sympathy for Czolgosz in public and was tarred, feathered, and run out of town on a rail.

And in St. Louis, Missouri, police swore out a warrant for the arrest of Emma Goldman, who had never met McKinley's assassin, but whose words had supposedly inflamed him to act. She fled to Chicago, where she gave herself up. She was thrown into jail, given the third degree, punched in the face by a policeman, and, after two weeks, was released. While she was in jail, her father was excommunicated from a synagogue in Rochester, New York. But once again, the nation healed. Vice President Theodore Roosevelt assumed the office of the Presidency, and set about reversing the conservative policies of McKinley. As they had with McKinley, some in the nation approved, and some didn't. It was part of the price of the Presidency.

Archduke Franz Ferdinand

POSITION:	*Heir to the throne of Austria*
DATE:	*June 28, 1914*
PLACE:	*Sarajevo, Bosnia*
HOW:	*Gunshot*
WHO:	*Gavrilo Princip*
CONVICTED:	*Yes. Died during 20-year prison sentence*
MOTIVE:	*Anger against repression of Serbian autonomy*
DIRECT CONSEQUENCE:	*World War I*

For all its prestige and foresight as the first multinational state, Austro-Hungary in the spring of 1914 was a powderkeg anxious to explode. The nobility flaunted its irresponsible lack of concern for a backward peasantry, thus setting the stage for the growth of a socialist working class. The Austrian-Magyar minority that ruled under the 83-year-old Emperor Franz Joseph of the house of Hapsburg governed many factions and former nationalities—among them Croatians, Slovenes, Bosnians, and Serbs, and seemed to have little care for or understanding of any of them.

Archduke Franz Ferdinand, the 55-year-old heir apparent to the Austrian throne, was a particularly unlikeable man, both in person and as a royal and political symbol. Paunchy and bullnecked, with cold, grey, accusatory eyes, an oversize moustache even for that day and age, and a tart tongue that insulted before it inquired, he had an enormous temper that led some in the court to whisper that he was actually insane.

In addition to this, he had broken court etiquette by marrying Sophie Chotek, a Czech of low nobility—a fact that would prevent their children from ascending to the throne. His interests were chiefly in things military, and in 1913, he made himself Inspector General of all the armed forces, a move that was seen by his enemies as an assurance that he would have the power to crush reform and impose centralized rule under himself in Vienna.

Add to this his well-known detestation of Hungarians and Slavs, and his well-advertised view that the introduction of a democracy and the expressions of minorities were ruinous to the Empire, and the formula was complete to ignite negative emotions, which ranged from mild dislike to murderous rage.

This rage was particularly rampant among those Serbs within the Austro-Hungarian empire who hoped for a federation with the independent South Slav nation of Serbia. As early as 1911, secret revolutionary societies of South Slavs, calling themselves Young Bosnians, were firmly planted within the recesses of the Empire. The cells had links with Serbia's Black Hand group, dedicated to unifying all Serbs through revolution if necessary.

To the less sophisticated members of any of these revolutionary cells, assassination was a path toward the overthrow of the government, and 19-year-old Gavrilo Princip, a Serb from a West Bosnian family of poor peasants, was one of these unsophisticates. When he heard that Archduke Franz Ferdinand was coming to Sarajevo to celebrate the Feast of St. Vitus, inspect army maneuvers in Bosnia, and generally assert his power over this particularly rebellious part of the Empire, Princip knew his opportunity had arrived.

Had he been of a more subtle mind, Archduke Franz Ferdinand might also have noted that the Feast of St. Vitus was the anniversary of two major Serbian battles which were symbols of Serbian bravery and independence. But he paid no more attention to this than he did to his own intelligence service, which warned him not to go to Sarajevo.

Meanwhile, the conspiracy grew. According to one version of the story, the slight, intense Princip gathered six bombs, four revolvers, and three accomplices: Milan Ciganovic, Nedelko Cabrinovic, and Trifko Grabez. According to another version, Colonel Dragutin Dimitrievich, known within the Black Hand as "Apis", planned the assassination, and recruited the four secondary school students himself. The truth is probably somewhere in between. There was certainly Black Hand involvement in the plot, since the conspirators hid out beforehand in the house of Danilo Ilic, a member of the Black Hand in Sarajevo, and all carried with them signature vials of cyanide, designed to be taken should they be caught.

The team practiced their marksmanship in a park in Belgrade during the week preceding the late June visit of Archduke Franz Ferdinand and his wife Sophie to Sarajevo, and by all accounts, Princip became a better marksman than the other three.

THE ROYAL couple arrived in the Bosnian city on June 26, attended a bazaar and a state dinner, and generally enjoyed themselves. The crowds were large and friendly, and Sophie assured a nervous local dignitary that his fears for their safety had been proven unnecessary.

At 10 a.m. on the morning of Sunday, June 28, 1914, the six cars of the royal motorcade rode rapidly through the city on the way to the town hall. Lining the route along the Appel Quay, a street on the embankment above the Miljacka River, seven potential assassins waited—the original four, plus three more backups, and Ilic, who had hired the second team in case the first failed.

At 10:10 a.m., the open car containing Franz Ferdinand and Sophie—he in a feathered helmet and imposing royal uniform, she in a white dress and gloves, and carrying a white parasol—drew parallel with the first two killers.

They did nothing. One, Mehmed Memedbasic, became confused, and the second, Vaso Cubrilovic, held his fire out of sympathy for Duchess Sophie. The third assassin, Cabrinovic, was less befuddled. He flung his bomb, which ricocheted off the hood of the royal car, rolled under the vehicle behind it, and exploded, wounding members of the royal escort and some spectators. Cabrinovic, pursued by spectators and police, dashed to the river, swallowing the contents of his cyanide vial on the way. Police caught up with him. He vomited up the poison, and was beaten to a bloody pulp by the police.

The royal caravan stopped momentarily, then continued on its way, confident that the assassination attempt had failed. And, in fact, the four remaining killers then did nothing. Popovic, the youngest, was frozen in fear. Grabez had a rush of conscience, deciding not to throw a bomb that could injure innocent bystanders. Princip failed to recognize the royal vehicle until it had gone past him and out of firing range. Disgusted, he walked to a coffee house on Franz Joseph Street, where he gloomily brooded over a cup of sweetened coffee.

And so the assassination attempt had turned into an abysmal failure. The royal procession proceeded to the town hall ceremony, which unfolded smoothly.

AND NOW, an important and portentous decision was made. Instead of returning to the museum by way of Franz Joseph Street, Franz Ferdinand decided to go to the military hospital to visit the men who had been injured in the bomb blast. The way to the hospital was along the Appel Quay, which had been cleared of crowds. And had Franz Ferdinand been able to follow this change in his planned route of return, history might have been enormously different, and two world wars might never have been fought.

But fate took a hand in two ways: First, a jealous disagreement between Sarajevo's chief of police and the provincial military governor had removed a police cordon that should have lined the streets—particularly Franz Joseph Street—and stood between the royal entourage and any would-be assassins. Second, when the caravan resumed its trip at 11:15, it did not proceed, as the Archduke had directed, back through the Appel Quay, but into Franz Joseph Street.

Sensing possible treachery, the military governor shouted to the lead driver to stop and take the other road. As chance would have it, this halted the royal vehicle so that it stood directly in front of the coffee house to which the frustrated Princip had retired. He had finished his coffee, exited the coffee house, and now stood just three yards away from the halted royal carriage. It was almost too good to be true. Without hesitating, he drew his revolver and fired two shots.

The first hit the Archduke in the chest. The second crashed into Sophie's abdomen. There was a moment of shocked silence, a flash of stillness, while the royal couple remained frozen and upright. Then, the car leaped forward, and Sophie plunged backward against her husband. "Sopherl, Sopherl, don't die," the Archduke pleaded. But she was already dead, and in a few more minutes, he would be dead too.

The conspirators were arrested, jailed, and beaten, Princip so severely that he lost an arm. The

Daily News & Leader

LATE LONDON ED[n]

No. 21,311. LONDON & MANCHESTER, MONDAY, JUNE 29, 1914. ONE HALF-PENNY.

ASSASSINATION OF AUSTRIAN HEIR TO THRONE

CONSORT ALSO SHOT DEAD.

TWO ATTEMPTS.

REVOLVER AFTER BOMB FAILS.

WARNING OF PLOT

DISREGARDED BY ARCHDUKE.

The Archduke Francis Ferdinand, heir to the Throne of Austria-Hungary, and his morganatic wife, the Duchess of Hohenberg, were assassinated yesterday at Sarajevo, the capital of Bosnia, which was annexed by Austria a few years ago.

This double crime is one of the most extraordinary in history. The Archduke's visit was in connection with the manœuvres. While the Archduke and his Consort were driving to the Town Hall through the gaily decorated streets, a bomb was thrown by a printer, named Cabrinovitch. The Archduke warded off the bomb, which fell and exploded, injuring the occupants of the next carriage, and some of the spectators.

After some delay the procession drove on. On the steps of the Town Hall, where the Burgomaster was to read an address, the Archduke protested against the outrage, and it was thought all danger was past. It was after leaving the Town Hall, however, that the august couple fell the victims of a second, and this time doubly fatal, outrage. Two revolver shots rang out, and both the Archduke and the Duchess were fatally wounded. They were carried to the Palace, but died before arriving there.

Both Cabrinovitch and the second miscreant, a student named Prinzip, were arrested, and had to be rescued from the crowd, which nearly lynched them.

The news was conveyed to the aged Emperor, whose life has been marked by a succession of tragedies. The possible effect of the latest sorrow upon Francis Joseph adds to the problems of a difficult situation in Austria-Hungary. The Archduke, on his morganatic marriage, renounced all rights on behalf of his wife and children. The new heir to the Throne is his nephew, Archduke Karl Franz.

In London the effect of the tragedy, which has caused great grief to the King and Queen, is the abandonment of to-night's State Ball. The Archduke and the Duchess were guests of the King and Queen at Windsor last November, and endeared themselves to all.

The Kaiser has cancelled all fetes at Kiel, and will attend the funeral at Vienna.

THE KING'S PLANS.

Abandonment of To-night's State Ball.

When the news was received in London at the newspaper offices during yesterday there were eager inquiries at the Austro-Hungarian Embassy. No official confirmation was obtainable immediately, but no doubt was thrown upon the story, and the flag was lowered to half-mast. Inquiries by telephone were pouring in from everywhere. The Ambassador was out of town, but he was immediately informed.

An early visitor was Sir Charles Cust, on behalf of the King and Queen, who were inexpressibly shocked, for the Archduke and his wife were last November the guests of their Majesties at Windsor, where they made themselves popular with everyone with whom they were brought into contact.

In the evening Sir Charles Cust again called at the Austrian Embassy on behalf of his Majesty to request that an expression of his deep sympathy and that of the Queen be forwarded to the Austrian Court. His Majesty also sent for Sir Douglas Dawson, Controller of the Lord Chamberlain's Department, and it was announced that the State Ball arranged for to-day has been abandoned. The other function arranged for to-day, the investiture, will not be affected.

It was officially announced last night that the English Court would go into mourning until next Sunday.

At Marlborough House the news came as an especial shock. One of Queen Alexandra's guests at the present time is Queen Olga of Greece, whose husband, Queen Alexandra's brother, also died by the hand of an assassin last year.

THE LATE ARCHDUKE FRANCIS FERDINAND. [Photo: C.N.

"THE WORK OF SERVIAN ENEMIES."

Assassin Nearly Lynched by the Crowd.

(From Our Own Correspondent.)

VIENNA, Sunday.

The Archduke Francis Ferdinand, the heir-presumptive, and his consort, the Duchess of Hohenberg, were assassinated in Sarajevo, Bosnia, this morning. The official account says that when the Archduke and the Duchess of Hohenberg were driving in a motor-car to a reception in the Town Hall, a bomb was thrown at their automobile, which the Archduke managed to ward off with his arm. The bomb exploded when the motor-car had passed, slightly injuring Count Boos Waldeck and Colonel Merizzi, and more or less seriously injuring six of the spectators. The bomb was thrown by a typographer named Cabrinovitch, of Trebinje, who was immediately arrested.

After the reception in the Town Hall the Archduke and his consort continued their drive through the town, when they were shot at by a student named Prinzip, of Grahova, who fired several shots with a Browning pistol. The Archduke was fatally injured in the face, and the Duchess of Hohenberg in the abdomen. They were taken to the palace of the Governor, where they succumbed to their injuries. Prinzip was arrested, and he and Cabrinovitch were nearly lynched by the embittered crowd.

PROTEST TO BURGOMASTER.

I learn that when the bomb was thrown the Archduke stopped his motor-car for some time. When he arrived at the Town Hall the Burgomaster wished to welcome him with an address, but the Archduke stopped him, saying, "Burgomaster, do you not know what happened? We have come to visit your town and bombs are thrown at us. This is iniquitous." After a pause he ordered the Burgomaster to deliver his address, to which he replied.

After the ceremony the Archduke expressed his intention of going to the hospital to see Colonel Merizzi, one of the officers who had been wounded by the bomb. The Archduke had been in Bosnia for several days to attend the military manœuvres there which terminated yesterday, and he was about to return to Vienna. The Emperor, who travelled to his villa in Ischl yesterday, on hearing of the death of his nephew and his wife at once decided to return to Schoenbrunn, where he arrives to-morrow.

The assassin Prinzip, who is 19 years old, has been studying for some time in Belgrade. In a statement made after his arrest he declared that for some time he had planned to kill a personage of high position. He hesitated for a moment to-day on seeing the Archduke's consort beside him in the motor-car, but he fired two shots in quick succession. He denies that he had any accomplices.

JUMPED INTO THE RIVER.

Cabrinovitch, who threw the bomb, received it from an anarchist in Belgrade, whose name he did not know. He also denies having accomplices. After he threw the bomb he jumped into the river to escape, but policemen jumped in after him and seized him.

A second bomb was found near the spot where the first was thrown.

The news of the dreadful tragedy has caused the greatest consternation here and throughout Austria-Hungary. It was made known to the public by the issue of flysheets. All concerts and afternoon performances at the theatres were at once cancelled.

It is believed here that the assassination was the work of Servian enemies of the monarchy, and it is said that the Servian Minister here warned the Archduke Francis Ferdinand, through Count Berchtold recently, not to go to Bosnia.

No private news has so far been received from Sarajevo. It appears that the telegraph and telephone are under the strict control of the authorities.

20 PERSONS INJURED.

Two doctors were immediately in attendance at the palace, but medical help was in vain, both dying a short time after the shots were fired. The bodies are still at the Palace.

After the outrage there was immense excitement in Sarajevo, many people weeping in the streets, and black flags were immediately hoisted.

The bomb was filled with nails and pieces of lead and iron. The shutters of several shops were struck, and in all about twenty persons were injured, most of them slightly.

The children of the Archduke are at Konopischt, and nobody dares inform them of the death of their parents.

The Bosnian Diet held a special sitting this afternoon, attended by all the members in black, except four Servian Opposition Deputies, who appeared in ordinary attire. A further remarkable fact is that the first news of the tragedy reached Budapest from Belgrade.

By the death of the Archduke Francis Ferdinand the succession falls to his nephew, Karl Franz Joseph, an extremely popular young officer, whose eldest child, Otto, was born two years ago.

The late Archduke enjoyed great popularity in clerical circles, but lived a somewhat retired life. He devoted his time to military and naval affairs, but of late years also exercised considerable influence in matters of foreign policy.

President Poincaré dispatched a telegram of sympathy to the Emperor Francis Joseph yesterday.—Reuter.

ARCHDUKE'S PROTEST TO MAYOR.

Came on Friendly Visit and Received by Bomb.

SARAJEVO, Sunday.

At ten o'clock this morning the Archduke and the Duchess left the military camp in their automobile for the town hall. The car halted for some minutes while a number of young girls presented flowers to the Royal pair, who spoke a few kindly words. The car had only moved on a few yards when a man, since identified as a printer named Cabrinovitch sprang out from the crowd and hurled a bomb full at the Royal couple. The infernal machine fell at the back of the car, where the Archduke was sitting, and, rebounding on to the road, exploded. The Royal car had by this time moved several yards, and the full force of the explosion fell on the following automobile, which contained four members of the suite—Count Boos Waldeck, Baron Rummerskirch, Countess von Lanjus, lady-in-waiting, and Lieutenant-Colonel von Merizzi, aide-de-camp to the Archduke. The last named received a splinter in the neck, and was badly hurt.

The Archduke, after ascertaining the extent of the injuries to the aide-de-camp, and seeing that he was medically attended to, gave the order to proceed, and the Royal car soon afterwards arrived at the Town Hall.

At the entrance to the building were the members of the Town Council, with the Burgomaster at their head. The Burgomaster was about to read an address to the Royal visitors, when the Archduke raised his hand and spoke, in a voice in which resentment was blended with emotion: "Mr. Mayor, We come to Sarajevo to make a friendly visit, and are greeted by a bomb. This is outrageous." Then, after a pause, the Archduke said: "You may now speak."

The city fathers stood thunderstruck, and could not conceal their chagrin. The Burgomaster, however, recovered himself and delivered his speech. The Archduke replied, and with his wife spent half an hour inspecting the Town Hall.

The Archduke then stated he was going on to the garrison hospital to see how Lieut.-Col. Merizzi was progressing. The Royal couple, escorted by the Town Councillors, descended the steps leading to the entrance to the building, re-entered their automobile, and drove off.

The car had reached the corner of the Franz-Josef and Rudolf streets, when two revolver shots, in close succession, rang out. The first struck the Archduke in the right cheek, inflicting a mortal wound, while the second penetrated the body of the Duchess, severing a main artery. She sank unconscious into the arms of her spouse, who a few seconds afterwards also fainted.

With all speed the car was driven to the Konak, but almost before a doctor could reach their side the Royal couple had expired.—Central News.

THE LATE DUCHESS OF HOHENBERG. [Photo: C.N.

KIEL FETES ABANDONED.

The Kaiser Returning to Berlin To-day.

KIEL, Sunday.

At five o'clock this afternoon, at a given signal, all the ships in the harbour hoisted the Austro-Hungarian flag at half-mast, including the British warships, although it was known only on the flagship that the Archduke Francis Ferdinand and the Duchess Hohenberg had been murdered.

The news as soon as received was sent to the Emperor by dispatch boat, his Majesty being on board the Meteor, which was in a race for yachts of A1 class. The Emperor and all the other yachts, including the English, at once stopped racing. His Majesty leaves for Berlin to-morrow.

The news arrived just in time to enable the reception Prince Henry was giving at the Castle for the British Admiral and the senior officers of the squadron to be cancelled.—Reuter.

Archduke Charles Francis, the new Heir to the Austrian Throne. [Photo: E.N.A.

Sarajevo, the capital of Bosnia, where the assassinations took place. The river which divides the town is the Miljacka. Sarajevo is known as the City of Palaces, and as the Damascus of the North. (Photo: E.N.A.

ARCHDUKE REFUSED TO HEED WARNING.

Recent Signs of a Serbophile Movement.

SARAJEVO, Sunday Night.

The greatest consternation prevails in the town, into which crowds of holiday-makers returning from a day's outing in the country have been pouring all the evening. All the theatres and places of amusement are closed. Although of a retiring disposition and little known to the masses of the people, the Archduke inspired confidence, for he approached all the great questions of the day with an open mind. The Duchess of Hohenberg was of Czech origin, and had many sympathies in Bohemia, and the dismay felt in Prague will, therefore, be readily imagined.

It is understood that the Servian Minister in Vienna in the name of his Government had officially warned the Austrian Government that the police had knowledge of plots against the life of the Archduke. The latter, however, refused to pay any heed. On the other hand, there have been signs of a Serbophile movement at Sarajevo for some time past, and there have been numerous demonstrations against Austrian officers and officials.

At the reception at the Town Hall the Archduke and Duchess, though still somewhat agitated, seemed much relieved after their narrow escape from the bomb that was first thrown. In his speech the Archduke expressed the greatest interest he felt in the development and prosperity of Bosnia. After the first attempt the extraordinary military measures which had been taken were suppressed by order of the Archduke, who expressed the wish that the program should be in no way modified.—Reuter.

THE NEW HEIR.

Future Empress Educated in England.

The new heir to the throne is Archduke Karl Franz. He is a son of Archduke Otto, brother of the murdered Francis Ferdinand. Until his death in 1906 Otto was next in the line of succession.

Karl Franz is 27 years of age and a major in one of the Austrian infantry regiments. He is devoted to his profession and is not unknown in England, having represented the Emperor at the Coronation of King George and Queen Mary. A brilliant linguist, he speaks German and Hungarian fluently, and has a thorough knowledge of the Slav tongues. Of athletic build, he is popular with both Austrians and Hungarians, and he has made a close study of the Slavonic and Balkan problems. Three years ago he was married to the Bourbon Princess Zita, of Parma, and a son was born to them in 1912 and named Francis Joseph Otto. There is also a baby daughter.

The wedding of Karl Franz and Princess Zita excited great interest, for it was a love match. She was then but 19, and part of her education had been received at Ryde, in the Isle of Wight. A few months after the wedding she accompanied her husband in his march across Galicia, meeting him in her motor-car at each halting-place.

DYNASTIC PROBLEM.

Who is the Heir to the Throne of Hungary?

The death of the Archduke Francis Ferdinand opens the thorny question of the Austro-Hungarian succession. The Archduke's marriage with Countess Chotek (Duchess of Hohenberg) being morganatic, his children, according to Austrian law, are debarred from succeeding him in his rights to the Austrian throne. But this disqualification does not extend to the Hungarian part of the Monarchy, where morganatic marriages are regarded as valid in every respect.

In these circumstances, if a division of the Monarchy had been possible, the eldest son of the late Archduke would have succeeded the Emperor Francis Joseph, on the latter's demise, in Hungary, while Archduke Karl Franz, the son of Francis Ferdinand's brother, would have become Emperor of Austria in virtue of his seniority in the collateral male line.

It is said, however, that in anticipation of this dynastic difficulty Francis Ferdinand signed on the day of his marriage a voluntary abdication on behalf of his future children of their prospective rights to the succession in Hungary. If true this would appear to leave the Archduke Karl Franz in sole possession of the title and rights of heir to the double throne, but it does not dispose of the point as to whether in view of the provisions of the law in Hungary the Archduke Francis Ferdinand could thus abandon the rights of his children.

3.30 A.M. EDITION.

LINER ON THE ROCKS.

FOG DISASTER ON THE IRISH COAST.

WIRELESS CALLS.

WAR VESSELS TO THE RESCUE.

The Anchor liner California ran on to the rocks at Tory Island, off the north coast of Ireland, yesterday. She sent out calls for help, and gunboats and destroyers were sent to her assistance. The latest news this morning is that the vessel is safe, but her position is serious. Another liner is standing by. The passengers and crew are still on board. There is no panic.

According to a Lloyd's message, the California's bows are badly stove in, and the two fore holds are full of water.

The accident is attributed to fog, but details are wanting. It is not known how many passengers the California was carrying. She was bound for the Clyde, having left New York on the 20th.

Six torpedo boat destroyers which have been patrolling the Ulster coast looking for gun-running steamers are hurrying to Tory Island. Of these, the Swift, the largest of the patrolling craft, has Captain Wintour, the officer commanding the flotilla, on board. Two destroyers from Lough Swilly and Lough Foyle are expected to reach Tory Island early this morning. The entire wireless and telephone stations along the coast from Bangor, County Down, to Bundoran, County Donegal, are being kept open all night, and the cruiser Hecla is in Lough Swilly awaiting orders to leave in the event of her assistance being needed for the stranded liner.

At 11 o'clock last night a little group of people was gathered in front of the Anchor Line office in Londonderry awaiting news of the California. They were expecting friends.

Telegraphing early this morning, a Londonderry correspondent stated that a very heavy fog hung over the entire Donegal coast yesterday afternoon and evening. When the correspondent drove from Gweedore yesterday he found Tory Island was invisible from the mainland. A thick rain also was falling. Little was known of the position of the California from Londonderry. The Irish passengers of the liner were due at 2.30 this morning.

The California is a steel twin-screw steamer of 8,662 tons gross, and was built in 1907 at Glasgow by Messrs. D. and W. Henderson, Ltd. Her dimensions are: Length, 470ft.; breadth, 58ft.; depth, 34ft.

Tory Island is a bleak and barren place north-west of Donegal, twelve miles from the coast of the mainland. It is 5½ miles long and a mile wide. The surface consists mainly of bare rock and sand.

The gunboat Wasp was wrecked on Tory Island in September, 1884, while on a mission to the North of Ireland in connection with the land agitation troubles in Donegal. Fifty-two of the crew perished. The wreck was attributed to bad navigation.

AVIATOR'S THRILL.

Mr. Hawker Saved from Death by Falling Among Trees.

Mr. H. G. Hawker, the aviator, had a thrilling experience at Brooklands on Saturday. While he was attempting to loop the loop his machine fell among some trees and was wrecked.

During the time the motor racing was in progress Mr. Hawker had looped the loop three times, and in the evening he went up again, but owing, it is stated, to insufficient speed, the machine slipped back and dived nose downwards.

It then span round and round and fell amongst the trees on St. George's Hill. There it came in contact with the limb of an oak tree and this righted it. Apart from a sprained wrist and a cut finger, Mr. Hawker was not much the worse for his adventure, and a little later he rode into the aerodrome on the carrier of a friend's motor-cycle.

ANTI-SALOON CAMPAIGN.

(From Our Correspondent.)

MONTREAL, Sunday.

The principal issue in the forthcoming elections for the Legislature in Ontario is "The Abolition of the Bar," and this is being strenuously urged by the Liberals. To-day many preachers throughout the province preached sermons on the subject, urging the election of Liberal candidates as the only visible advance that could be made in the temperance cause.

The nomination of several clergymen as Liberal candidates and the taking up of the question by some of the Churches have already afforded evidence of serious trouble, especially among the Methodists and Presbyterians, over the mingling of politics and religion.

KING RECEIVES BOER FARMERS

The King received at Buckingham Palace on Saturday morning the South African farmers who are now on a visit to England. The party, numbering about fifty, drove to the Palace in motor-cars, and were presented to his Majesty by Sir Owen Philipps, the proceedings taking place in the grounds. The South Africans left later in the day for Oxford, where they lunched at Magdalene College.

The farmers rested yesterday at Cheltenham after their strenuous week.

A full story of the dead Archduke's career and his morganatic marriage with Countess Chotek will be found on Page Two.
On Page Six a well-informed correspondent discusses the effects of the Sarajevo disaster on the political situation in the Dual Monarchy. On Page Seven is reviewed the tragic story of the House of Hapsburg during the reign of the Emperor Francis Joseph.

TO-DAY'S WEATHER.

London and Channel Forecast.—Light, variable breezes; fine; warm.
Lighting-up time, 9.19.

Police arresting suspected conspirators in Sarajevo on the day of the assassination

adults were sentenced to death; Princip, who was now really 20 years old, but, through a clerical error in his papers, was still officially considered to be 19, was given 20 years hard labor. He would die within two years, of tuberculosis. Danilo Ilic and two more conspirators were condemned to death.

THE ASSASSINATION was treated at first in a low key manner in Bosnia, in Austro-Hungary, and throughout Europe. Even the funeral was small and private, and Sophie was buried with two white gloves on her grave—a mark of a mere lady in waiting. The old and ailing Emperor Franz Joseph reportedly sorrowed only for his nephew's orphaned children, and rivals of Franz Ferdinand in the Imperial Court secretly rejoiced.

But then, an accusation that there had been Serbian involvement in the planning of the assassination began to surface. The weapons, the story went, had originated in the Serbian army, and a Serbian army major was deeply involved in the plot. Then it spread. According to the augmented story, the Serbian cabinet, including the Prime Minister, knew of the plot and could have prevented the assassination, but chose to remain silent and allow it to happen.

The rumors were only that, but they were enough for Emperor Franz Joseph to contact his ally Kaiser Wilhelm II of Germany and forge an alliance to go to war with Serbia—ostensibly to avenge the assassination, but incidentally to satisfy Austria's territorial imperative.

It was a risk-filled venture. Serbia's most powerful ally was Russia, who in turn had potential allies in the United Kingdom, France, and Italy. But Austria and Germany nevertheless formed a fateful alliance, and demanded that Serbia cease anti-Austrian propaganda, dismember the Black Hand and any other nationalist groups that advocated the incorporation of the South Slavs into Serbia, fire all anti-Austrian officials, allow Austrian police into Serbia to round up the last of the conspirators involved in the assassination, and cease arms smuggling. All in 48 hours.

The reply came back on July 25, two minutes after the deadline, and it was more than accommodating. It only refused to fire anti-Austrian officials and let in the Austrian police—two absurd requests anyway. But Austria and Germany had apparently only made the demands in the expectation that they would be rejected out of hand, so that war could be blamed on Serbia. The Austrian ambassador had already packed his bags when the acceptance arrived. He ignored it and left for Vienna.

On July 28, Austria-Hungary declared war on Serbia. By August 1, Germany had declared war on France and Belgium. On August 4, the United Kingdom declared war on Germany, and by the end of the month, World War I was a reality.

It would rage until November 11, 1918, kill 10 million people, destroy the Hapsburgs, form the country of Yugoslavia (translated, it means "Land of the South Slavs") and lay the groundwork for Nazi grievances that would lead to World War II.

And when the cold war between the western and eastern blocs ended in 1991, and Yugoslavia began to come apart, Serbs and Croats would, in the playing out of an ancient enmity, enter into a civil war, and that war would threaten the peace of the rest of the world.

It is doubtful that the 20-year-old Gavrilo Princip dreamed that his two pistol shots would ignite that much horror. He only saw a tyrant sitting beyond the barrel of his gun. But the dominoes of fate and ambition were set to falling that June morning in Sarajevo, and the world would never be the same again.

GRIGORII RASPUTIN

POSITION:	*Adviser to Czarina Alexandra Feodorovna*
DATE:	*December 16, 1916*
PLACE:	*Petrograd, Russia*
HOW:	*Poisoning, gunshot, stabbing, beating, drowning*
WHO:	*Aristocratic conspirators*
CONVICTED:	*No*
MOTIVE:	*The salvation of Russia*
DIRECT CONSEQUENCE:	*The Russian Revolution of 1917-1918*

SPEAKING of the assassination of Grigorii Yefimovich Rasputin (reconstructed LEFT in a scene from the film *Nicholas and Alexandra,* with Tom Baker as Rasputin), Trotsky opined, "It was carried out in the manner of a scenario designed for people of bad taste."

Then again, Rasputin's entire career might well be interpreted as a scenario designed for people of bad taste. A semiliterate peasant who preached a doctrine of salvation which included varying amounts of religious and sexual fervor, he nevertheless possessed a personal magnetism that attracted women to him in large, eager numbers. One of the women he attracted was czarina Alexandra Feodorovna, the wife of czar Nicholas II.

Nicholas himself was something of a mystic, and so was probably partially responsible for Rasputin's omnipresence at court. But the heavily bearded, wild-eyed Rasputin endeared himself enduringly to the czarina by checking the bleeding of the czarevich Alexis, who suffered from hemophilia. To the czarina, this was a gift from the Beyond, and Rasputin represented it.

To others, his position of power was assured by another dimension of devotion. When Princess Murat asked Rasputin, "By what means are you able to exert such an influence upon the mighty ones of your country?" he answered, "It is love, my little dove," and, taking out a piece of paper, wrote, "Love is your solace, your melancholy, your pain. The joy of love is given to all. Grigorii."

THROUGHOUT most of the years of the reign of Nicholas II, Rasputin exerted enormous influence in court, dispensing favors to those who curried them and bringing ruin upon the heads of those who opposed him.

Thus, there were those who opposed Rasputin early in the Romanov reign, and among them were those who urged Russia's involvement in Europe. Rasputin was passionately opposed to war, and continually petitioned the czar not to become involved in the 1913 conflict between southern Slavs and Turks in the Balkans. Patriots argued that Holy Russia should come to the aid of her co-religionists, and they were furious that Rasputin, through newspaper articles and personal contact with the czar, prevented Russia's involvement.

OUT OF this dispute rose the case of the mad monk Iliodor, which culminated in the first, nearly successful assassination attempt upon Rasputin. Ambitious and unstable under the best of circumstances, Iliodor, an advocate of Russia's involvement in the Balkan Holy War, launched a campaign of petition to the Synod of the Russian Orthodox Church to have Rasputin defrocked. He painted lurid details of Rasputin's sexual misdeeds and cursed Over-Procurator V. K. Sabler for being sympathetic and therefore blind to Rasputin's sins. "You are a traitor and an apostate," he wrote to Sabler, "Your corrupt hands are unworthy to hold the most holy tiller of God's church, the bride of Christ. They should be shining the devil's boots in hell . . ."

Then, in a burst of unwise passion, Iliodor called upon the synod to unfrock either Rasputin or himself: "Either indict Rasputin for his horrible crimes, committed on religious grounds, or unfrock me . . ." he wrote, and Sabler obliged, expelling Iliodor from holy orders.

Iliodor resumed his secular name, Sergei Trufanov, and, although placed under house arrest in his native village in southern Russia, he gathered around him some fanatical followers, among them women who believed they had been wronged by Rasputin. In early 1913, this odd group conspired to entice Rasputin to a Petrograd house with the promise of sex, and then castrate him. Rasputin found out about it, and failed to show up.

But in the spring of 1914, Chionya Gusyeva, a once-beautiful young woman who had been a prostitute and was now disfigured by syphilis, visited Trufanov, told him it was her sacred duty to destroy Rasputin, and asked for his blessing. He gave it to her with alacrity. Disguising herself as a beggar, she followed Rasputin to his vacation home in Pokrovskoe.

ONE MORNING that spring, a telegram was delivered to Rasputin's home by the postman. One of Rasputin's relatives received it and failed to tip the postman. Rasputin rushed out to catch the mail deliverer and give him his rightful gratuity. As he reached the sidewalk, a beggar woman asked him for money. He reached into his pocket, and faced a knife. Gusyeva stabbed Rasputin once in the stomach, driving the knife blade up to the rib cage.

The monk staggered, but had enough strength to avoid the second thrust and hold her off until an angry mob grabbed her.

It took the doctor six hours to reach his patient, and by that time, the risk of infection had accelerated. The doctor performed an emergency operation on the spot. Rasputin refused anesthetic, but fainted as soon as the operation began.

It was a stopgap measure, and the doctor insisted on transporting Rasputin for six hours over rutted roads to the nearest hospital. The trip was the first of two major tests of his extraordinary constitution. He survived this one, but spent a long and painful summer and autumn recovering.

The czarina, informed of the attempt on his life, acted swiftly. Gusyeva was arrested, after narrowly escaping a lynch mob. She was interrogated immediately. Her defense: Rasputin had abused his so-called sainthood, had committed heresies, and had raped a nun.

No trial was held; Gusyeva was declared insane after a short imprisonment and placed in an asylum in Tomsk, where she remained until after the February revolution, after which she disappeared. Meanwhile, Trufanov disguised himself as a woman and, accompanied by his sister, escaped across the border into Finland.

And so ended the first conspiracy on Rasputin's life. There were some who saw a wider plan to it. Gusyeva attacked Rasputin only hours after Gavrilo Princip's successful assassination of Archduke Ferdinand, several thousand miles to the west in Sarajevo (see page 34), and Rasputin, after all, had for some time now tried to prevent the czar from becoming involved in the events that would eventually culminate in World War I. But it was probably just coincidence; no historian has been able to fortify the suppositions with facts.

AND RASPUTIN continued to plead with the czar to stay out of the conflict. In the summer of 1914, he wrote an impassioned letter to Nicholas that was part prophecy and part petition:

> Dear friend,
> Again I say a terrible storm cloud hangs over Russia. Disaster, grief, murky darkness and no light. A whole ocean of tears, there is no counting them, and so much blood. What can I say? I can find no words to describe the horror. I know they all want you to go to war, the most loyal, and they do not know that they will face destruction. Heavy is God's punishment; when he takes away men's understanding it is the beginning of the end. You are the czar, the father of your people, don't let the lunatics triumph and destroy you and the people, and if we conquer Germany, what in truth will happen to Russia? When you consider it like that there has never been such a martyrdom. We all drown in blood. The disaster is great, the misery infinite.
>
> Grigorii

The monk's passion notwithstanding, Russia entered the war. Nicholas spent more and more time away from the Palace.

In 1915, with the country in poverty-induced turmoil and with Nicholas off fighting World War I, Rasputin ran the country virtually on his own authority. Nicholas had left the czarina in charge, but she was scarcely able to run a household, much less a country, and she allowed the opinions and appointments of Rasputin to shape the government of Russia.

Competent men who disagreed with the peremptory monk were dismissed; sycophants who agreed with him were appointed. Rumors

Rasputin—probably in 1914—with some of the women his mystic fervor inspired.

abounded that the czarina and Rasputin were involved in planning a secret, separate peace with Germany.

FINALLY, sensing that the future of Russia was being directed by a mad mystic who had the royal family of Russia in his thrall, a group of conservative patriots headed by Prince Felix Yusupov and the czar's cousin, Grand Duke Dmitri, decided to do away with Rasputin.

Yusupov recruited V. M. Purishkevich, a member of the *Duma*, or parliament, who was known as being "so right-wing that the only thing further right was the wall." Unstable, he was nonetheless vitriolically opposed to Rasputin's presence and influence, and had delivered, in the *Duma*, a powerful attack against the dynasty. On November 19, 1916, he urged the members of the *Duma* to ". . . go to Imperial headquarters, throw yourself at the czar's feet, and beg permission to open his eyes to the dreadful reality, beg him to deliver Russia from Rasputin and the Rasputinites . . ."

Joined by two other assassins, a young officer named Sukhotin and Doctor Lazovert from Purishkevich's medical team, the group met and planned the assassination of Rasputin for the night of December 16.

The scheme was to invite Rasputin to Felix's palace on the Moika Canal, ostensibly to introduce him to Felix's wife, Irina, who would really be in Yalta. While Rasputin was waiting to meet the absent Irina, he would be fed poison. Then, the conspirators would take his body by train to a battlefield and dump it. This last detail was later revised. For the assassination to have effect, they reasoned, the body of the murdered Rasputin would have to be found, so they decided to throw the corpse into the waters of the Moika.

Meanwhile, Rasputin had presentiments of death. In the second week of December, he bade goodbye to several intimate friends, including the czar, who was home for a week from the war. "This will be for the last time," he said to each of them. Yusupov extended his invitation to Rasputin, who accepted it. The time set for the meeting was 11 p.m. on December 16. Rasputin would be told that Irina was entertaining some friends but would join them shortly. Then, Rasputin would be guided to a room where three cakes and two glasses of wine would be laced with potassium cyanide. If the cakes did not finish him off, it was reasoned, the wine would.

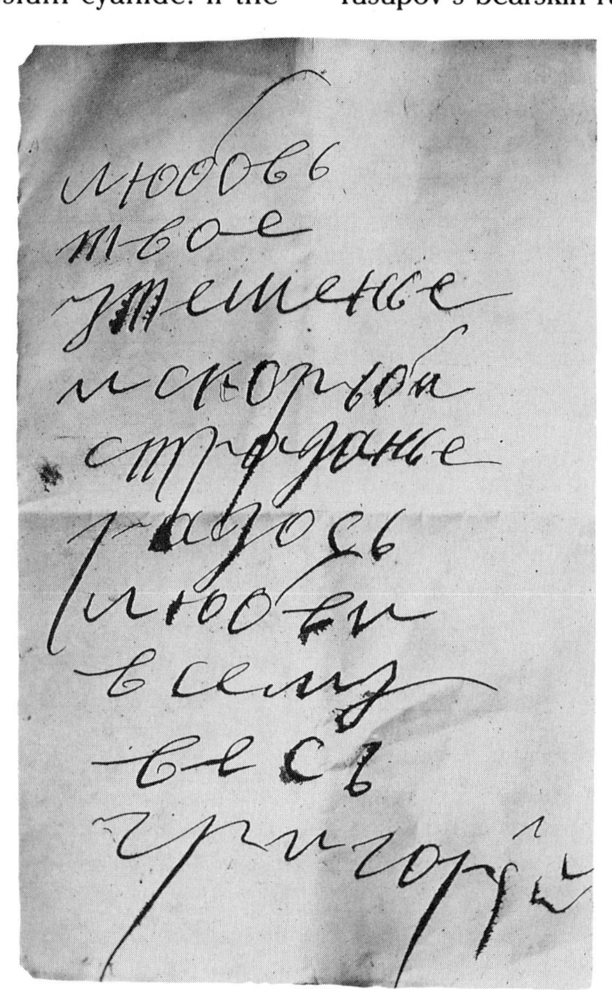

The slip of paper on which Rasputin wrote his message about love to Princess Murat (see page 41). Rasputin is said to have "painted the letters with apparent difficulty, like a peasant who plows the ground."

The object of the plot did, in fact, eat two poisoned cakes and did drink two glasses of poisoned wine. And they had no effect whatsoever on him, except to make him thirsty and vaguely discontented. Time passed, while the incredulous Yusupov made small talk and waited for the poison to take effect. At intervals, he went upstairs to report to the other conspirators, who grew increasingly nervous.

Lazovert fainted, and had to be revived in the snow that was heaped around the palace. Time ached by. By 2:30 a.m., it had become nearly impossible for Yusupov to pretend that Irina was still entertaining guests. He took leave of the monk, went up the stairs, supposedly to check on Irina, and conferred with the other conspirators. Rasputin would have to be shot, and a pistol was pressed into Yusupov's hand. He concealed it and rejoined Rasputin, who asked for more Madeira, drank it, seemed to cheer up, and suggested a trip to the gypsies.

Yusupov demurred, and instead, stood by the fireplace, examining a crystal and bronze Italian crucifix. Rasputin joined him, commenting on the inlaid chest upon which the crucifix lay. Yusupov drew his revolver, held it momentarily behind his back, then brought it in front of him and shot Rasputin in the chest. The monk's eyes gaped wide in astonishment; he opened his mouth as if to speak, clutched at his chest and fell to the carpet.

As soon as they heard the shot, the others ran into the room. It was 3 a.m. The victim of their plot was motionless, and bleeding profusely on Yusupov's bearskin rug. They lifted the body from the rug and dumped it onto the bare floor in a corner of the room.

The second phase of the plot was now put into action: Sukhotin gathered up Rasputin's hat and coat and put them on. He went up the canal to Purishkevich's home. Purishkevich's wife was to burn the clothes. Then, Sukhotin was to return to the palace, wearing his own hat and coat, and help carry Rasputin's body to the canal.

Purishkevich went upstairs and Yusupov returned to the library. He walked across the room, to the inert body of the slain monk, and leaned over it. To his horror, first one eye, then the next opened. Rasputin leaped to his feet with a roar and he attempted to grab Yusupov by the throat. "Felix, Felix," he hissed while he tried to strangle his assailant. Terrified, Yusupov twisted out of Rasputin's grasp and ran upstairs for his revolver.

Left alone, Rasputin dashed into the courtyard, yelling, "Felix, Felix, I'll tell the czarina!" Told the unbelievable news by Yusupov, Purishkevich drew his own revolver and ran out into the snow-filled courtyard, firing four shots. The first two missed; the third caught Rasputin in the back and stopped him, and the fourth flung him to the ground. Purishkevich sprinted across the snow, and delivered a massive kick to Rasputin's head.

The commotion in the courtyard attracted the attention of a policeman, S. F. Vlassyuk, who was passing by on the other side of the Moika. By the time Yusupov joined Purishkevich, the policeman had crossed the canal and was banging on the palace door.

Yusupov opened it and explained that he and his friends had been having a riotous, drunken evening, and at the end of it they had amused themselves by shooting Yusupov's dog. The policeman expressed understandable incredulity, and Yusupov invited him into the house, where he explained that he had just shot Rasputin, and the policeman had best hold his tongue, for czar and country. The shaken officer agreed, and did not report the incident to his supervisor.

Now, it was time to dispose of the body. Yusupov set upon it with a blackjack, beating it over and over, until it was battered almost beyond recognition. At around 5:30 a.m., Sukhotin, Lazovert and the Grand Duke returned for the body. Tying it in a canvas covering and placing it in a car, they drove it to the Petrovksy bridge over the Neva River, and dumped it into the icy waters. When the police recovered the body two days later, water in the lungs indicated that Rasputin had been alive when he was thrown into the river.

REPORTS of the powerful monk's death were greeted with rejoicing in government and royal circles. To some aristocrats, the assassins were considered heroes. But to the peasants, Rasputin was a martyr who had come from the people, represented the people, and was killed by the aristocrats.

The czar, summoned by a distraught Alexandra, was not appreciative of the assassination, and put the conspirators under house arrest. For all he knew, a palace coup was in the making. He was right. There was, but the events of the coming revolution would make it moot.

The investigation of the assassination would drag on and also be consumed, eventually, by the revolution, whose first shot, according to many, was fired at Rasputin. The assassination proved to many that, even at the highest levels, there was moral corruption, and the czar was no longer in charge.

To most historians, the damage had already been done, long ago, by the Romanovs themselves, and the czar and his family would only have 18 months to live themselves (see page 46). Dmitri Purishkevich's sister wrote, shortly after Rasputin's assassination:

> His death came too late to change the course of events. His dreadful name had become too thoroughly a symbol of disaster. The daring of those who killed him to save their country was miscalculated. All of the participants in the plot, with the exception of Prince Yusupov, later understood that in raising their hands to preserve the old regime they struck it, in reality, a fatal blow.

Rasputin would not remain in his grave for long. In March, 1917, while the czar and his family were being held prisoners in the palace, preparatory to being redistributed to various hiding places, the body was dug up and burned at a roadside, a quarter of a mile from the forest of Pargolovo by members of Russia's anti-aircraft battery.

CZAR NICHOLAS II

POSITION:	*Czar of all the Russias*
DATE:	*July 16, 1918*
PLACE:	*Ekaterinburg, Russia*
HOW:	*Firing squad*
WHO:	*Bolshevik soldiers led by Jakov Yurovsky*
CONVICTED:	*No. Five men wrongly executed.*
MOTIVE:	*To eliminate the living symbols Russian monarchy*
DIRECT CONSEQUENCE:	*Official terror as a tool of Soviet government*

WHEN White Russian and Czech troops overran the town of Ekaterinburg in 1918, the forest nearby yielded a gruesome legacy of the town's recent Bolshevik occupation. In an abandoned mineshaft LEFT, were the dismem-bered remains of czar Nicholas II and all of his family.

Nicholas's grandfather, Alexander II, was a czar who seemed to be aware of the needs of all of his people. He overhauled ancient legal and military systems that had sent peasants into the army for up to 25 years and had decreed barbaric punishments for their minor crimes. He created the *zemstvos*—rural councils that were the first, hesitating steps toward representative government.

But Alexander, for all his reforms, was a Romanov and a czar, and thus, doomed. In the early afternoon of March 13, 1881, while returning to the Winter Palace along the Catherine Canal in Petrograd, he saw some of the Cossacks in his entourage fall to the snow after a bomb had been thrown at the royal carriage by a young terrorist named Rysakov.

Alexander left his carriage to minister to the fallen, and when he did, a second terrorist, Ignacy Grinevitsky, threw a better aimed bomb, which landed at the czar's feet. It exploded, mutilating him horribly. He was carried to his bedroom, where, in unceasing pain, he slowly died.

Among those present at the death watch were the future czar Alexander III, his wife, Maria Feodorovna (who was told of her father-in-law's state while she was ice skating, and carried the skates into the deathroom), Princess Yurievskaya, (the czar's mistress for many years and his wife of only nine months), and 12-year-old Nicholas. Nine of the Romanovs gathered in that room that afternoon in 1881 were destined to be assassinated.

NICHOLAS was a quiet, introspective, not very bright boy, who, under his father, led a spartan and sheltered life. Those who knew him lovingly described his "frank blue eyes" and "tender, shy, slightly sad smile." Small wonder he smiled sadly; he was forced to sleep on a camp bed and ordered by his father to be up and out by 6 a.m. every morning for military drill.

And yet for all of the discipline that Alexander ordered for his son, he apparently cared deeply for him. Seven years after the assassination of Alexander II, the imperial train was derailed at Borki. Twenty-one were killed, and the coach in which the royal family rode was reduced to splintered timbers. Alexander held back these timbers so that Nicholas could crawl to safety, but the wounds the czar received from the wreck and the effort he expended in saving his son eventually resulted in his own death, in 1894, at the age of 50.

By that time, Nicholas was an extraordinarily handsome young man of 26, hopelessly and thoroughly in love with Princess Alix of Hesse. The granddaughter of Queen Victoria, Alix hesitated to reject her Protestantism for the Orthodox Russian Church, but a combination of persuasive interviews with her grandmother, pleas from Nicholas, and the imminent demise of his father, made up her mind. The couple were married in the czar's bedroom a few days before he died and Nicholas ascended to the throne of the Russias soon afterwards.

THE NEW czar and his czarina, now known as Alexandra Feodorovna, had little concept of ruling so vast a country, and particularly one that was already well on its way toward revolution. Alexandra loathed pomp and parades, and avoided them, thus slighting, and perhaps even insulting her people. In May of 1898, she thoughtlessly shortchanged the populace during a ceremony in which it was customary to dispense presents to the masses. Word spread that the gifts were running out, and a riot ensued in which hundreds were suffocated or crushed to death. Alexandra went to a ball and danced the night away, apparently oblivious or immune to the carnage she had caused.

No matter that she and her husband may not have been informed of the extent of the tragedy. They were perceived as careless and isolated, and this was further reinforced by her apparent inability to give Nicholas and Russia a male heir. This was corrected in 1904, when Alexis Nicholaevich was born. But even that joyous occasion contained seeds of its own discontent and danger. Born a hemophiliac, Alexis wasn't expected to live beyond his 18th year.

The mad monk Rasputin, called in desperation by Alexandra, apparently cured the young prince, but caused endless grief for his parents. Fiercely religious (she had embraced Russian Orthodoxy as fervently as she had her original Protestantism), Alexandra now thoroughly offered herself up to the monk's brand of mysticism, which Nicholas himself also embraced. Rasputin's influence at court began to grow.

RASPUTIN'S was not the only influence at work in Russia at the turn of the century. Something far more powerful and inexorable was growing throughout the country. Revolutionary opposition to the monarchy, fed by poverty in the populace, was beginning to take root. The Social Democratic Labor Party came into being in 1898. The Socialist Revolutionary Party was founded in 1901, and calls for a constitutional government increased.

Alexander III had been a complex and strong ruler; Nicholas was not. Well-intentioned and perhaps personally courageous, he had no heart for either discussion or compromise, and when crises arrived, he would frequently escape with his family to their palace in the country at Tsarskoe Selo.

"Nicholas recoiled in hostility before everything gifted and significant," wrote Trotsky, in his not necessarily clear-eyed *History of the Russian Revolution*. "He felt at ease only among completely mediocre and brainless people, saintly fakers, holy men, to whom he did not have to look up . . . This 'charmer' without will, without aim, without imagination, was more awful than all the tyrants of ancient and modern history." As revisionist as this is, it *is* a vision that the poor and alienated—and hence, those who fought revolutions—held of their czar.

In 1904, this relationship between the ruled and their ruler was further aggravated by Nicholas's decision to enter into the two-year Russo-Japanese War. The last adventure of the Romanovs, a manifestation of Nicholas's vow upon coronation to press for the Russification of the borderlands, it was an unmitigated disaster, characterized by scandal, bungling, and humiliation. Russia's prestige in the world was damaged by it, and the underground, composed of those who had chafed against the autocracy that had suppressed strikes, tormented Jews, and exiled thousands to Siberia, now erupted above ground, into the streets.

ON SUNDAY, January 22, 1905, a group of metal workers, led by a socially activist priest named Father Georgi Gapon, marched to the gates of the Winter Palace in Petrograd. Gapon had written to the czar the day before, in the mildest kind of language, asking him to speak to them at 2 p.m. "Do not fear anything," he wrote, "Stand tomorrow before the people and accept our humblest petition. I, the representative of the workingmen, and my comrades, guarantee the inviolability of Thy person."

But Nicholas chose not to meet with the workers, who had just engaged in an ineffectual four-day strike. As usual, the czar packed up his family and went to Tsarskoe Selo, 15 miles from the city.

Unaware of this, the marchers entered the great square before the Winter Palace, bearing icons and singing. The soldiers left behind to guard the palace apparently panicked, and, from a distance of 20 yards, fired volley after volley directly into the crowd. Defenseless women, children, and men died in agony. Five hundred of them were killed and several thousand were wounded. Blood stained the snow of the square, giving the name "Bloody Sunday" to the massacre.

It was a historic turning point. No matter how much he regretted what happened—and it appears that he did—Nicholas became, from this moment forward alienated from his people, and the 1905 revolution began. By the end of that year, more than 1,500 government officials would be killed.

KERENSKY IN LONDON—"RUSSIA TO JOIN IN"

The Daily Mirror

CERTIFIED CIRCULATION LARGER THAN THAT OF ANY OTHER DAILY PICTURE PAPER

No. 4,578 | Registered at the G.P.O. as a Newspaper. | THURSDAY, JUNE 27, 1918 | One Penny.

EX-TSAR MURDERED?

In pre-Revolution times. The Tsar with General Brusiloff.

Ex-Tsar Nicholas II.

Ex-Tsaritza in Uhlan uniform.

The Tsar, with sacred ikon in hand, blessing his troops.

The reports of the assassination of the ex-Tsar at Ekaterinburg by Red Guards still lack authoritative confirmation, but all the evidence points so strongly to their truth that there is little reason for doubt.

BRITISH AIRMAN'S DIRECT HIT.

Aerial photograph taken during a Royal Air Force raid over enemy territory showing a direct hit on a troop train. Such targets are so minute when seen from a great altitude that the number of hits scored on them is astonishing.—(Official photograph.)

"HAPPY ENDING" OF A WAR ROMANCE.

Major H. Lloyd Williams, D.S.O., M.C., Welsh Fusiliers, of Bangor, married to Miss Dorothy Marian Le Poer Trench at Weston-super-Mare. The bridegroom, who has been through some of the hottest fighting in France, first met his bride on a sad mission from her dead brother, who had confided to him messages and articles to deliver to the home folk.

V.C. WINS M.C.

Lieutenant Frederick M. W. Harvey, V.C., of the Lord Strathcona Horse, who has just been awarded the M.C. He is reported to be wounded.

GENERAL STAFF

Capt. G. R. P. Roupell, V.C., appointed to the General Staff and to be temporary major while so employed.

Czar Nicholas II with his four daughters (left to right: Tatiana, Olga, Marie, and Anastasia) and the czarevitch (far right). The other four boys are nephews of the czar.

Riots, naval mutinies, and assassinations roared through Russia, culminating in a general strike in October. Sensing the power of change, Count S. Y. Witte induced Nicholas to sign a manifesto promising representative government and basic civil liberties. The *Duma*, an elective body, was instituted, along with an upper chamber of deputies. But two months later, Nicholas dissolved it by locking its meeting rooms and surrounding them with troops. It was the first of a series of confrontations. The *Duma* was reinstated, sputtered forward, was organized and reorganized, while opposition grew against the czar both in the country and in the palace.

THE COMING of World War I in 1914 calmed the domestic situation. Patriotic fervor united sworn enemies.

In 1915, Nicholas took command of the army and left the country in the control of the czarina—which to many in the palace meant that it was Rasputin who was really running the country. Some nobles, in fact, let it be known publicly that the descending order of influence in the government began with Rasputin and ended with Nicholas. And the government indeed deteriorated; Rasputin was fiercely opposed to the war and tried to dissuade Nicholas from participating. Rumors were rampant that the czar was entering into a secret treaty with Germany in order to come home and suppress revolutionary movements. And then, in 1916, Rasputin was assassinated by noblemen (see page 40), and became, for some of the masses at least, a martyr.

By January of 1917, Nicholas, called home by the death of Rasputin, had become almost totally isolated from not only his people but his court. Some who sought an audience with him were let into a room that was screened at one end by a curtain, and they swore that the empress was sitting on the other side of it, listening to every word that was said.

Anti-Romanov plots were rampant in the *Duma* and the drawing rooms of Petrograd, all planned by nobility. The empress was to be arrested on her visit to the country. The czar was to be waylaid on his train. The royal family was to be kidnapped. None of this happened, but unrest was clearly the predominant atmosphere at the top, as well as elsewhere.

Meanwhile, arctic temperatures brought about huge food shortages in Russia, further aggravating the populace. Lenin arrived in early 1917. The *Duma* was a place of constant chaos. On March 1, bread rationing was introduced and there was a run on the bakeries, followed by another metal workers' strike. On March 8, true to form, Nicholas left Petrograd for the country. And on March 8, the Russian Revolution began. For a solid week, violent demonstrations raged across the country. The army mutinied. Strikes and marches became riots. Police stations were attacked, looted, and burned. Law courts were invaded and sacked.

BY MARCH 15, it was clear that the House of Romanov was collapsing. Accepting the inevitable, Nicholas abdicated, turning over the succession to Grand Duke Michael Alexandrovich. Under open arrest, for their own protection, the royal family was escorted to the Tsarskoe Selo palace. Within a few days, their arrest became real. Word came that the provisional government had allowed envoys from England to arrange passage for the royal family to reach asylum in England, but "Citizen" Romanov was not going to get away. Security tightened upon Nicholas and his family, who were now kept under constant surveillance and allowed to use only a corner of their gardens.

There they remained until August 14, when, since there was talk of the Kronstadt sailors raiding the palace, they were moved for their own safety to the provincial town of Tobolsk, in Siberia. And here, for nearly a year, with the irony that only real life can provide, they lapsed into the same sort of anonymity that Lenin had experienced when he had been exiled to Siberia.

Meanwhile, the revolution grew more complex and bloody. The Bolsheviks, led by Lenin, and his second in command, Trotsky, assumed power. Once more, in April, 1918, Nicholas and his family were moved, this time to Ekaterinburg (now Sverdlovsk), in the Ural Mountains near Czechoslovakia. In Tobolsk, they had enjoyed limited freedom, and were even allowed to attend the local church. Ekaterinburg, however, had a hostile soviet in control, and the royal family was treated with no respect whatsoever. They were imprisoned in a merchant's house, and placed on soldier's rations.

The guards were not ungenial, despite the fact that their chief, Andyev, was generally drunk, and had a habit of thrusting himself between the czar and czarina and drinking from their common pot. But on July 4, these guards were replaced by a group of cold and correct soldiers, led by Jakov Yurovsky, who had been trained in the secret police. They of course weren't guards at all, but executioners, and Nicholas, according to his diary, sensed danger.

BACK IN Moscow, there was contention over the fate of the czar. Trotsky argued for a trial at which Trotsky himself would be the prosecutor. Lenin balked, fearful that Nicholas, given the public forum of a trial, would conduct himself with enough dignity to gain sympathy with the populace.

While Moscow fretted, there was no doubt in the minds of the Ekaterinburg Soviet. They were determined to kill not only the czar, but also his family—thus collapsing, in one movement, the hated House of Romanov. Isiah Goloshchekin, representing the Ural Soviets, traveled to Moscow to argue their case.

But even before the arguments began, history took a hand, and sealed the fate of the royal family. Czechs, strengthened by anti-Bolshevik Russian officers and soldiers, began to close in on Ekaterinburg. On July 12, Goloshchekin returned from Moscow with the news that the fate of the Romanovs had been placed in the hands of the Ural Soviet. On July 13, Yurovsky was given the order to execute them.

Plans for the massacre went forward swiftly. Yurovsky and Goloshchekin explored and settled upon an abandoned mine shaft 14 miles from Ekaterinburg for the disposal of the bodies. Other members of the Ural Soviet set about buying drums containing 150 gallons of gasoline and 400 pounds of sulfuric acid.

On July 14, Father Storozhov, a local priest who was allowed to conduct worship with the family, noticed and remarked upon the deep depression into which the Romanovs had sunk. The young prince Alexis, in steadily failing health, was unable to move from his bed. The others were unbrokenly sad and distracted.

On the afternoon of July 16, Yurovsky ordered all of the help except the guards away from the house. At 7 p.m., he asked for and received 12 revolvers, and collected his closest men, all members of the Cheka, or secret police, around him. At 10:30, Nicholas and his family, innocent of what

Under arrest in Tobolsk, left to right: Olga, Anastasia, the czar, Tatania, the czarevitch, Marie.

was about to happen, went peacefully to bed. At midnight, Yurovksy awakened them.

The Czechs and the White Army were approaching, he said, and they would have to dress and come downstairs immediately. They were to be moved. The family drew on their clothes rapidly, and, still unsuspecting, descended the stairs, with Nicholas carrying the weak and sleeping Alexis in his arms.

Yurovsky led them to a small, semi-basement room with a heavy iron grille over its single window. He asked them politely to wait until their transport arrived. In fact, to make them comfortable, he had three chairs brought in. Alexandra sat in one, Nicholas in another, Alexis reclined in the third. The four girls—the grand duchess Olga, Tatiana, Marie, and Anastasia—stood behind the chairs.

Alongside them, silently waiting for their escape to safer quarters, were their family physician Dr. Eugene Blotkin, Trupp the imperial footman, and the cook Kharitonov.

Bustling among them was Demidova, the empress's parlormaid. She attempted to make her mistress more comfortable by stuffing a pillow behind her back. Another pillow, into which were sewn some of the imperial jewels, she clutched tightly to her body.

The door opened, and Yurovsky and his Cheka squad entered. "Your relations have tried to save you," he said, evenly and absurdly. "They have failed and we must now shoot you."

Nicholas rose to protest, but before he could speak, he was killed by a single, well-aimed bullet to the head from Yurovsky's revolver. A fusillade erupted from the Cheka guards, cutting down Alexandra, Olga, Tatiana, Marie, Blotkin, Kharitonov and Trupp. Demidova had been missed by the bullets, and now, screaming, she ran from one wall to the other, trying to escape. The guards rushed into the next room and returned with rifles fixed with bayonets. They drove the bayonets into her body 30 times, then crushed the head of Jimmy, the family cocker spaniel, with a rifle butt.

Alexis, still in his father's arms, had only been wounded, and he stirred. One of the assassins walked over to him, and smashed his head with his boot. Yurovsky, following, placed his revolver in the boy's ear and fired two shots.

According to legend, Anastasia was the one daughter who escaped the bullets. For nearly 75 years, various women would emerge from international shadows, claiming to be the lost Princess Anastasia, heiress to the considerable, remaining Romanov fortune. Books, plays, and movies were written. But in 1992, the truth emerged from official Soviet records. Anastasia did not escape. On that morning in 1917, the entire band of executioners turned on her with bullets, rifle butts and bayonets. No one was spared.

THE BODIES were wrapped in sheets and transported to the abandoned mine shaft. Before dawn, the work that would take three days began: The bodies were dismembered, sawn up, and burned, and the larger bones were dissolved in sulfuric acid. The powdered remains of the humans were thrown into a pool at the bottom of the mine shaft. The charred body of the dog was tossed in whole.

Eight days after the massacre, Ekaterinburg fell to the Czechs and White Russians. A group of officers searched the house in which Nicholas and his family had been held, and found evidence of the killings. It would be the following January before bits and pieces of clothing, jewelry, and bodies were exhumed from the mine.

There was no doubt that the Supreme Soviet had known of the mass murder, and had tacitly approved it. At first, they admitted only to the shooting of the czar. But as evidence accumulated, they conducted a show trial, in which 28 Social Revolutionaries who apparently had nothing to do with the assassination were charged with wholesale murder. Five were found guilty and executed.

The massacre of many of the remaining Romanovs spread, and continued for the next two years. Trotsky would eventually explain away the carnage. "The execution of the czar's family was needed not only in order to frighten, horrify, and dishearten the enemy," he wrote, "but also in order to shake up our own ranks to show that there was no turning back, that ahead lay either complete victory or complete ruin . . ."

It was an attempt to make every Bolshevik in Russia an accomplice in the crime, and spur on each to kill every White Russian who still lived. But the horrors and the privations of the revolution had dulled the public consciousness. There was neither acclamation for the assassination nor renewed energy in the revolution.

Still, there was one far-reaching effect of the murder of Nicholas and his family. It was an object lesson in terror. It showed the Bolsheviks that they were capable of it, and that it was a weapon they could wield with great success.

What they didn't realize at the time was that it was a double-edged weapon. In the hands of Josef Stalin, it would be turned upon the Soviet Union itself. And, irony of ironies, the terror realized in the cellar in Ekaterinburg in 1918 would eventually be responsible for the assassination of one of the two authors of the revolution (see page 66), as well as thousands and thousands of Soviet citizens.

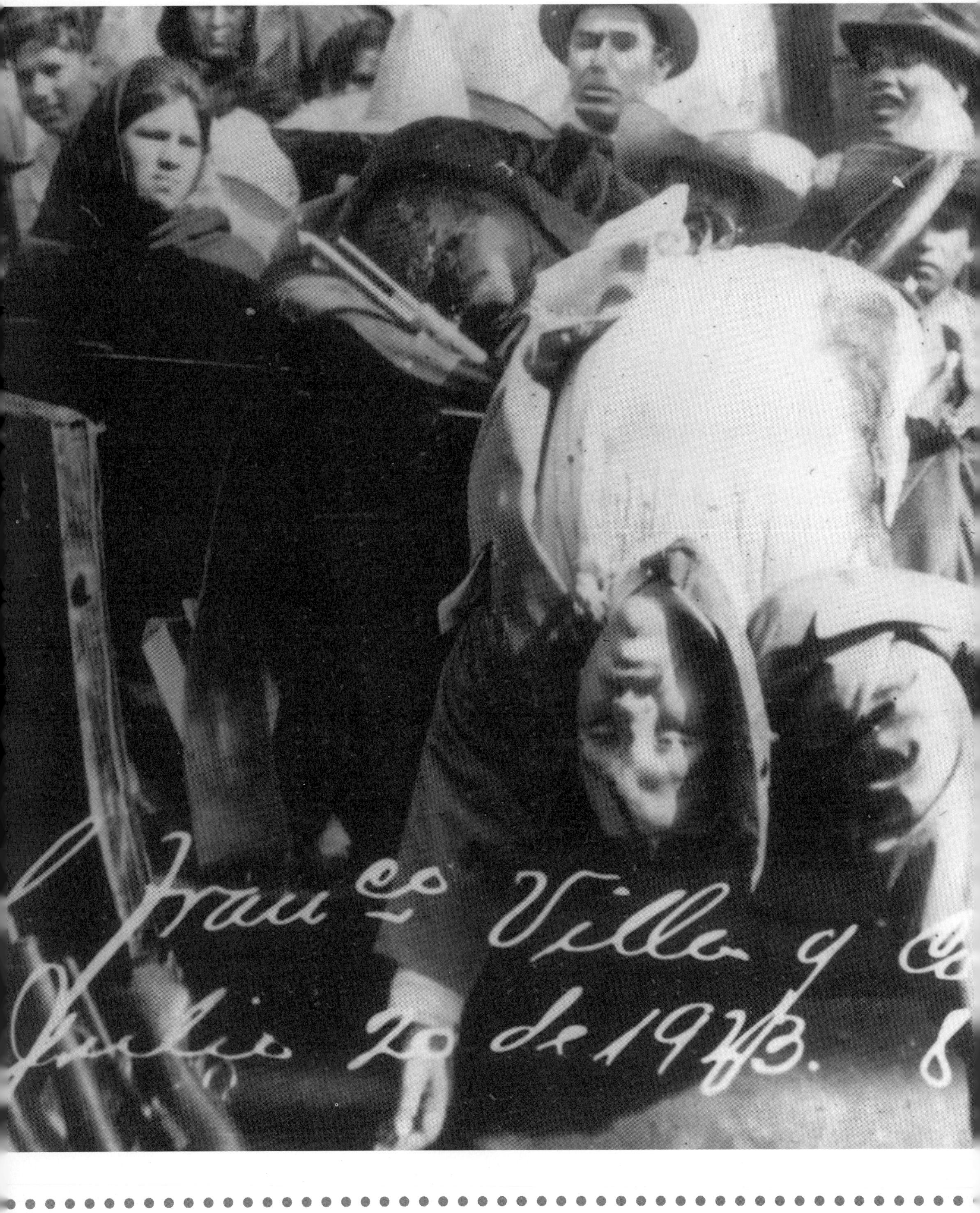

Franco. Villa y
Julio 20 de 1923.

Pancho Villa

POSITION:	*Mexican bandit leader and political activist*
DATE:	*July 20, 1923*
PLACE:	*Parral, Mexico*
HOW:	*Multiple gunshots*
WHO:	*Jesus Salas and accomplices*
CONVICTED:	*Yes, but released*
MOTIVE:	*Political gain through revenge*
DIRECT CONSEQUENCE:	*Disappearance of a romantic figure*

TO THE peasants of northern Mexico, Francisco Villa, popularly known as Pancho Villa, was a Robin Hood, stealing from the rich and dispensing the spoils to the poor. To his political enemies—and there were many—he was a menace. One of these enemies, Jesus Salas, a member of the State Legislature of Durango, organized a group of followers who, for days, staked themselves out in a house in the town of Parral, on the way to Guanajuato, at the southern tip of the northern province of Chihuahua. There, one July morning, they killed the 55-year-old bandit leader who had managed to survive scores of previous assassination attempts, rival bandits, and even the U. S. Army, led by General "Black Jack" Pershing.

IT MAY be that the life and motives of Pancho Villa have been romanticized by film-makers and the myth-makers among the poor in Mexico, but both had rich material from which to spin their tales. The facts read like a feverish adventure-action novel.

Villa's real name was Doroteo Orango, and he grew up poor in the tiny mining town of Las Miras, in the state of Durango. Unable to receive an education because of his family's poverty, the future bandit leader's first job was as a village butcher. Mexican tradition has it that he traded the butcher block for a life of butchery when he discovered that one of the owners of an estate on which he worked had raped his sister. Orango killed the man, rode off into the hills, and changed his name.

Another version of the story advances his age to 21, when he was well known for his absolute devotion to poker. One night, in a Chihuahua sporting fraternity, a cowboy questioned his honesty. In this version, Villa drew out a revolver and shot the man, leaped on a horse, and fled into the mountains. And his bandit career began.

However it happened, Pancho Villa rose swiftly to the status of legend. A man who neither drank nor smoked but had no moral compunctions about killing, he soon gathered a well-disciplined army around him, and began a systematic series of raids on the wealthy landowners and mining men of northern Chihuahua. After each raid, he would share some of the loot with the local peasantry.

IN 1910, he became a military leader, fighting under General Francisco Madero in the revolution that unseated President Porfirio Diaz and replaced him with Madero. Villa's skill as an organizer gained him the rank of colonel, and a huge army. When Madero assumed power, Villa, feeling that his military mission had been accomplished, left the army and became a businessman.

But his civilian life, as anyone who knew him could have predicted, was destined to be short-lived. Generals in the Mexican army systematically lusted for power; General Pascual Orozco conducted a rebellion to overthrow Madero in 1912, and Villa rejoined the Mexican army, pitting himself against a general who had once been a former companion in arms.

A few months into the rebellion, Villa was accused of insubordination by General Victoriano Huerta, under whom he was serving. Villa was ordered to be executed by firing squad, but at the last minute, as he was about to be shot, Raul Madero, the president's brother arrived and stopped the proceedings.

It was too close a call for the mountain man. He knew an enemy general when he saw one, and so he escaped from military prison, where he was still incarcerated, and fled to the United States. There, a year later, he heard of Madero's assassination and Huerta's self-proclamation as dictator. Villa returned, and joined with General Emillio Carranza and Emiliano Zapata to form a revolution to overthrow Huerta. His 35,000-man cavalry was chiefly responsible for the success of the revolution. In 1914, Huerta resigned and Carranza assumed the presidency.

Villa, however, was never altogether enchanted by Carranza, and in the chaos that erupted after the change of government, he, with his cohort Zapata, briefly occupied and ruled Mexico City. That was overreaching, even for Pancho Villa, and the two outlaws and their army were soon driven back into the northern hills of Mexico by an army led by General Alvaro Obrigan.

FOR A WHILE, Villa dropped out of sight, busying himself with his people, the residents of Chihuahua. He redistributed land there and further endeared himself to the poor of Mexico. Then, on March 6, 1916, he resurfaced. Angry at recognition of the Carranza government by the United States and also in need of basic supplies, he and his men attacked Columbus, New Mexico, a border town. Several Americans were killed, and President Woodrow Wilson dispatched an expeditionary force into Mexico under the command of General Pershing, to bring back Pancho Villa, "dead or alive."

Into every hill and haunt that might have contained the bandit and his men, Pershing and his expeditionary force searched and pursued. They persistently came up empty-handed. Peasants were peculiarly uncooperative; the federal forces of Mexico were either incompetent or corrupt.

And then, with an irony and coincidence that only nonfiction can provide, Villa appeared, and engaged in a pitched battle in Parral, very near the spot at which he would eventually die. It was an ambush. He knew the area well. He waited for the arrival of the soldiers with several hundred of his men, and when they arrived, the bandits attacked.

Pershing's men had been forewarned against just such a plan. They fought back ferociously, routing Villa's forces and seriously wounding Villa himself. Shot three times in the leg, he was carried to a cave in the nearby mountains, where he hovered between life and death for weeks.

Meanwhile, the expeditionary force encountered increasingly hostility from peasants and government representatives alike. Their presence, which had now extended to nine months, was looked upon as an incursion onto Mexican soil. And so, after conducting a fruitless campaign that had cost the U.S. government $100,000,000, Pershing and his men retreated across the northern border.

Recovering, Pancho Villa again reappeared. But his brush with death had produced a noticeable diminishment of enthusiasm, both in him and his men. Older, perhaps wiser, he and 900 of his followers surrendered peacefully, in July of 1920, at Sabinas, to a force of nearly 10,000 federal soldiers led by General Eugenio Martinez.

Villa was wanted for murder in the United States, but extradition for a folk hero would have been unthinkable, and he and his band knew that. He was still popular, Carranza was gone, and so the interim government of Adolfo de la Huerta awarded Pancho Villa a sentence of internal exile in Mexico, two million dollars in gold as a pension, and a small farm in Canutillo. There, the former brigand settled down, bought the latest American farm equipment and a Ford (some stories say a Dodge), and took up the life of a farmer.

It was a remarkable change from his former life, when he was described by historian Samuel H. Mayo as ". . . warm and friendly at one moment and ferocious the next. He could invite you to dinner and then order your execution—rescind the order and offer you coffee."

This bandit, who commanded so many villistas and had once ordered the cold-blooded slaughter of 300 prisoners, now built a hospital, chapel school, and telegraph office in the quiet little town of Parral.

STILL, even with all this peace and largess, Villa found it impossible to remain silent about the affairs of Mexico. He had been involved too long and too deeply. Presidential elections were in the offing. He let it be known that he favored his old friend Adolfo de la Huerta, or possibly General Raul Madero, over the favorite, Plutarco Callas.

He was setting himself up for danger, and his friends warned him against becoming involved too deeply in the sometimes lethal practice of Mexican politics. He ignored the warnings and followed his own lights.

Ironically, it would not be national, but local politics that would eventually account for his

Villa in January 1911, leading rebel troops against the government of Porfirio Diaz.

demise. Jesus Salas, the man who organized the plot to assassinate Pancho Villa, did it not because of Villa's impending reentrance into national politics, but to avenge a massacre, years ago, by Villa and his men, of residents of the small village of El Oro, in the state of Durango. Salas, himself up for reelection, became convinced that this master dramatic stroke would turn him into a hero in the eyes of the voters of Durango. There is no evidence that he had ambitions beyond that.

Salas worked diligently for months, assembling a band of conspirators. At the beginning of April, 1923, he rented a house at the corner of Benito Juarez and Balbino Barredo Streets, a location past which Villa rode constantly on trips from his ranch in the hills to the village of Parral.

In this anonymous house, Salas and six assassins studied the retired bandit leader's habits, his riding and walking routes, and the best positions for firing on him. Almost unbelievably, they were not discovered by any of Villa's friends during the three months they spent in hiding.

Once during that time, the group of seven assassins had a clear shot at Villa, but at the last minute, a group of school children on their way home dashed between them and the bandit.

Villa and Emiliano Zapata (holding sombrero) in the presidential palace during their 1914 occupation of Mexico City.

But at 8 a.m. on the morning of July 20, 1923, there were no children present as Pancho Villa and his secretary, Colonel Miguel Trillo, came into sight in Villa's slow-moving Ford. The conspirators, who had been waiting since dawn on either side of the road, opened fire. Over a hundred shots blasted the walls of the houses lining Benito Juarez Street. Forty of them slammed into and through the car; nine of them tore through Pancho Villa. He had no time to fire his famous twin pistols, which he always carried with him. Nor did Trillo, who was likewise armed. Daniel Tamayo, Villa's assistant, Rosario Rosales, Villa's chauffeur, and an unidentified passing civilian who happened to wander into the crossfire were all cut down instantly.

The murderers, much as Villa had in his heyday, leaped onto horses and fled into the hills. Salas's later confession noted that there were plenty of sympathetic citizens of Parral who aided in their escape and who would have provided them with shelter in the village itself. But in the heat of the moment, he said, the assassins chose to head for the hills.

A few days later, Salas wandered down out of his very temporary hideout, and was taken to Mexico City for trial. He announced, during the proceedings, that he would donate the reward money for the capture, dead or alive, of Pancho Villa by the United States toward the establishment of a charitable institution for the families of Villa's numerous victims.

There were certainly enough children already claiming money from the bandit's estate. No fewer than five wives and an army of offspring, plus his brother Hipolito and his sister Mariana showed up, claiming rights to it.

On September 20, 1923, Salas was sentenced to 20 years in prison, but he served only a fraction of that time. Obregon, the new president, made it known in public that there was a danger that Salas would be killed in prison.

He was right. Villa's death was about to be avenged. Salas survived, but all but one of his co-conspirators died violent deaths, one of them in an ambush at the exact spot at which Pancho Villa had met his own.

The state now took over the doling out of Villa's estate, and the continued war between those who idolized and those who condemned Pancho Villa raged on, unabated. Forty years later, the Mexican congress voted to preserve forever his name in gold on its chamber walls, along with other heroes of the Mexican Revolution. Once again the man was accorded the forgiving soft focus of legend.

LONG, FOLLOWED BY BODY GUARDS, LEFT THE HOUSE CHAMBER FOR THE GOVERNOR'S OFFICE DOWN THE HALL
CROWD WHICH SURGED FROM HOUSE CHAMBER SCRAMBLED BACK WHEN FIRING COMMENCED.
IN FRONT OF THE GOVERNOR'S DOOR, LONG TURNED TO TALK WITH WHITE AND FOURNET.
FOURNET GRABS WEISS' ARM, DEFLECTING AIM.
BODYGUARD RHODIN CLOSED WITH WEISS. THEN BACKED OFF FIRING FIRST SHOTS INTO HIS BODY.
AS LONG TURNED, WEISS STEPPED FROM BEHIND POST, DRAWING GUN FROM SIDE TROUSER POCKET.

HUEY LONG

POSITION:	*U.S. Senator from Louisiana*
DATE:	*September 8, 1935*
PLACE:	*Baton Rouge, Louisiana, U.S.A.*
HOW:	*Gunshot*
WHO:	*Carl Weiss*
CONVICTED:	*No. Killed by Long's bodyguards*
MOTIVE:	*Never determined*
DIRECT CONSEQUENCE:	*Termination of Long's run for the Presidency*

"WITH KNOWLEDGE aplenty and friends galore, he is bound to go out and make the world take notice," read the inscription under the class photo of Carl Weiss in the Tulane year book.

And the world did take notice, but not in the way the editorial writers had imagined.

On the afternoon of September 8, 1935, Dr. Carl Weiss, now a practicing and respected ear, eye, nose, and throat specialist, intercepted Louisiana dictator Huey Long in the rotunda of the state capitol in Baton Rouge and shot him. Within a minute, according to the most accepted version of the incident, he would be cut down with a fusillade of over 60 bullets from Long's bodyguards. Huey Long would be removed as a potent force in the politics of not only Louisiana, but the United States, and possibly the world.

THE WRITER Robert Penn Warren would make all of this indelible in his masterful, Pulitzer Prize winning novel *All the King's Men*, in which he moved the assassination outdoors and set up a love triangle as one of the assassin's motives. But aside from some literary license, his portrayal of the character and the influence of "the Kingfish," as Huey Long was called in his native state, was essentially and chillingly correct.

Born in Winnfield, Louisiana in 1893, Huey Long, with his brother Earl, seemed destined from the cradle for politics. Originally a farm boy, then a salesman, and finally a lawyer (he attended Tulane, the same university from which his assassin graduated), Huey Long became an attorney for the state of Louisiana shortly after being admitted to the bar.

In 1928, on his second try, he was elected governor of the state on a populist platform of reform to help the working family. Early in his term, he brought about the construction of badly needed roads and bridges, the expansion of state-owned hospitals, and the erecting of schools in rural regions. He achieved much of this by heavily taxing big businesses, especially the oil companies.

And so, his aims were, on the surface at least, noble ones. But his method of achieving them was anything but noble. He seemed impatient with the democratic process.

He used patronage to ramrod his programs past the state legislature, and he enlisted the aid of unsavory characters and organizations to help enforce his plans. Organized crime was one of them, and when New York City Mayor Fiorello H. LaGuardia forced the Mafia's slot-machines out of the Empire State, Long invited mob-leader Frank Costello to talk. Within a short time, New Orleans had become the slot-machine capital of the country, and the Long political machine was several millions of dollars wealthier.

Most of the time, his strong-arm tactics worked. Sometimes, however, democracy won, but only after a battle. In 1929, Long called a special session of the legislature to pass a new tax on the oil industry. Fist fights broke out on the floor of the Louisiana House of Representatives, which not only threw out the bill, but impeached Long for the crimes of bribery and gross misconduct. He was never convicted.

In 1930, he was elected to the U.S. Senate, but for nearly two years, he refused to take his seat. Afraid that Lieutenant Governor Paul N. Cyr would succeed to the Louisiana state governorship and dismantle the Long political machine, he didn't assume his duties in Washington until a year and a half after he won them.

During that time, Cyr swore himself into office twice, but a cordon of national guardsmen, under Long's orders, surrounded the highway commission, the capitol and the executive mansion, preventing the succession.

This sort of police-state behavior caused apprehension among those not altogether enchanted with this undeniably charismatic political leader. His stratagems echoed uncomfortably those of another ascending leader in Germany named Adolph Hitler. Hitler had also increased the efficiency of government by doing away with representation and forging a police state. And his fellow dictator, Benito Mussolini in Italy, had begun by building roads and other public projects, and making the trains run on time.

It was a chilling parallel, particularly considering Long's political evolution. Early in his career as a U.S. senator, he supported the New Deal policies of Franklin D. Roosevelt. They, after all, were designed to help the same constituency that he himself commanded. But when it became apparent that Roosevelt was planning to be in office for multiple terms, Long, aspiring to the Presidency himself, became a fierce foe of Roosevelt and his New Deal policies, and founded and espoused his own set of social reforms.

Early in 1934, he introduced his plan for national and social overhauling. Called the "Share the Wealth" plan, it proposed a guaranteed family income and a homestead allowance for every family in the United States. Needless to say, Long began to gather wide support among voters hard-hit by the Depression.

BUT, AS most demagogues do, he overreached. In that same year of 1934, he began a restructuring of the state government of Louisiana which would give him virtually dictatorial powers. He effectively did away with local government. It became a crime punishable by imprisonment for federal agents to enter Louisiana to advocate New Deal reforms and put them to work in the state.

He gerrymandered election districts, dividing the state's electoral map with convenient boundaries which guaranteed that anti-Long candidates would be defeated in coming elections and pro-Long candidates would be elected.

One of these gerrymandered districts would politically disable Judge B. H. Pavy of Opelousas. Judge Pavy was the father-in-law of Long's assassin, Dr. Carl Weiss. The jurist had been one of Long's principal opponents in St. Landy Parish for some time, and it may have been loyalty to the judge, an inflamed sense of injustice, or—as Robert Penn Warren suggested in *All the King's Men*—both of these plus the final straw of some sort of relationship between Long and Dr. Weiss's wife that finally determined his actions on September 8, 1935.

LONG SPENT much of that day in the Louisiana state legislature, which met in the five-million-dollar Baton Rouge state house. He strode up and down the aisles, interrupting speakers, joking, cajoling, bullying his ideas and programs through what was now a puppet legislature anyway.

Early that evening, Dr. Weiss, attired in a white linen suit, left his home, explaining to his wife that he had to make a few house calls. Instead, he drove to the capitol building, parked his car, and ascended the building's steps. He stationed himself in the corridor outside the office of Long's handmaiden governor, Oscar O. K. Allen. Later, some witnesses would swear that, as he paced agitatedly up and down the hallway, Weiss muttered, "It won't be long now,"—which sounded a little too literary to be true.

Shortly before 9:30 p.m., the legislature recessed, and Senator Long, accompanied by his armed bodyguard and Supreme Court Justice John B. Fournet, strode from the floor of the House of Representatives. "Everybody be here in the morning," he shouted, gruffly, to his cohorts. "Tell everybody to be here."

The Senator had a habit of striding aggressively forward, as if he were wading into a fight. It was difficult to keep up with him in moments like these, and his bodyguards spread out in a phalanx behind him, guarding the rear. Thus, they did not see Dr. Weiss step from the side of the corridor and swing into line alongside Senator Long.

A FEW steps, and Dr. Weiss drew out a Belgian .32 caliber pistol, jammed it into Huey Long's right side, and fired. Long staggered, Justice Fournet snatched at Weiss's arm, and Murphy Roden, a bodyguard, dived at the assassin. They grappled for an instant, then fell free of each other. Seconds later, sub-machine gun and pistol fire erupted from the bodyguards. It was like a small war, and it didn't cease when the doctor fell to the floor. State

"All the News That's Fit to Print."

The New York Times.

LATE CITY EDITION
WEATHER—Rain today, temperature unchanged; tomorrow rain.
Temperatures Yesterday—Max., 77; min., 59.

VOL. LXXXIV....No. 28,352. Entered as Second-Class Matter, Postoffice, New York, N. Y. NEW YORK, MONDAY, SEPTEMBER 9, 1935. PPP TWO CENTS In New York City. | THREE CENTS Within 200 Miles | FOUR CENTS Elsewhere Except in 7th and 8th Postal Zones.

DOCTOR SHOOTS HUEY LONG IN LOUISIANA STATE CAPITOL; BODYGUARDS KILL ASSAILANT

Times Wide World Photo.

SENATOR HUEY P. LONG.

ITALY SEEN PLAYING FOR TIME IN GENEVA AND INTENT ON WAR

League's Efforts May Turn on Making Peace Rather Than Preventing Conflict.

ROME IS STILL NOT BOUND

Assembly Meets Today, but Is Not Expected to Consider the African Problem.

'ON THE MARCH,' SAYS DUCE

Mussolini Asserts Italy Wants 'Peace With Justice'—Rome Raises Rediscount Rate.

The Italo-Ethiopian Crisis.

GENEVA—War seems probable in Africa before the League can achieve any settlement, as Italy apparently is playing for time. International police control for Ethiopia is one proposal being considered. The League Assembly convenes today but is not expected to take up the Ethiopian problem at this time.

ROME—Premier Mussolini in one speech yesterday said Italy wanted "peace and justice" and in another said "Italy is now definitely on the March." The Bank of Italy for the second time in a month raised the rediscount rate, this time from 4½ to 5 per cent.

ADDIS ABABA—Ethiopian troops were dispatched to the south to be ready for any Italian offensive from Italian Somaliland. The Emperor's advisers counseled firmness in the face of various proposals broached at Geneva. The Italian Minister protested against alleged arrests and annoyances of consulate members.

Sparring by Italy Seen.

By FREDERICK T. BIRCHALL.

Wireless to THE NEW YORK TIMES.

GENEVA, Sept. 8.—In the lull that has fallen upon the Italo-Ethiopian negotiations here it is possible to take account of the progress that has been made so far. It is impossible to escape the conviction that this progress has been more apparent than real.

The Italians, it should be emphasized, have not agreed to the formation of a new conciliation committee, set up by the League of Nations Council. By refraining from voting they have merely consented to ignore its establishment. Whether they will negotiate with the committee as a whole still remains to be seen.

They have said their sole object in remaining here is to pay to the great powers remaining in the League the courtesy of talking with them. But they take the position that their proposed war on Ethiopia is justified by their citation of Ethiopian shortcomings and that the League will exceed its prerogatives if it attempts to prevent that war, because, the Italians assert, Ethiopia is unworthy of membership and ought to be thrown out.

Italy Held Playing for Time.

However, it is quite obviously to Italy's advantage to prolong the negotiations here until the time is ripe to attack in East Africa. There are six divisions of Italian troops and half of the proposed equipment and airplanes still on their way to their base or only newly arrived there.

Eritrea and Italian Somaliland are still waterlogged from rains and in no condition for the movement of troops. It will be at least a fortnight before this condition changes. The probability is that the Italian advance in force may be delayed almost to October.

There must, however, be quick action in Geneva if an Italian invasion of Ethiopia proper is to be prevented. So the coming week will doubtless witness an intensification of the efforts to reach a settlement.

The first problem will be to find a basis on which to negotiate. The only basis in sight is that of the Paris proposals, which Italy has already rejected. It is contended by Rome that those proposals were presented as the maximum that could be obtained. The British and French assert, on the other hand, that they were offered merely as a basis for negotiation. The one certain fact is their rejection.

Obviously, therefore, the proposals must be expanded if they are to become even a basis for further talk. It is also pretty clear that they must be expanded in the direction of giving Italy greater political and military control over Ethiopia than the original proposal contemplated.

How that can be brought about while preserving even a remnant of Ethiopian sovereignty and independence is not clear at present. That will be the committee's problem.

The one thought in the minds of some members—it is said, inciden-

Continued on Page Four.

Thieves Free 'Gas' Flood, Imperil Chicago Area

Special to THE NEW YORK TIMES.

CHICAGO, Sept. 8. — Thieves took an automobile and a tank truck at the plant of the Red Flash Petroleum Corporation early today. In filling the tank truck from an electric gasoline pump they broke the pump, thereby endangering hundreds of lives and millions in property.

Sixteen thousand gallons of gasoline flooded streets and alleys, six inches in depth in many places, over a wide area. A spark from a locomotive or from an automobile, or a lighted cigarette stub, would have started a conflagration.

The petroleum company has many tanks at its plant. Abutting the plant are many homes and factories.

The police, hastily summoned, shut off the broken pump, and diverted all traffic until the gasoline had been washed into the sewers with fire hose.

DOHENY, OIL MAN, DIES IN WEST AT 79

Figure in Teapot Dome Case Had Spectacular Rise From Poverty to Wealth.

PROSPECTOR FOR 20 YEARS

Then He Turned From Gold to Petroleum and Started the Los Angeles Boom.

By The Associated Press.

LOS ANGELES, Sept. 8.—Edward Laurence Doheny, who wrested one of the world's largest fortunes from the oil fields of California and Mexico, died at 8 o'clock tonight at his home here. He was 79 years old.

Mr. Doheny's death was caused by age and complications after an illness that kept him bed-ridden for almost three years. At his bedside were his widow, Estelle, and five grandchildren.

Discoverer with the late Charles A. Canfield of one of the first oil fields of California, Mr. Doheny had a career that was one of the most picturesque in the history of American industry. In Tampico, Mexico, he reared a vast industrial empire that came to be known as one of the greatest concentrated oil holdings of private capital in the world.

Tragedy and sorrow stalked him at the very zenith of his career, however, because of his operations in Elk Hills, Calif. He was indicted in 1924 in connection with naval reserve leases. Albert B. Fall, former Secretary of the Interior, also indicted in this case, was convicted, but Mr. Doheny was acquitted.

Only recently a Doheny-controlled corporation here foreclosed on the New Mexico ranch of Mr. Fall, who disclosed that he had received orders to vacate. Mr. Doheny and Mr. Fall were reported to have remained close friends through the years, but Doheny made no comment on the foreclosure.

Waited Years for 'Strike.'

Edward Laurence Doheny left home when 16 years old to be a muleteer. He spent the next twenty years tramping plains, deserts and mountains as a prospector, with the "big strike" always just around the corner. In 1892, while walking the streets of Los Angeles, a mere chance caused him to shift his quest from gold to petroleum, and a few years later he was one of the greatest oil operators in the world. He spent his youth in hardship, his middle age in a phenomenal rise to wealth, power and fame, and much of his old age in grief and humiliation through the notorious oil scandals of the Harding administration.

Mr. Doheny came of Irish pioneers. He was born on Aug. 10, 1856, to Patrick and Eleanor Elizabeth (Quigley) Doheny at Fond du Lac, Wis., which was then in frontier territory. His boyhood surroundings were similar to those described in the old dime novels. He knew plainsmen and Indians, and at the early age when he left home to take charge of the mules in a government surveying expedition in Indian territory he already knew how to fend for himself.

No Future as Muleteer.

He saw no future in caring for mules but his trip to the Southwest gave him a taste for the sort of work to which he was to devote his youth. He had no technical training, but he observed the government surveyors, picked up the elements of their trade, and practiced for a while, but soon decided that it offered little better chances for wealth than did mule-driving, and it was wealth that Doheny wanted. He talked to prospectors and decided that prospecting was the life for him.

He spent twenty years looking for gold. Sometimes he found it. Repeatedly he built up mines, knew temporary affluence, "went broke" and started out again. The Black

Continued on Page Thirteen.

BIGGEST BUSINESS SINCE '30 FORESEEN THIS FALL BY LABOR

A. F. of L. Asserts Upswing Is Healthiest So Far and Is Not Due to Federal Spending.

FINDS STEEL 'OUT OF RED'

Higher Buying Power Created by NRA and AAA Has Been Felt at Last, Says Report.

Special to THE NEW YORK TIMES.

WASHINGTON, Sept. 8.—In the most optimistic statement on the recovery movement it has yet made, the American Federation of Labor today said that business was showing greater vitality than in any upswing since 1933 and that "the last four months of 1935 may well bring the highest level of industrial operations and earnings for any similar period since 1930."

"The present business upswing," the federation said, "is the healthiest thus far; it is the first not due to government spending or currency action; the first which seems due chiefly to inherent economic strength. Dividend payments in August exceeded last year by $11,000,000, or 4 per cent; the steel industry is out of the red for the first time since 1930. With these signs of increased industrial earnings, much depends upon the workers making a new drive now for higher incomes."

Buying power of the workers, lifted to higher levels in 1934 by the NRA, and the income of farmers, raised by the AAA, the report said, "at last have made themselves felt in sufficient degree to stimulate production."

The federation stated that orders for automobiles in the first half of 1935 were 75 per cent above last year and that, "as a result of increased buying and production and growing confidence, industry is beginning to order new machinery. Machine-tool orders in the first half of 1935 were 47 per cent above last year."

Big Expansion Outlays Cited.

"All these lines of activity," the survey continued, "have continued through July and August. The automobile industry is spending $100,000,000 on production equipment; the steel industry, $130,000,000, it is estimated. This new life in the heavy industries should mean more jobs where unemployment has been particularly severe."

The federation said that the trend had started strongly upward after a five months' waiting period, and that from the week of July 6 to Aug. 24 THE NEW YORK TIMES index recorded a gain of 8 per cent to 88 per cent of normal.

"This striking gain," it said, "was made in the short space of seven weeks; it leaves business well over half-way back to normal. Employment, however, has not kept pace with gains in business."

Stressing that the income of wage-earners had lagged, the survey quoted Department of Commerce figures in contending that workers lost three-fifths of their income from 1929 to 1933, and had regained a little over one-tenth by 1934.

The only important increase in employment since recovery started, the survey said, came in 1933, this being due largely to the shortening of work hours under NRA.

"In the Summer of 1933, 1,800,000 men and women were put to work by dropping five hours from the work week," the survey continued. "Since September, 1933, there have been no further significant gains in employment in spite of increasing production. This has been especial-

Continued on Page Two.

A.F. du Ponts Race by Air To Daughter Ill in Jamaica

By The Associated Press.

WILMINGTON, Del., Sept. 8.—A. Felix du Pont Jr. said tonight he had received word from his parents that they had arrived at Kingston, Jamaica, after a 2,000-mile airplane dash, to be at the bedside of their daughter, Miss Lydia du Pont.

Mr. du Pont said his parents informed him Miss du Pont was ill with tonsilitis in a Jamaica hospital. It was at first reported she was suffering with tropical fever.

The elder du Pont, who is vice president of E. I. du Pont de Nemours & Co., and Mrs. du Pont were taken from Wilmington to Washington yesterday in an airplane piloted by their son. At Washington they boarded a transport plane to Miami. The trip from Miami to Jamaica was made in another transport. Young du Pont said his parents arrived at Jamaica late today.

Miss du Pont was taken ill while working with a Philadelphia scientific expedition in the Colombia jungles.

$200,000 IN LIQUOR SEIZED ON VESSEL

British Ship and 3 Speedboats Captured by Coast Guard Near Atlantic City.

20 PRISONERS ARE TAKEN

Cutters Halt the Transfer of Cargo With Shot—Largest Haul Since Repeal.

Special to THE NEW YORK TIMES.

CAPE MAY, N. J., Sept. 8.—Three American boats, a British ship, twenty men and a cargo valued at $200,000—one of the largest captures since prohibition was repealed—were seized by Cape May Coast Guards shortly before last midnight ten miles southeast of Atlantic City.

Led by Lieutenant R. L. Burke, in charge of the Coast Guard air base here, three cutters on regular patrol observed the British oil schooner Popocatapelt anchored. Alongside of the 103-foot craft were the three American boats, with liquor aboard.

The smaller boats were listed as the Theresa of Margate, N. J.; Nampahc of Point Pleasant and the Dreadnaught. All the boats, about forty feet long, are equipped with high-powered motors.

Eight members of the crew were on the British boat, which was listed as a "British oil screw," equipped with a Diesel driving engine. Its capacity is 153 tons.

One shot was fired by the Coast Guards when they approached the schooner. This, the officials said, was the regulation warning. The rum-runners did not put up a fight, Lieutenant Burke said. The four boats and the prisoners were brought to the local base. The prisoners were segregated and questioned.

The Dreadnaught, Coast Guards said today, was leaking badly and every effort was being made to keep her afloat.

Liquor seized on the three American boats, it was reported, already had been unloaded from the British craft. When the American boats caught sight of the Coast Guardsmen an attempt was made to make for shore, but the cutters were soon alongside and the crews surrendered.

The cargo, consisting of 5,000 cases, was estimated to be worth $200,000. It was composed of British liquor, alcohol and assorted brandies.

The capture, Coast Guards

Continued on Page Two.

Panama Assemblyman Holds Police at Bay; Wanted Following Theft of U.S. Army Guns

Special Cable to THE NEW YORK TIMES.

PANAMA CITY, Sept. 8.—A member of the National Assembly, Victor Florencia Goytia, is holding at bay at his residence policemen who have an order for his arrest in connection with the recent theft of machine guns and other arms and of ammunition from the United States Army at Corozal.

Detectives have been guarding his house since yesterday, but Goytia refuses to leave and has announced that he will not be taken alive and will shoot the first man who touches him.

A former Chief of Police, Homero Ayala, who had been held by the Canal Zone police after his arrest by the Panama police yesterday and delivered to the Canal Zone authorities, was released in $1,500 bail today. He was one of the leaders of the revolt of 1931. After the overthrow of President Arosemena he became Chief of Police, but resigned later and joined the opposition to the present government.

The theft from the United States Army post included four machine guns, valued at $4,000; four automatic rifles, valued at $1,000, and small arms and ammunition valued at $400, all of which were believed to have been taken for possible revolutionary use.

Both Goytia and Ayala are prominently identified with the reformed Liberal party, which has been attacking the Arias government through the newspaper Panama American, edited by Goytia.

An investigation into the theft by Canal Zone police and the army, assisted by the Panama police, has resulted in the arrest of three Americans—Eddie Payne, a former soldier and former Canal Zone policeman; Ellis M. Stevens, an employe of the Panama Railroad, and Sergeant Carl Dumpke, a soldier of the Corozal Ordnance Depot—two Nicaraguans and two Panamanians.

The stolen arms have not yet been found, but the police say they have clues that are expected to lead to discovery of the cache.

'TOTAL REST CURE' IS BUSINESS NEED, SAY REPUBLICANS

'Breathing Spell' From Roosevelt Only Breeds Fear, National Committee Asserts.

CITES PLANS FOR NEW NRA

Howard Letter 'Stunt' Evaded Budget Balancing and Inflation Issues, It Charges.

Special to THE NEW YORK TIMES.

WASHINGTON, Sept. 8.—The Republican National Committee declared today that the business, financial and industrial interests of this country do not want "merely a breathing spell" from President Roosevelt's régime—"they want a complete rest cure."

In its weekly "Facts and Opinions" the committee, commenting on the exchange of letters last week between the President and Roy W. Howard, said that the Roosevelt-Howard correspondence failed to state the administration's position on inflation of the currency, balancing the budget and getting the government out of business.

"The Howard-Roosevelt question-and-answer stunt has changed no one's opinion of the Roosevelt administration or the policies and program of the New Deal," the committee asserted.

"It probably was not expected to do so. More likely it was designed to afford Mr. Howard a freshly laundered alibi for keeping his newspaper chain narrowly partisan in its support of the President and furnish an excuse in advance for advocating his renomination and re-election.

Charges 'Partisan Propaganda.'

"It was a good piece of partisan propaganda, even though perfectly transparent. The collaboration was perfect. The President did not dare run the risk of having such a prominent publisher publicly ask him any embarrassing questions to which he was expected to make a public reply. For that reason Mr. Howard avoided bringing up questions about inflation, return to a sound currency, balancing the budget, getting the government out of private business and, particularly, about the President's determination to make the United States Constitution conform to his socialistic program rather than abandon that program because it runs contrary to the United States Constitution. In other words, the political significance of Mr. Howard's letter is measured not by what it asked but by what it conspicuously failed to ask.

"On the other hand, Mr. Howard had something to protect. He could not afford to take his newspaper chain out on a limb by blindly hazarding a reply from an administration that had been as erratic as a weather vane in a whirlwind.

"Ghost writer No. 1 of the New Deal may not have composed both the letters, but he must be given due credit for a good job of editing. The President knew in advance the questions that would be asked. Mr. Howard knew in advance the answers that would be made.

Business Man 'Not Reassured.'

"Other than easing Mr. Howard's journalistic conscience and furnishing the President opportunity to offer a very abridged and very lame defense of his policies and motives, the correspondence has accomplished nothing.

"It is obvious the 'frightened business men,' out of solicitude for whom the correspondence was ostensibly initiated, are not going to be reassured regarding the Roosevelt program until they obtain some definite and dependable answer to the questions which Mr. Howard did not ask.

"There is nothing in the President's letter to which the confidence of men of affairs can make fast. He reiterates the fundamental fallacy of the New Deal—that it is impossible to distinguish between recovery and reform.

"Because of that blind obsession the Roosevelt administration in the name of reform unloosed forces destructive of our sound and legitimate economic structure, which made it impossible to have business recovery and which are justifiably accountable for the hostility and fright which Mr. Howard himself admits now pervade the world of business, finance and industry.

Holds Situation Aggravated.

"The President's letter aggravates the very situation it is supposed to alleviate by insisting that the policies of the New Deal are 'in conformity with the basic economic purposes which were set forth three years ago.'"

Some of the alleged rejections of his promises and of the party's platform pledges cited by the committee are:

Failure to maintain a sound currency.

Going off the gold standard contrary to predictions in his speech

Continued on Page Fifteen.

HELD IN 8 MURDERS, ENDS LIFE IN CELL

Gang Leader Hangs Himself After Confessing Murder of a Patrolman.

BETRAYED BY ASSOCIATES

Habit of Having Accomplices Slain Led Ex-Aides to Put Police on His Trail.

Anthony Cugino, Philadelphia desperado, sought for many months in connection with eight murders, committed suicide shortly before midnight last night in his cell at police headquarters.

Cugino had been subjected to fifteen hours of relentless questioning and, according to the police, had finally confessed to one of the eight murders—the killing of a policeman.

The gunman, known as the Stinger, whose arrest, according to the police, was brought about by the fear and hatred he had inspired in his own former associates, apparently had been resting quietly in his cell in the basement of the headquarters building. Patrolman Hugh O'Connell had seen him a few minutes earlier as he paced the lighted corridor in front of the cell group.

The next time the patrolman saw the prisoner Cugino was hanging from a water pipe in his cell.

He had torn his shirt into strips, fashioned a rope with the skill of a sailor, tied one end around the pipe and the other about his own throat and then had jumped from the edge of a wash bowl.

Cugino also used his necktie in fashioning his hangman's noose. The police investigation centred last night around the question as to why Cugino was allowed to keep an article with which he so easily improvised a rope.

O'Connell at once called for help, and Inspector James McGrath hurried to the cell. A few minutes later a police emergency squad arrived with pulmotors and then Dr. Wright, a police surgeon, and Dr. Louis Liccirdi from Columbus Hospital.

Both oxygen and adrenalin were administered in vain. The prisoner was pronounced dead at 2:25 A. M. after the police and physicians had worked nearly an hour over him.

O'Connell went on duty at 11:15 he informed Inspector McGrath and at that time Cugino seemed to be all right. At 11:30 two other prisoners in cells across the narrow aisle from that of Philadelphia's "Public Enemy No. 1," called to the policeman and asked for a drink of water. When he brought it they pointed out that Cugino seemed to be standing in a peculiar position.

"I called to him to get down," O'Connell said, "and there was no answer."

The patrolman then saw that the gangster had hanged himself.

Among the effects found on the

Continued on Page Two.

LONG PREDICTED HE WOULD BE SHOT

He Told Senate Aug. 9 That Plot to Kill Him Had Been Overheard in New Orleans.

ALWAYS HAD A BODYGUARD

Thomas Recalls Inquiry in Louisiana Revealed Hate and 'Almost Mob Desires.'

By The Associated Press.

WASHINGTON, Sept. 8.—News of the attempted assassination of Senator Huey Long in Baton Rouge startled the capital late tonight, with officials recalling instantly that only a month ago tomorrow he told the Senate a plot to kill him was afoot.

As word spread through the city, telephone calls to newspaper offices for information increased with the minute.

Until details of the shooting and his condition were known, officials and political leaders had little to say.

Senator Thomas, Democrat, of Utah, attributed the shooting of Senator Long to "an irresponsible and thoughtless person."

Recalls Overton Hearing.

Mr. Thomas is familiar with the Louisiana political situation, having presided at hearings there on the seating of Senator Overton of the Long faction.

"It is most unfortunate," Mr. Thomas's statement said. "I had first had acquaintance with the tense feelings and almost mob desires expressed by partisans on both sides when I presided in the Overton hearing two years ago.

"I cannot help but feel that the act was one of an irresponsible and thoughtless person, because no matter how hateful controlled government may become in the minds of its antagonists, the minute force is used confusion is instant.

"Shooting always invites more shooting. It cannot bring better conditions by shooting. The American system of recall is to use ballots and not bullets."

Others Took His Fears Lightly.

The committee of which Mr. Thomas was a member excoriated some of the methods involved in the conduct of Louisiana elections, but Mr. Overton kept his seat.

Many of the Senate, at the time of Long's speech, had taken the Louisianan's fears lightly.

The Louisianan, on Aug. 9, took the floor during a dull afternoon and said two of his supporters had sat in a hotel room in New Orleans adjoining an apartment where the reported plot was discussed. Some

Continued on Page Three.

SENATOR'S WOUND GRAVE

Pistol Pressed to Body, Bullet Goes Through His Abdomen.

ATTACKER A POLITICAL FOE

Would-Be Assassin a Relative of a Judge Whose Defeat Long Was Planning.

OPERATION IS PERFORMED

Follows Transfusion in Which Lieutenant Governor Gives Blood to the Senator.

Surgeons' Bulletin on Long.

Special to THE NEW YORK TIMES.

BATON ROUGE, La., Monday, Sept. 9.—The surgeons attending Senator Long issued the following bulletin at 2 o'clock this morning (4 A. M. New York time):

"Senator Long was wounded by one bullet entering the upper right side, emerging from the back. The colon was punctured in two places.

"The first blood transfusion has been given the Senator, with good results.

"The condition of Senator Long is thoroughly satisfactory. It will be seventy-two to ninety hours before further developments can be expected.

"Another bulletin will be issued at 7 A. M."

In an emergency operation the surgeons sutured veins to stop internal bleeding and cleansed the wound to prevent infection.

Special to THE NEW YORK TIMES.

BATON ROUGE, La., Sept. 8.—United States Senator Huey P. Long was shot through the stomach and gravely wounded tonight as he walked from the chamber of the Louisiana House of Representatives, where he had been directing the passage of bills aimed to strengthen his grip upon the politics of the State and to fight the New Deal and Roosevelt policies.

It was about 9:30 o'clock (11:30 New York daylight saving time), and the Legislature had just recessed until morning.

The would-be assassin, shot down and killed instantly by three members of the State police acting as bodyguards for Louisiana's senior Senator, was identified as Dr. Carl A. Weiss, an eye, ear, nose and throat specialist of Baton Rouge.

Dr. Weiss, who was 29, was the son-in-law of Judge B. H. Pavy of Opelousas, a leader of an anti-Long faction in St. Landry Parish.

One of the bills scheduled for passage at this special session of the Legislature was designed to gerrymander Judge Pavy's judicial district so that his re-election next January would have been well-nigh impossible.

The bill would have added the parishes of Acadia, Lafayette and Vermilion, where Long majorities are heavy, to Judge Pavy's home parish.

Lieut. Gov. Noe Gives Blood.

The most skilled surgeons in the State were summoned to the Senator's side at Our Lady of the Lake Sanitarium, to which he was rushed by automobile, conscious but bleeding profusely.

A blood transfusion was decided upon, and scores of friends volunteered to give their blood. Ten volunteers were selected for tests. Lieut. Gov. James A. Noe, a close friend of Senator Long, was accepted and the transfusion was made an hour and a half after the shooting occurred.

"Go ahead and clean it," Senator Long said through gritted teeth to the surgeon when they informed him that his wound would have to be cleaned. Tests were being made, physicians said, to determine whether the bullet which pierced Senator Long's abdomen was poisoned.

Soon after the transfusion was made it was reported that surgeons had decided to perform an emergency operation.

About an hour later the operation was carried out.

While the House gallery was crowded with spectators, there were few witnesses to the actual shooting. Senator Long had been strid-

Continued on Page Three.

Senator Huey Long lying in state in Baton Rouge.

troopers continued to pump bullets into the prostrate body that was now leaping, not from the suspiration of breath, but the impact of bullet after bullet burrowing into it. Thirty bullets entered his chest, 29 drove into his back, and two struck him in the head. The wall and floor of the state house were pitted beyond restoration.

THERE ARE two other reported versions of Long's and Weiss's last moments. One claims that Weiss never got off a shot, but was gunned down by the guards, who, in their enthusiasm, also killed their boss. The other insists that Weiss never really wished to kill Long, only injure him in public. He approached the Kingfish and punched him in the mouth, whereupon the guards opened up, killing both Weiss and Long. Neither of these has the ring of authenticity that the first version contains.

Meanwhile, as the guards continued to shoot the dead body of his assailant, the unnoticed Senator Long, with blood streaming from his mouth, staggered down a stairway from the main foyer of the capitol and fell into the arms of Public Service Commissioner James O'Connor. "Jimmy, my boy," he groaned, "I'm shot."

O'Connor, drawing his pistol, dragged the stricken Senator to a taxicab and stuffed him into it. At the hospital, physicians worked feverishly, transfusing the Senator with blood and performing emergency surgery without anaesthetic. "Go ahead and clean the wound," said the Senator, waving way the anaesthetist.

The bullet had made two puncture wounds in his stomach and had pierced a kidney. Two blood transfusions failed to rally the Senator, and at 4:10 a.m., he died.

THE NEXT day, the Louisiana legislature, with Assistant Attorney General George Wallace and several of Mr. Long's aides steering it, passed all of the legislation

Long had wanted. Much of it was, of course, unconstitutional, and was soon reversed. A thousand people, including many political notables, attended the funeral of Dr. Weiss the following day. Later that week, a state funeral for Huey Long would attract 30,000 mourners.

The Senator, it was revealed, died a relatively poor man. He left no will, a few oil stocks of uncertain value, a heavily mortgaged home in New Orleans, and life insurance policies worth about $130,000. The rest of the millions he had made over the years had, many theorized, been pumped into his Presidential campaign and to finance his newspaper, *The American Progress*. A Senate inquiry into the slaying was convened, but no proof of a conspiracy was ever proved. Dr. Weiss's reasons died with him, and the rest was speculation, and therefore subject to literary license.

LONDRES PIDE AYUDA A WASHINGTON

LEON TROTSKY

POSITION:	*Co-founder, with Lenin, of the Russian Revolution*
DATE:	*August 20, 1940*
PLACE:	*Mexico City, Mexico*
HOW:	*Blow from an ice-axe*
WHO:	*Ramon Mercador*
CONVICTED:	*Yes. Sentenced to 20 years' imprisonment*
MOTIVE:	*Execution, ordered by Stalin*
DIRECT CONSEQUENCE:	*Josef Stalin's power further consolidated*

IT IS doubtful that life in the U.S.S.R. would have been much better had Leon Trotsky won his power struggle with Josef Stalin. Both were, by all accounts, heartless men, and, indeed it was Trotsky who founded and commanded the same secret police who were blamed for carrying out an execution order from Stalin upon the exiled Trotsky.

Born Lev Davidovich Bronstein of Jewish parents in the Ukraine, Trotsky lived a violent and stormy existence, and the grisliness of his death was thought by many to be merely consistent with his way of life.

IMPRISONED and exiled over and over for his beliefs and activities, Trotsky took his name from the head jailer of the prison in Siberia from which he escaped in 1902. Henceforth, Leon Trotsky would work tirelessly to realize, on a grand scale, the ism of Karl Marx.

It was in 1905 that he adopted from Marx a theory of "permanent revolution" that would spread beyond Russia's borders to the world. He argued that the revolution should result in an immediate establishment of a so-called "dictatorship of the proletariat"—which became the basis of power for the Communist elite in the U.S.S.R. after 1918.

In Finland when the October 1905 general strike occurred in St. Petersburg, Trotsky hurried back to Russia, where he was elected to the executive committee of the soviet of St. Petersburg, later to be renamed Leningrad.

In 1907, after the collapse of the revolution, he was exiled to Siberia for life with the loss of all civil rights. He escaped on the way to Siberia, and, from then until 1917, when, with Vladimir Ilyich Lenin, he brought about the Russian Revolution of 1917–18, Trotsky remained a potent but exiled force for a world revolution for the proletariat.

Once more distanced by necessity from the country in which he foresaw the working out of his ideas, he lived first in Paris, then Vienna, then Zurich and finally New York City. All the while, he maintained contact with Lenin and the planners of the revolution.

IN MAY of 1917, with the revolution already three months old, he landed in Petrograd and immediately set about uniting workers under Lenin. Later that year, he became people's commisar for foreign affairs, and, in 1918, commissar of war.

He built the Red Army from a force of fewer than 10,000 to one of five million during the civil war that followed the revolution, and it was here that he began to clash with Stalin. His first argument with the future leader of the U.S.S.R. was over the status of trade unions—Trotsky wanted them controlled by the state; Stalin did not.

THE TWO existed in sustained and unrelieved enmity, and as Lenin's health declined and palace intrigue accelerated, the battle for succession became joined. It was bitter and heated. Stalin gathered all of the many enemies Trotsky had strong-armed to gain power, and they proved formidable.

At Lenin's funeral in 1924—which Trotsky did not attend—Stalin declared himself Lenin's successor. He saw to it that Trotsky was first expelled from the Communist party, and then, in 1929, exiled from the U.S.S.R. to Alma-Ata in Central Asia.

The banished revolutionary remained there for only a short time, proceeding first to Turkey, then France, then Norway.

Back in the U.S.S.R., where Stalin was busily purging dissent and dissenters, Trotsky was tried in absentia, and, in the trials of 1936, he was accused of treason, a charge he vigorously denied.

NOW THE long arm of Stalin extended into Norway, forcing his exile from that country, and he fled to Mexico City, where he continued to write the fierce anti-Stalinist tracts that enfuriated the Communist dictator, and to foment unrest among students and workers in the Soviet Union, among whom the tracts were circulated.

His writings were as fierce and vicious as the man. George Bernard Shaw said of them, "When he cuts off his opponent's head, he holds it up to show that there are no brains in it." This Trotsky did to Stalin, over and over, in such works as *The Stalinist School of Falsification*, *Stalin's Crimes*, *The Real Situation in Russia*, and an unfinished "antibiography" called, simply, *Stalin*.

For a while, Trotsky lived in the home of the famed Mexican muralist Diego Rivera, but the two volatile geniuses soon argued over radical theory, and Trotsky moved out and into his own home. It was here, in Mexico City, that he founded the Fourth International, a small but articulate group of theorizers who advocated world revolution and the triumph of pure Communism.

It was hardly a low profile activity, and Stalin accelerated his efforts to eliminate what had become a very large thorn in his side.

First, in 1938, the dictator's assassins gained entrance to a Paris hospital, where Trotsky's 32-year-old son was a patient. They kidnapped and then murdered him.

Then, in the early hours of May 24, 1940, 21 men, dressed in Mexican police uniforms, burst into Trotsky's home in Mexico City, set off dynamite, then flung his bedroom door open and proceeded to spray the room with 300 rounds of machine gun fire. Miraculously, Trotsky and his wife escaped injury by prostrating themselves flat on the floor. The conspirators escaped, taking with them one of Trotsky's guards, a New Yorker named Robert Sheldon. It would be weeks before his riddled body would be found in a deserted house not far from the Trotsky home.

Life was obviously going to continue in its accustomed, tumultuous way for the revolutionary leader. Shortly after this first attempt on his life, a group of men whom Diego Rivera identified as agents of Stalin's secret police, surrounded the painter's home as he was working on a portrait of the film star Paulette Goddard. Rivera escaped in a station wagon, then charged Lombardo Toledano, the leader of the CTM, Mexico's labor group, with anti-American, pro-Stalin, pro-Nazi activities, and planning attempts on both his and Trotsky's lives. None of the charges was ever proven.

Now, during the late spring and early summer of 1940, Trotsky supervised the transformation of his home into a fortress. Three-gun pill boxes were mounted on 15-foot-high brick walls. A steel door was added to the front entrance of the villa, and an army of guards was hired to police the grounds.

IT WAS a little like the barricading of exiled royalty behind their palace walls in the 17th and 18th centuries, and, like that royalty, Trotsky neglected to protect himself from his friends. In March 1940, an American girl from Brooklyn, Sylvia Ageloff, introduced him to Frank Jackson, a friend whom she had met two years before in Paris. The two hit it off well—or as well as anyone did with the steel-trap minded revolutionary. Jackson was a willing listener, an eager student, and a skilled flatterer. He became a regular dinner guest in Trotsky's home, and a member of his inner circle of acquaintances. In April, Miss Ageloff returned to her job as a home relief welfare investigator, but Jackson stayed on in Mexico City, where he developed his skills at using an ice axe by climbing the volcanoes near Mexico City.

Incredibly enough, no one seemed to question what Jackson did for a living, or why he seemed to have a seemingly inexhaustible supply of money. He was, it appears, an extraordinarily skilled fake, and apparently attractive enough to cause Sylvia Ageloff to return to Mexico City on vacation on August 1. The two spent a great deal of time together, but it was not until after the assassination of Trotsky that Miss Ageloff realized that her new friend Frank Jackson was actually a Soviet assassin named Ramon Mercador. He had been convinced by his mother, who held the Order of Lenin for masterminding Stalinist assassinations, that the elimination of Trotsky was a necessary and glorious mission.

AND SO, at 5:30 on the afternoon of August 20, armed with a revolver and a dagger, and hiding an ice axe beneath his rain coat, Jackson/Mercador

Average net paid circulation for July exceeded
Daily---1,925,000
Sunday-3,400,000

DAILY NEWS

Copr. 1940 by News Syndicate Co. Inc. NEW YORK'S PICTURE NEWSPAPER Trade Mark Reg. U. S. Pat. Off.

FINAL

Vol. 22. No. 50 | New York, Thursday, August 22, 1940★ | 60 Pages | 2 Cents IN CITY LIMITS | 3 CENTS Elsewhere

TROTSKY IS DEAD

Story on Page 2

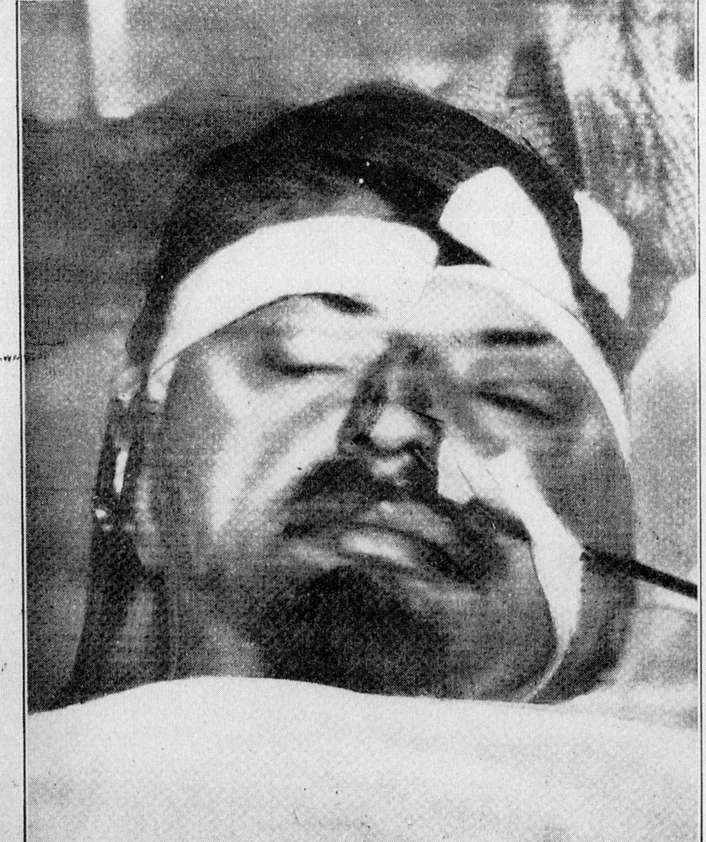

(Wide World Wired foto)

(Associated Press Wirefoto)

↑ Trotsky Death Weapon

Mexican policemen show short-handled pickax with which Frank Jackson fatally wounded the exiled Leon Trotsky, military genius of the Russian Revolution. Jackson, beaten by police, is recovering in hospital where Trotsky died. —*Story p. 2.*

← Dying, He Blamed Stalin

In pain-wracked hours of his battle for life in Mexico City hospital, Trotsky knew death was coming, and said: "Stalin has finally accomplished the task he unsuccessfully attempted before."

Josef Stalin, with members of his government, meeting wives of army officers in a propaganda painting of the 1940s.

entered the Trotsky home. He went to the empty study and concealed the ice axe in it. Then he joined Trotsky in the patio near the chicken yard. He had asked the older man to help him with an article he had written, and Trotsky, always delighted to dispense advice, had agreed.

The two talked for a while, then entered the dining room, where Mrs. Trotsky was sitting, reading. Jackson asked for and received a glass of water. Mrs. Trotsky got it for him, and the two men, still talking earnestly, entered the study.

Within a few minutes, loud arguing was heard by the guards in an adjoining room, then several thuds. The guards and Mrs. Trotsky ran to the study. They flung open the door to a scene of bloody mayhem.

In his later confession, Jackson described what had happened:

> I put my raincoat on the table on purpose so that I could take out the ice axe which I had in the pocket . . . I took the *piolet* [a synonym for ice axe] out of my raincoat, took it in my fist and, closing my eyes, I gave him a tremendous blow on the head . . . The man screamed in such a way that I will never forget as long as I live. His scream was . . . very long, infinitely long, and it still seems to me as if that scream were piercing my brains.

The ice axe sank deeply into Trotsky's brain, and the assassin apparently expected his victim to die silently, then and there.

INSTEAD, Trotsky remained standing. He whirled, wild eyed, and fought his way past his assailant, toward the study door. The assassin pulled out his revolver, and aimed at Trotsky's back. But before he could fire, the door burst open and two of Trotsky's guards dashed in, chopping the revolver from Jackson's hand, slamming him to the floor and beating him mercilessly.

The profusely bleeding Trotsky staggered into the dining room and collapsed. Mrs. Trotsky cradled his head while a guard called an ambulance. Both assassin and victim were rushed to the central hospital in Mexico City, where they were installed on the same floor. Mercador recovered quickly. Trotsky lingered for 26 hours, then died at 7:25 p.m. on August 21, 1940.

Mrs. Trotsky and Albert Goldman, the family attorney, announced that the former Russian leader's body would be brought to New York for a memorial service and burial.

That same day, the U.S. State Department issued an order barring his entrance, dead or alive, into the United States. Goldman announced an immediate appeal. But Mrs. Trotsky apparently had neither the heart nor the stomach to go through protracted legal proceedings. Five days later, on August 27, she had her husband cremated in Mexico City.

SYLVIA AGELOFF was arrested as an accomplice, and brought to trial with Mercador in Mexico City. The trial inched forward for months, then years. Partway through the first year, Miss Ageloff was freed, and all charges against her were dropped. She had been, the court was satisfied, as deceived as anyone else about the identity and purpose of her one-time fiancé. Mercador, who first identified himself as Jacques Monard van den Dreshd, a native of Teheran and the son of a Belgian diplomat, testified that the money he always carried was an inher-itance, and his motive for the killing was Trotsky's adamant efforts to prevent his marriage to Miss Ageloff.

As the years ached by, the truth and his real identity slowly emerged. In 1943, a Mexican court sentenced Mercador/Jackson/van den Dreshd to 20 years in prison.

Now, all pretense was abandoned. It was revealed that his mother was Caridad, the great Soviet heroine, and that she had been waiting outside the Trotsky compound in a car, to aid in her son's escape.

Negotiations between Mexico and the U.S.S.R. continued, first to make Mercador's stay in prison comfortable, and then, to secure his early release. He was freed in 1960, and departed for communist Czechoslovakia, where he lived for a while and was declared, like his mother, a hero of the Soviet Union. By the 1970s, he had emigrated to Cuba, and he died in Havana on October 18, 1978.

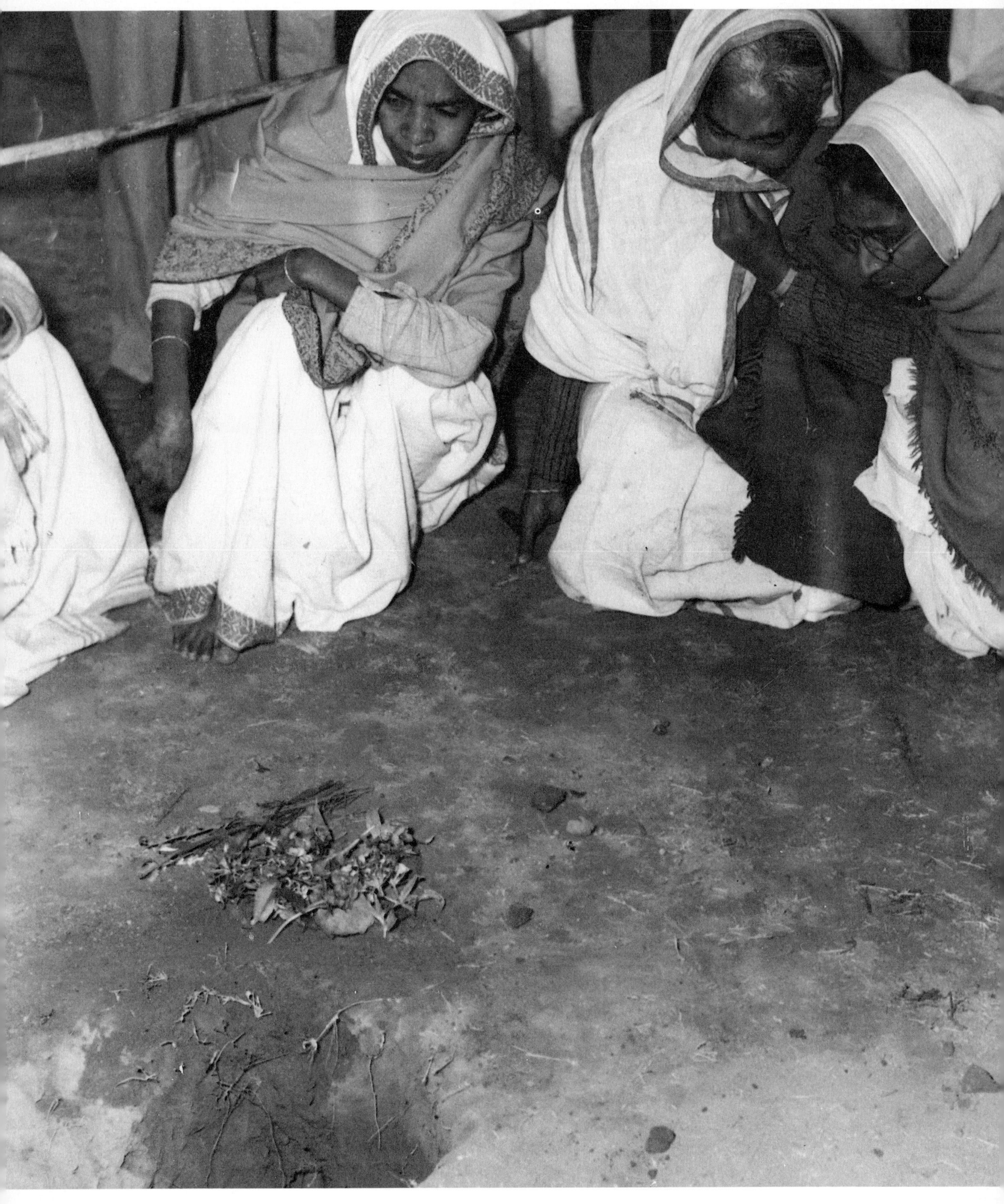

MOHANDAS GANDHI

POSITION:	*Spiritual leader of India*
DATE:	*January 30, 1948*
PLACE:	*New Delhi, India*
HOW:	*Gunshot*
WHO:	*Nathuran V. Godse*
CONVICTED:	*Yes. Hanged November 15, 1949*
MOTIVE:	*To provoke religious conflict in India*
DIRECT CONSEQUENCE:	*Escalation of religious strife and division in India*

IN A tearful, trembling voice, Indian prime minister Jawaharlal Nehru spoke to the people of India via radio on the night of January 30, 1948. "Friends and comrades," he said, "the light has gone out of our lives and there is darkness everywhere." At the same moment, people who revered Mohandas Gandhi were scooping up earth, as a relic, at the spot where their great spiritual leader had fallen earlier that day, fatally wounded by an assassin's bullet. They left the excavation that appears LEFT.

At almost precisely 4 o'clock that afternoon, as Gandhi was entering his prayer pavilion, connected by a long stone walk to Birla House, his residence in New Delhi, Nathuran V. Godse, a Hindu extremist and the editor of the newspaper *Hindi Rashtra*, had stepped in front of the frail and tensile man and killed him with three shots from a Beretta automatic pistol.

It was the end of a long life, and a dramatic pause in a monumental spiritual journey. Gandhi was a symbol to the world of nonviolence, and what it could accomplish. Fifteen years later, Dr. Martin Luther King would practice the technique of passive resistance he had learned from Gandhi's long life of nonviolent opposition to British rule and the division between Muslims and Hindus in his country. And 20 years later, Dr. Martin Luther King would also be dead of an assassin's bullets.

MOHANDAS Karamchand Gandhi was born in Porbandar, India, on October 2, 1896, studied law in London in the late 1880s, and then returned to India, where he practiced law for several years. But his calling was far beyond this, and, when, in 1893, he went to South Africa, it was clear that his mission was more spiritual than legal—though he never lost sight of the political gains that could be achieved through his practice of passive resistance. His first test of it was in South Africa, where he utilized passive resistance to protest what he considered unjust and discriminatory laws aimed at Indians.

After long spiritual study in South Africa, and the securing of an agreement with the South African authorities that alleviated anti-Indian discrimination, he returned to India in January, 1915, to begin his long campaign to bring about India's independence from Great Britain—a campaign that led to the formation of the *satyagraha* (literal translation: holding to the truth), a movement which advocated noncooperation with British authorities.

GANDHI was a moderate presence in India until the appalling Amritsar massacre of April 13, 1919, in which British troops, led by Brigadier General R. E. H. Dyer, fired upon several thousand unarmed Indians who had gathered, in defiance of a British ban on public meetings, in the Sikh Holy Shrine of Jalianwala Bagh.

Civil unrest had followed the imposition, earlier that year, of the Rowlatt Acts, which provided for the arrest and imprisonment of political agitators without a trial. On April 10, in Amritsar, two nationalist leaders were arrested and deported. Riots resulted, and the ban on public assembly was imposed by Dyer and Sir Michael O'Dwyer.

When word reached Dyer that several thousand Indians had gathered in the enclosed park of Jalianwala Bagh, he gathered 90 Gurkhas and Baluchi soldiers and two armored cars and descended upon the park, blocking its only exit with the cars.

Then, without warning, he ordered his troops to open fire on the crowd: 1,605 rounds were

LARGEST NET SALES of any Daily Newspaper Printed in Northern, Southern, Central or Western India. REGD. No. B111

The Times of India

ESTABLISHED 1838

NO. 27. VOL. CX BOMBAY: SATURDAY, JANUARY 31, 1948. PRICE TWO ANNAS DO NOT PAY MORE

MAHATMA GANDHI ASSASSINATED AT DELHI

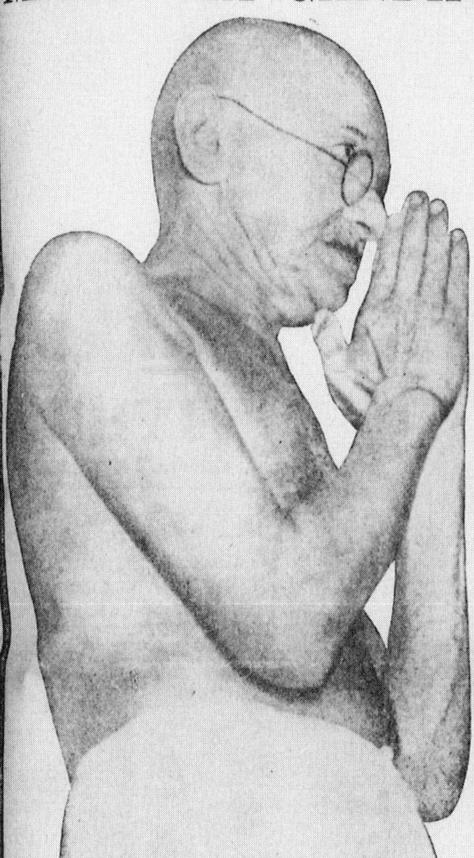

MARATHA FROM POONA FIRES AT POINT-BLANK RANGE

Outrage On Way To Prayer Meeting

FUNERAL TODAY AT JUMNA GHAT: COUNTRY-WIDE GRIEF

From Our Special Representative

NEW DELHI, Jan. 30.

MAHATMA GANDHI WAS ASSASSINATED ON FRIDAY EVENING.

While on his way to the prayer meeting, the Father of the Nation was shot four times at point-blank range by a man who sprang out of the congregation.

Three bullets struck the Mahatma, and he was immediately taken to Birla House. He passed away at 5-40—35 minutes after the crime.

The alleged assassin is Nathuram Vinayak Godse, a 36-year-old Maratha Hindu from Poona. He is stated to be a fairly well-known Marathi litterature and his writings are reported to show his pronounced communal feelings. He had arrived in Delhi on Thursday evening.

Mahatma Gandhi's funeral procession will leave Birla House tomorrow at 11 a.m. The cremation will take place according to Vedic rites at Jumna Ghat about 4 p.m.

Mahatma Gandhi's death shocked Delhi and the whole of India with "the impact of atomic force." The Governor-General, Lord Mountbatten, the Prime Minister, Pandit Jawaharlal Nehru, the Deputy Prime Minister, Sardar Vallabhbhai Patel, and other Cabinet Ministers were immediately informed of the tragedy.

Pandit Nehru and Sardar Patel and other Ministers rushed to Birla House.

The Military Secretary to the Governor-General, Col. D. H. Currie, and General Bucher, Commander-in-Chief of the Indian Army, and the Jam Saheb of Nawanagar also arrived immediately at Birla House.

An A. P. I. correspondent who was present when Mahatma Gandhi was assassinated says:

The congregation of about 500 was anxiously waiting for Mahatma Gandhi to arrive at the prayer meeting at five o'clock. Mahatma Gandhi was delayed five minutes. He emerged out of Birla House supported by his grand-daughters Ava Gandhi and Manu Gandhi and walked briskly, as was [illegible] to the prayer platform. [illegible] the congregation, they split into two parts to make a passage for him.

When Mahatma Gandhi was 15 yards from the platform, I heard a shot about two yards ahead of me. I spotted the man who fired the shot and saw him hold a revolver in his right hand at right angle. Three more shots followed in succession.

MAHATMA COLLAPSES

I saw Mahatma Gandhi collapse. He appeared to be hit in the stomach and I was shocked to see blood oozing out and staining his white 'dhoti'. There was immediate panic. For a minute I was dazed.

Immediately those who were behind the assailant overpowered him and seized him by the wrist. His revolver dropped to the ground. The assailant was dressed in a khaki shirt of military design and in a pair of trousers. The police who were on sentry duty took hold of the man. I rushed to the spot where Mahatma Gandhi had fallen.

I saw Mahatma Gandhi bleeding. His eyes were closed and his head bent. His hands were folded as if in prayer. He was helped up in a sitting posture by his grand-daughters. Immediately Mahatma Gandhi was carried by four or five persons into Birla House.

The doors of his room were closed and no visitors were allowed. I waited among a large, anxious crowd in Birla House. I saw Dewan Chamanlal coming from inside the house at 5-35. Five minutes later a member of the camp, pale and grief-stricken, emerged out of Mahatma Gandhi's room. He said, "Bapu is dead."

By the Mahatma's bedside were Mr. Devadas Gandhi, his wife and children.

Around his bed were the Governor-General, members of the Cabinet and his intimate colleagues. As Mahatma Gandhi breathed his last, recitations from the *Bhagwad Gita* were rendered. This was followed by the singing of his favourite hymn *Vaishnava Janaho.*"

CABINET CONSULTATIONS

A few minutes later, Lord Mountbatten and members of the Cabinet retired to an ante-room and behind closed doors held consultations.

It is believed that it was the desire of the Government that Mahatma Gandhi's body should be embalmed and kept in State for a few days. However, they consulted Mr. Devadas Gandhi and Mr. Pyarelal, his secretary. Both of them desired immediate cremation and it is learned that it was Mahatma Gandhi's wish that he should be cremated promptly.

Immediately instruction was given to the departments concerned to make the necessary arrangements for the cremation.

It was also suggested that at 4 p.m. tomorrow people throughout India should congregate on the banks of rivers, wherever there are rivers, or in other appropriate places in revered remembrance of the departed leader.

Till late in the night, despite the leaders' persuasion, crowds lingered on in Birla House and more people streamed in with a determination to have a last *darshan* of the Mahatma.

About 9 p.m. the Mahatma was put on a plain bier, draped in white khadi, and carried to the terrace of Birla House. The body was placed near the end of the terrace and kept in a slightly slanting posture. Floodlights were lit and the body was visible to the crowds below.

Shouts of "Mahatma Gandhi ki Jai" rent the air. People wept and sobbed.

A few minutes later, the body was carried back to the room where Mahatma Gandhi had died. The lights were dimmed. The crowds silently melted away.

Members of Mahatma Gandhi's ashram and other intimate associates will sit beside his body throughout the night and chant hymns.

The news of Mahatma Gandhi's death flashed throughout the city in a few minutes. Business houses, shops, restaurants and cinema houses were immediately closed. A marriage procession, proceeding along Connaught Place, halted and dispersed silently. Traffic in the city came to a standstill. Men, women and children who were on their evening walk in Connaught Circus were visibly moved and many of them broke into tears. Crowds of people hurried to Birla House on [illegible] filled the compound.

About 8 p.m. somebody shouted "Mahatma was not dead and his doctors were hopeful of his recovery." Though the news was incorrect, many persisted in believing that Mahatma Gandhi was not dead and tried to get into Birla House to get the Mahatma's *darshan*.

Pandit Nehru came out of the room, climbed the outer gates and addressed a few words. He was choked with emotion. He told the gathering in a faltering voice that Mahatma Gandhi was dead. He was shot by a mad man. In this crisis we should not lose our balance of mind.

All programmes of All-India Radio went off the air at five minutes to six and the announcer said: You will now hear a very important announcement" and in solemn words broke the news of the death of Mahatma Gandhi. He repeated it four times both in English and Hindustani.

The announcement was followed by recitation of Mahatma Gandhi's favourite hymns *Vaishnava Janaho*, *Ram Dhun* and verses from the *Gita*.

(*Life-Sketch on Page 6 and Tributes on Page 7*)

ARRANGEMENTS FOR FUNERAL

Running Commentary By A.I.R.

NEW DELHI, January 30:

The funeral procession of Mahatma Gandhi will start from Birla House at 11 a.m. tomorrow, pass through a number of localities reaching Jumna Ghat at 4 p.m.

[illegible] arrangements will be [illegible] have a last look at the Mahatma.

All-India Radio, Delhi will cover the funeral procession tomorrow from 10-30 a.m. onwards. The running commentary on the procession will be relayed by all stations of A.I.R.—A.P.I.

"PRINCE AMONG MEN"

Gen. Smuts's Tribute

CAPE TOWN, January 30: When he received the news of the death of Mahatma Gandhi, Field Marshal Smuts, the South African Premier, said: "I have heard of the assassination of Gandhi with the deepest grief, which I am sure will be shared all over the world.

"Gandhi was one of the great men of my time and my acquaintance with him over a period of more than 30 years has only deepened my high respect for him, however much we differed in our views and methods.

"A prince among men has passed away and we grieve with India in her irreparable loss."—Reuter.

IRREPARABLE LOSS TO MANKIND

The King's Message

LONDON, January 30.

HIS Majesty the King has sent the following message to the Governor-General of India, Lord Mountbatten:

"The Queen and I are deeply shocked by the news of the death of Mr. Gandhi. Will you please convey to the people of India our sincere sympathy in the irreparable loss which they, and indeed mankind, have suffered."—Reuter.

Delhi Takes Swift Security Steps

ARMY CHIEFS ASKED TO STAND BY

NEW DELHI, January 30.

WITHIN five hours of Mahatma Gandhi falling a victim to an assassin's bullet, security measures were speedily put into force by the Government of India throughout the country, and commanding officers in army units were ordered to be prepared to assist the civil authorities.—A.P.I.

DISTURBANCES IN BOMBAY

Curfew Imposed On Affected Areas

"Thirty-two knife-attacks, six of them fatal, were reported in Bombay on Friday evening," states a communique issued by the Assistant Director of Publicity, Bombay, on Friday.

The communique added: "Immediately on hearing the news of the outbreak of disturbances, the Home Minister, Mr. Morarji Desai, called on the police headquarters and later toured the affected areas.

"Full police and military precautions, including the enforcement of curfew where it is necessary, have been taken to maintain peace in the city. The situation is now reported to be under control."

On Other Pages

13 DAYS STATE MOURNING

NEW DELHI, January 30.

State mourning will be observed for 13 days from today, states a "communique" issued from the Prime Minister's secretariat tonight. Flags will be flown half mast. There will be no public entertainments during this period.—A.P.I.

Regret In Czechoslovakia

PRAGUE, January 30: News of Mahatma Gandhi's death was received in leading Czechoslovak circles with great regret, for he was held in high esteem in all spheres of Czechoslovak life.—Reuter.

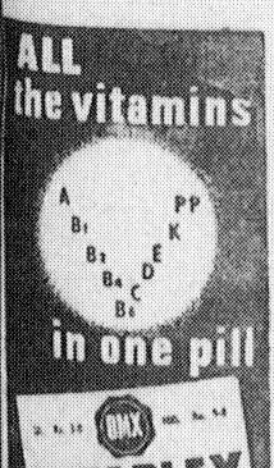

"Most Dastardly Attack On One Of Greatest Men"

QUAID-I-AZAM JINNAH'S SYMPATHY

KARACHI, January 30.

"I WAS shocked to learn of the most dastardly attack on the life of Mr. Gandhi, resulting in his death," said Quaid-i-Azam Mohammad Ali Jinnah, Governor-General of Pakistan, on hearing the news of death of Mahatma Gandhi. "There can be no controversy in the face of death," he added.

"Whatever our political differences" he continued, "he was one of the greatest men produced by the Hindu community and a leader who commanded their universal confidence and respect.

"I wish to express my deep sorrow and sincerely sympathise with the great Hindu community and his family in their bereavement at this momentous, historical and critical juncture, so soon after the birth of freedom and freedom for Hindustan and Pakistan".

Quaid-i-Azam Jinnah concluded: "The loss to the Dominion of India is irreparable and it will be very difficult to fill the vacuum created by the passing away of such a great man at this moment".

"TRAGIC NEWS"

The Prime Minister of Pakistan, Mr. Liaqat Ali Khan said: "The tragic news of Gandhiji's assassination has come as a terrible shock to me.

"It is a most dastardly act and I am sure it will be condemned unreservedly, in the strongest terms, by everybody.

"He was a great figure of our times and was working unceasingly to bring back sanity to the people and to establish communal harmony. His loss will be felt and mourned by all.

"For the last many years he had been the soul of the Congress Party and it would be no exaggeration to say that he was the father of the Congress. It is a strange irony of fate that a man who had been preaching all his life the doctrine of non-violence should himself be made the tragic target of violence. His recent efforts for communal harmony will be remembered with gratitude by all lovers of peace. His removal from the stage of Indian politics at this juncture is an irreparable loss.

"I send my sincere and heart-felt sympathy to his relatives and to all those who mourn him."

Qazi Fazlullah, Revenue Minister of Sind, said: "Mahatma Gandhi was the greatest man in the world. I am sure that Mussalmans all over Sind was sorrow-stricken."

The Governor of Sind, Shaikh Ghulam Hussain Hidayatullah has sent the following telegram to Pandit Nehru: "Shocked to hear of the great tragedy of Mahatma's assassination. Deepest condolences and sympathies."

The Mayor of Karachi, Mr. Mohammed Ahsan, who toured the city late tonight, in the company of the Revenue Minister of Sind, said: 'The average man in the street is stunned and shocked."

Kazi Fazlullah said: "We found that several groups of Muslims in different localities of Karachi were anxiously listening-in to the radio. They are shocked and grieved."

"TOO TERRIBLE FOR WORDS"

The news soon spread throughout the city and drew expressions of horror from all sides.

The Governor-General had left the capital for the week-end and was not at first available on the telephone. The Prime Minister was in conference with the Finance Minister and the Premier and certain other Ministers of East Bengal when the report was received. A senior official of Pakistan Foreign Ministry, conveying Mr. Liaqat Ali's reaction to the press, said that the news was "too terrible for words."

China's Condolence

New Delhi: The Chinese Ambassador called at Birla House and expressed on behalf of the Chinese Government and Generalissimo Chiang Kai-shek deepest grief and conveyed sincerest condolences. He also bowed before the body of Mahatma Gandhi. He said "Gandhiji is dead. He lives for ever."

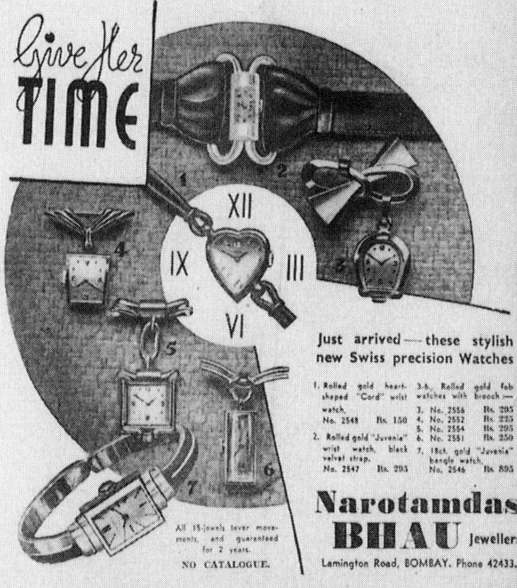

pumped into the panicking mass of people. Officially, 379 were killed and 1,200 injured, but the Hunter Commission, convened after more killings and more riots had forced martial law on Amritsar, set the figures at 1,200 killed and 3,600 injured. Not only this. After the shooting, Dyer kept his armored cars in place, preventing medical personnel from entering the park or survivors from carrying out the wounded.

Wholesale humiliation of Indians followed. Public floggings took place for, according to the Hunter report, "the contravention of the curfew order, failure to salaam to a commissioned officer, for disrespect to a European, for taking a commandeered car without leave, refusal to sell milk, and for similar contraventions." Indians were forced to crawl on all fours past a place where a woman missionary had been attacked.

If the Hunter Commission had reacted strongly to the massacre and its aftermath of excesses, Gandhi might have remained a quiet and respected figure of much spiritual strength and some political force in India. But a defiant Dyer who testified that if he had had more ammunition, there would have been more casualties, was merely condemned with such mild admonishments as "unfortunate" and "injudicious." And O'Dwyer's intemperate statement that "There is another force greater than Gandhi's soul force" assured the polarization of the country. Indians turned toward Gandhi and his doctrine of passive resistance, which now became the most effective weapon of all against British colonialism.

"If blood be shed," Gandhi told his followers, "let it be my blood. Cultivate the quiet courage of dying without killing. For man lives freely only by his readiness to die, if need be, at the hands of his brother, never by killing him."

TO GANDHI'S distress, however, passive resistance was not the weapon of choice for all Indians seeking independence from Britain, and in the 1920s, he temporarily abandoned his work. But even this suspension of public activity furthered his quest for equal independence and dignity for all human beings, regardless of race or nationality. His quiet disavowal of violence raised him to the position of spiritual leader of India, and the title of Mahatma (great soul).

His program of reform, articulated at this time, was three-pronged: a free and united India, the revival of cottage industries such as weaving, and the abolition of the caste system. He was arrested and imprisoned in 1922 and sentenced to six years in prison for sedition, but was released after two years for "reasons of health."

In 1930, he led the famous 200-mile march to the sea to make salt on the shore in protest against the British salt tax. He was imprisoned for his leadership of this march but was released in 1931 to attend the London Round Table Conference on India, as the representative of the Indian National Congress.

Even then, all Indians were not in favor of his reforms or his ideas. And so, in 1934, he resigned from the Congress, preferring to utilize his method of fasting and *satyagraha* to bring about democratic reforms in several Indian princely states. His influence remained strong, and his protegé and lifelong friend, Jawaharlal Nehru, became the leader of the Indian National Congress.

As a result of his continued opposition to British rule during World War II, Gandhi was imprisoned from 1942 to 1944. But again, upon his release from prison, he became a major figure in the negotiations that Britain conducted in its plan to commence its pullout from India in 1945.

BRITAIN'S determination to create Pakistan, a separate Muslim state, was opposed by Gandhi, who believed in and advocated the complete equality and peaceful coexistence of all peoples and religions. Ironically, as with so many religious leaders, this advocacy of equality would ultimately lead to his death.

Britain now left India, and violent confrontations erupted between Muslims and Hindus after Independence Day, August 15, 1947. Gandhi used his spiritual influence to quiet them. His fasts unto death finally sobered both sides, and brought about a pact by the Indian government guaranteeing the safety of the Muslim minority, represented by the Muslim League. A relative calm settled over India and Pakistan by January of 1948.

But, as in Gandhi's earlier crusades, there were some of his own Hindu faith who opposed his efforts to bring peace to everyone. They felt he had betrayed his fellow Hindus by criticizing the anti-Muslim riots, and so a group of nine Hindu extremists planned his assassination.

65-year-old Vinayak Damodar Savarkar, who had headed the once-powerful anti-Muslim and anti-Gandhi Mahasabha, was the mastermind. He recruited eight younger men. The group met in early January, and, on the 19th, they planned to kill the Mahatma. It was an ill-organized attempt; there was confusion over who would carry guns and who would carry the grenades, and, as they approached Gandhi's dwelling, their confused suspiciousness revealed them. One was arrested, and there were reports later that he confessed the entire plot, naming his co-conspirators. If this were so, the police knew about the danger to Gandhi, but never told him, and thus they were partially responsible for what eventually occurred. But this culpability would never be proved. What is definitely known is that the conspirators met again on January 29, when they chose 36-year-old Nathuran Godse to carry out their plans.

That same night, Gandhi recited a homely Gujarat couplet which had been well known in Porbandar during his youth: "This is a strange world; How long have I to play this game?"

To those who did not believe in the transcendent spirit and spiritual development of Mahatma Gandhi, it would emerge as ironic. But to those who understood the Guru principle, everything that occurred during the next 243 hours had an explanation, and that explanation was contained in the Bhagavad-Gita, in which Lord Krishna explains to Arjuna the qualities of a great saint: ". . . The sage whose mind is unruffled by suffering, whose desire is not to rouse by enjoyment, who is without attachment to anger or fear . . . who accepts good and evil alike, neither welcoming the one nor shrinking from the other—take him to be one who is merged in the infinite."

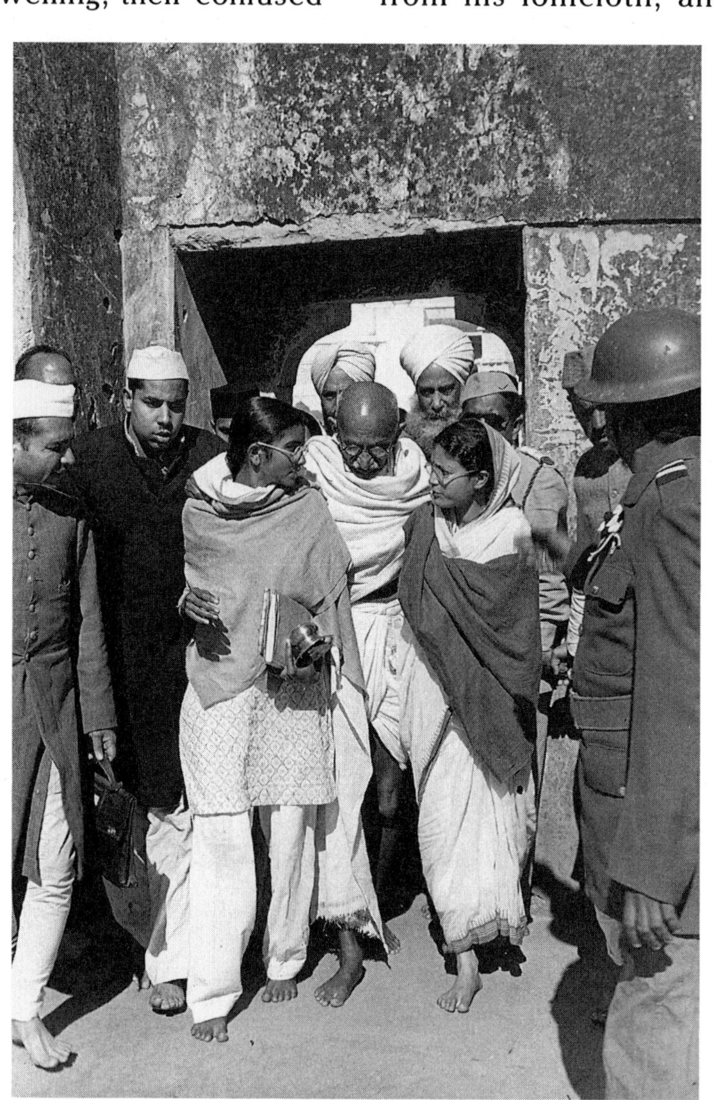

Gandhi in 1948 at Meherauli, a Muslim shrine, in a public appearance—one of his last—that was dedicated to the same principle of religious tolerance that his assassins so bitterly opposed.

A few minutes before his death, as he was walking from Birla House to the prayer pavilion, Gandhi looked at the dollar watch that dangled from his loincloth, and said to his walking companion, deputy prime minister of India Sardar Patel, "Let me go now. It's prayer time for me."

Then, supported by his grandnieces Ava and Manu, he made his slow way to the vine-clothed prayer pavilion. As he reached the top of the structure's three steps, Nathuran Godse approached him. "You are late for prayer today," he said to the Mahatma.

"Yes, I am," Gandhi answered.

Godse drew the tiny revolver he had concealed in his shirt, and fired three times at point blank range. One bullet entered Gandhi's chest; two ripped into his belly. With no surprise, and no apparent pain, Gandhi folded his hands in prayer and murmured, "Ai Ram, Ram," a greeting to Rama, one of the Hindu manifestations of the God who dwells within and without. He fell backwards, and spoke no more. Godse was immediately seized by police. Gandhi was carried, by two male secretaries, into Birla House, where he would die two hours later.

The nation would go into a 13-day mourning period. The next day, Gandhi's body would be transported to the banks of the sacred river Jumna, where it would be put on a funeral pyre composed of sandalwood and ghi, incense, coconuts, and camphor. At each corner was a stump of the sacred peepul tree. The fire was lit by his son Ramdas; Nehru, Patel, Governor General Earl Mountbatten, and Lady Mountbatten threw last rose petals onto the pyre.

Gandhi's devotees knew the best of it—that their Mahatma had already broken the Hindu wheel of birth and death and rebirth and redeath. He had, as Lord Krishna described it, ". . . merged into the infinite."

FOUR MONTHS later, the nine conspirators would be tried in a courtroom of Delhi's massive 17th-century Red Fort. Godse submitted a 92-page, handwritten statement to the court, in which he denounced Gandhi as "a political and ethical imposter" and a "curse to India, a force for evil" who would eventually bring about Muslim dominance of the entire country. Godse and one other were convicted and hanged at Ambala jail on November 15, 1949. The others were sentenced to life in prison.

And the conflict between Muslims and Hindus, exacerbated by the petitioning of the country into Pakistan and India, and opposed to his last moments by Mohandas Gandhi, continued. Throughout the next 50 years, terrible riots and unrest would erupt again, and two more Gandhis would be assassinated. The words and the deeds and the monumental accomplishments of the Mahatma would pass from actuality to legend, and manifest themselves more beyond India's borders than within them.

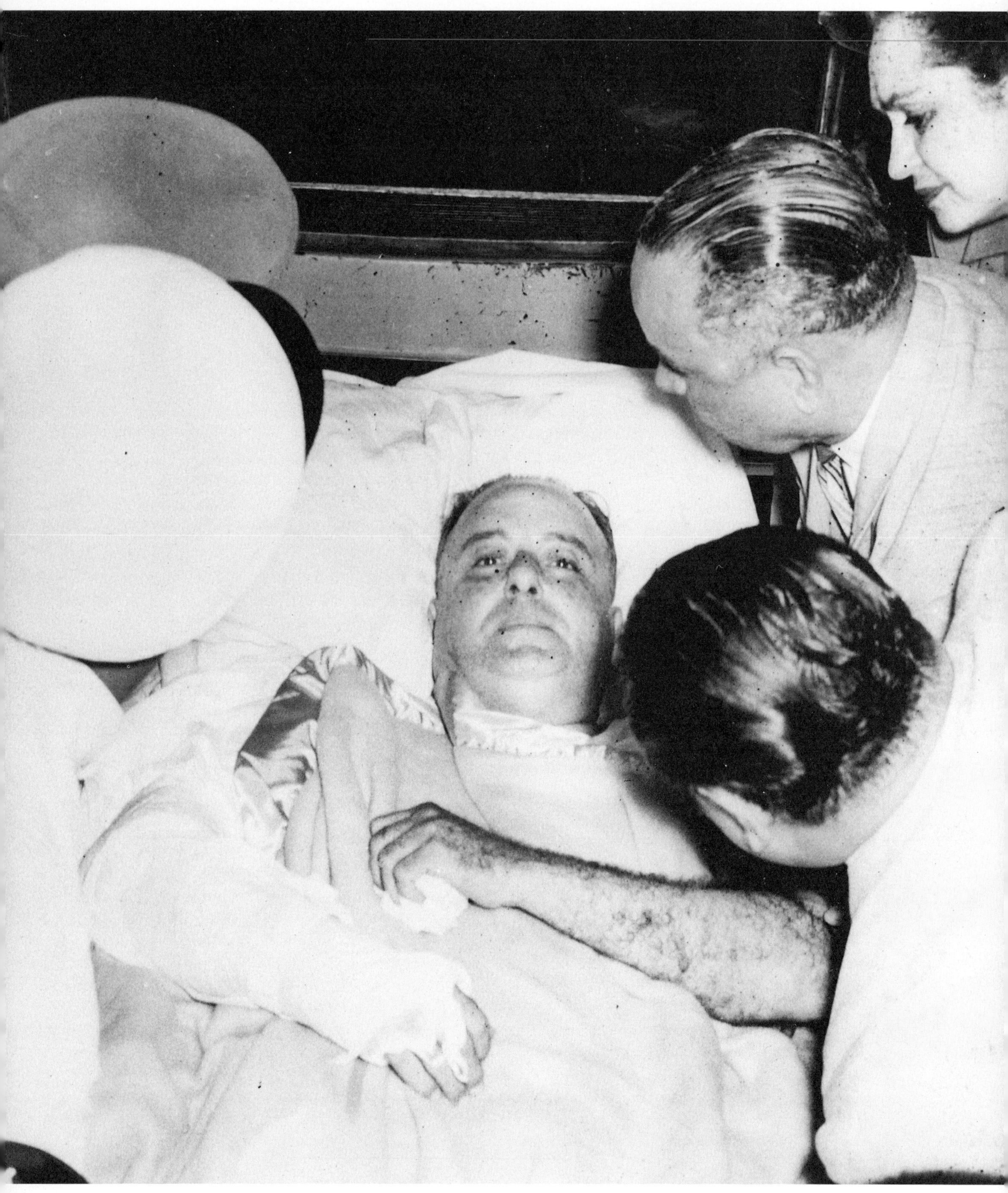

ANASTASIO SOMOZA

POSITION:	*Dictator of Nicaragua*
DATE:	*September 21, 1956*
PLACE:	*León, Nicaragua*
HOW:	*Gunshot*
WHO:	*Rigoberto Lopez Perez*
CONVICTED:	*No. Shot by Somoza's bodyguards*
MOTIVE:	*Personal hatred of Somoza*
DIRECT CONSEQUENCE:	*Continued excesses leading to Sandanista Revolution*

LIKE Rafael Trujillo, Anastasio, "Tacho" Somoza, the undisputed and inventive dictator of Nicaragua for 22 years, was reputed to be a creation of the United States of America. And, like Trujillo, Somoza, seen LEFT on his way to hospital, died of an assassin's bullets.

Whether this evaluation was true, whether the dog wagged the tail or the tail wagged the dog, has become something of a historical contention. Large events create large myths, and the long reign of Tacho Somoza was rife with myths. There was, for instance, the often reiterated evaluation of Somoza, attributed over and over to President Franklin D. Roosevelt: "He's a son of a bitch, but he's our son of a bitch."

Historical research confirms that not only did F.D.R. not say this, he probably *couldn't* have said it. Its choice of words was distinctly non-F.D.R. But the choice was definitely one that Somoza himself would—and probably did—make, as easily as a greeting. The quote, in fact, was often proudly referred to by the dictator to show his toughness and the toughness of his partner, the U.S.A.

That sort of convenient hyperbole and public relationship led to dire consequences for the U.S.A. in the 1980s, when the Sandinistas, who succeeded Somoza, turned the myth on its ear and aroused much of the Nicaraguan populace against what the Sandinistas were able to picture as a hostile, manipulative U.S.A., a world power that had a history of supporting despotic Central and South American dictators just because they were anti-Communists.

And to Americans of the 1980s, Nicaragua became either Vietnam or Cuba, depending upon their loyalties and political orientation. The truth, more complex than either slogan or myth, lay somewhere in between.

ANASTASIO SOMOZA was born in San Marcos on February 1, 1896, the son of Julia Garcia and Anastasio Somoza, a coffee planter. The young Somoza received a private education in his village, attended the *Instituto Nacional de Oriente* in Granada, Nicaragua, then went to Philadelphia, where he honed his business skills at the Pierce School of Business Administration. It was in Philadelphia that he met his future wife, Salvadora Debayle, who belonged to a prominent Nicaraguan family.

Somoza and his new wife returned to Nicaragua, where he experimented with a business career, without noticeable success. And so, he followed the path of many failed businessmen, into politics.

IT WAS a time of enormous North American influence in the hemisphere. At the end of the 19th century, America intervened in the Spanish Civil War in Cuba, then set about excluding other powers from the Isthmus of Panama, in order to build a canal. Nicaragua offered an alternative canal route between the Atlantic and Pacific Oceans, but Nicaragua was a notoriously unstable country.

In 1907, President Theodore Roosevelt convened a Central American Conference to solve disputes in the area. Two years later, Nicaragua commenced negotiations with Japan and Great Britain for a canal through Nicaragua. But they were short-lived. Financed by some U.S. companies and some other Central American governments, a revolution, led by General Juan Estrada, erupted in October, 1909, in Bluefields, on the Atlantic coast.

The rebels were seriously outnumbered by the troops of President Zelaya, and they asked for U.S. intervention. Under the guise of protecting

Tempo Backstage with the Lyric's new opera
In Section 2

Chicago Tribune

5 Star Final ★★★★★

Thursday, September 18, 1980

134th Year—No. 262 © 1980 Chicago Tribune — 9 Sections 20¢

Inside
Illinois QB loses in court *In Sports*
Snow lease nullified *Page 3*

Saudis hike oil price $2 to mend OPEC rift

By William Mullen
Chicago Tribune Press Service

VIENNA—Saudi Arabia, the largest oil supplier to the United States, agreed suddenly late Wednesday to immediately increase its price for a barrel of crude oil by $2 to $30.

The surprise move came at a meeting of the Organization of Petroleum Exporting Countries in an apparent attempt to close a serious rift in the cartel. The other OPEC nations will freeze their oil prices at current levels for three months.

The move came as a shock because Saudi Arabia agreed to the increase without asking for any preconditions or concessions from the other OPEC members. The Saudis earlier had maintained that any price increase must be tied to a unified OPEC pricing policy.

EARLIER WEDNESDAY, the three-day meeting of OPEC foreign, oil, and finance ministers broke down after strong disagreements on a long-range pricing strategy.

The breakdown in the talks was so serious that there is some question whether all 13 member-nations will attend a summit meeting early in November in Baghdad, Iraq, to celebrate OPEC's 20th anniversary. There are indications that Iran, Libya, and Algeria could boycott that meeting.

After the week's meetings failed to come to a long-range pricing agreement, the Vienna OPEC session had come to an abrupt end Wednesday afternoon.

THE OIL MINISTERS reconvened Wednesday night, however, announcing they were going to discuss possible recommendations to make to their respective governments on pricing.

Sheik Ahmed Zaki Yamani, Saudi Arabian oil minister, attended only the first 40 minutes of the six-hour night meeting. But he apparently made the offer to increase Saudi prices to paper over the differences between members.

In a draft resolution after the 11th-hour meeting, OPEC announced that the new price for the Saudi oil would go into effect immediately. All other OPEC prices will remain frozen until the next ordinary pricing meeting, scheduled for Dec. 15 in Indonesia.

AT THE heart of the split was a fight over future policy on the timing and size of oil price increases. Yamani has been urging an orderly index of price increases

Continued on page 16, col. 1

Somoza slain in ambush

UPI Telephotos

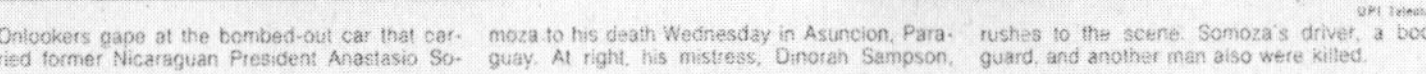

Onlookers gape at the bombed-out car that carried former Nicaraguan President Anastasio Somoza to his death Wednesday in Asuncion, Paraguay. At right, his mistress, Dinorah Sampson, rushes to the scene. Somoza's driver, a bodyguard, and another man also were killed.

Blast in Paraguay kills ex-dictator

From Tribune Wire Services

ASUNCION, Paraguay—Ousted Nicaraguan leader Anastasio Somoza was assassinated Wednesday in a barrage of bullets and explosives that tore apart his automobile in central Asuncion, Paraguayan authorities reported. His driver and another man with Somoza also were killed, they said.

Police said there were as many as nine assassins and they all escaped. One report said one of the assassins was believed to be wounded seriously when Somoza's bodyguard returned fire before being killed.

Joyful Nicaraguan revolutionaries said in Managua the attack was carried out

• Tribune reporter Mark Starr recalls an interview with Somoza. Page 5.

by Paraguayan "freedom fighters." The Nicaraguan government took no direct responsibility.

POLICE SOURCES SAID Somoza's white Mercedes-Benz was caught in a well-planned ambush between attackers firing automatic weapons from a pickup truck that had been following his car and from others in a nearby house firing a weapon variously identified as a bazooka, machine gun, or rocket launcher.

After bursts from the house halted Somoza's car, his bodyguards, traveling behind the Mercedes, returned fire. But they were attacked by three gunmen traveling behind them in a pickup truck, police said.

The attackers in the truck fled. Six people ran from the house and escaped by commandeering a passing car, the sources said.

Police found weapons and unused rockets in the house.

Police identified two of the suspects as

Continued on page 16, col. 1

Anastasio Somoza

Almost 24 years after his father, it was the turn of Anastasio Somoza Jr.

Americans in Bluefields, 400 U.S. marines landed. But Zelaya's highly trained troops won the battle and executed two North American demolitions experts. It was only a battle, not the war. The U.S. broke diplomatic relations with Nicaragua, which forced Zelaya out of office.

It was the beginning of a sustained relationship between the U.S. and Nicaragua, one described by a *New York Times* correspondent in 1929 as "the U.S. [taking] a bear by its tail."

America succeeded in maintaining Conservative governments in Nicaragua for some time, broken by varying degrees of unrest. Juan Estrada was replaced by Adolfo Diaz, who, faced by increasing Liberal opposition, requested and received American military intervention: 2,700 U.S. troops landed on both coasts in August of 1912, and by October, the rebels were defeated and dispersed. For the next 23 years, with the exception of a two-year period when Calvin Coolidge withdrew them, marines remained in Nicaragua, ostensibly to prevent the nation from tearing itself apart, but also to sustain the Central American pact of 1907 and to safeguard the 1914 Bryan–Chamarro Treaty, which granted the United States exclusive rights to build a canal in Nicaragua.

By 1927, Nicaragua was weary of fighting anyway, and, with the exception of a small band led by General Augusto Cesar Sandino, the warring factions laid down their arms.

On November 24, 1928, the United States supervised the first "free" election in Nicaraguan history. The Liberal José Maria Moncada won; President Herbert Hoover reduced the U.S. marine presence from 5,000 to 1,300, and, in the hills, Sandino and his men carried on like the bandits they had become.

MEANWHILE, Anastasio Somoza was rising in Nicaraguan politics. Supporting the Liberals in the 1926–27 revolution, Somoza was a natural when they returned to power in the elections of 1928. Active as an interpreter during the negotiations that ended the revolution and led to the elections, Somoza became administrator of taxes, then governor of the department of León, then minister to Costa Rica, then undersecretary, and finally secretary for foreign relations.

In 1932, Liberal leader Juan Sacasa won the election, and in January, 1933, the U.S. marines, their mission accomplished and their presence an embarrassment to a U.S. that no longer wished to be a Goliath in a Central America populated by Davids, left—so rapidly, it was reported, that General Calvin B. Matthews, the head of the marine legation and the *Guardia Nacional*, barely had time to pack.

What Matthews *did* have time for, however, was to appoint Anastasio Somoza head of the *Guardia Nacional*, a U.S.-created peacekeeping force. Somoza accepted with alacrity, assuring General Matthews before he left that "I'll give this country peace if I have to shoot every other man in Nicaragua to get it."

And that was perhaps the first tip-off of the man and his methods. He would soon take control of the Liberal Party while solidifying his control of the *Guardia Nacional*. With the departure of U.S. forces, the guerrilla chief Sandino made peace with the government. But Somoza was unsatisfied, and on February 21, 1934, he ordered members of the *Guardia Nacional* to abduct and assassinate Sandino.

It was the sort of brutality that would eventually climax in yet another Somoza myth, that he had a habit of executing his enemies by tossing them alive into the active volcano of Masaya.

SOMOZA now proceeded inexorably toward the presidency of Nicaragua. Tall and gregarious, a hearty host and a notable drinker, he was easily able to push his uncle, President Sacasa, out of power. Sacasa repeatedly asked for U.S. intervention, or at least advisement. But the new policy of nonintervention instituted by Hoover and carried on by the Roosevelt administration prevented this.

In June, 1936, Sacasa was forced into exile, and, in December of that same year, Somoza was elected president. Two weeks later, he reassumed control of the *Guardia Nacional*. At the end of his term, he changed the constitution to allow him another "transitory" term, until May, 1947.

World War II came, and the United States needed military bases in Nicaragua, which Somoza provided. A friendly relationship existed between the two countries, at least on the surface. As the war ended, and the necessity for these bases dimmed, and as dictators fell in Guatemala, El Salvador, and Venezuela, it became necessary for the United States to take a stand against Somoza. This they did by dispatching Nelson Rockefeller, in his capacity as assistant secretary of state for inter-American affairs, to the Nicaraguan ambassador, to suggest that Somoza's reelection in 1947 might seriously affect relations between the two countries.

SOMOZA obliged by nominating 70-year-old Leonardo Arguello, a previous opponent, as the Liberal candidate. The fix was in. But the victorious Arguello, who won an election reportedly stolen by the *Guardia Nacional*, proved hard to handle. First, he tried to take control of the *Guardia*. Then, he asked for Somoza's resignation. Two days later, he was deposed by Somoza, who remarked to the chargé d'affaires at the U.S. embassy, "Can you imagine what a stupid bastard? I took him out of León where he couldn't earn a dime, and he does something crazy like that."

A tenuous relationship with the U. S. followed, leading Somoza to step down once again in favor of his elderly uncle, Victor Manuel Roman y Reyes. The Organization of American States extended recognition to the Reyes government. A month later, Reyes died, and a new constitution—the 10th since Somoza first ascended to power—allowed Tacho to seek and win election yet again as president. He was inaugurated on May 1, 1951.

And now, in 1953, with Dwight Eisenhower as U.S. president, and a fear in the U.S. over the growth of Communism in the hemisphere, Somoza once again began to present himself as a Communist fighter and friend of the U.S. He aided the U.S. in the overthrow of the Communist Guatemalan government by providing the C.I.A. with a place to train Guatemalan rebels. Then, he provided weapons and training for a group of 500 Costa Rican exiles.

This was more public and more than the U.S. wished, and when these exiles invaded their homeland, aided by air drops from Nicaragua, the U.S. was forced to halt the war. Somoza was publicly distressed. "What advantage do we get from being friendly?" he asked an American reporter. "You treat us like an old wife. We would rather be treated like a young mistress."

In all fairness, Somoza improved the lot of Nicaraguans by importing tractors, launching a land-clearing program, and introducing such lucrative new crops as cotton and rice. But he also improved his own lot by acquiring coffee *fincas* and cattle ranches and parlaying them into a fortune estimated at $60 million—which, by the end of his reign in 1956, was $20 million more than the entire annual budget of Nicaragua. In fact, by that time, he reportedly owned a tenth of the country's farmland, plus interests in 430 other properties, and all at a time when the average per capita income of the rest of the population of Nicaragua hovered around $245 a year.

Somoza loved being with the people, proving to his enemies that the populace loved him. And on the night of September 21, 1956—he always boasted that the number 21 was his lucky number—he attended a party in his honor at the *Casa del Obrero*, a Workers' Club in León, 45 miles north of Managua. Shortly after 11 p.m., he stood in a crowd watching the other dancers.

IN THAT same crowd lingered 27-year-old Rigoberto Lopez Perez, a slight and short salesman of phonograph records in neighboring El Salvador. He was known among his acquaintances as a constant grumbler about President Somoza. A mere mention of the dictator's name would bring forth non-stop mutterings. Nothing specific. Nothing overtly threatening. But Perez was obviously no fan of Somoza.

That night, he carried with him a Smith and Wesson .38 caliber revolver. He worked his way through the crowd of celebrants. Somoza and his bodyguards were relaxed, swaying with the music, laughing among themselves. Tacho, in an open-necked shirt and wearing his trademark wide brimmed hat, was absorbed in the scene.

Perez got close enough not to miss, then drew his revolver. He got off four shots before he was cut down with a fusillade from the bodyguards. There would be 20 bullet holes in his dead body when it was later taken to the León morgue.

Screams and shouts of outrage stilled the music. A swirl of bodyguards and the curious ran like a tidal pool around the stricken dictator. All four of the assassin's bullets had plowed into his imposing frame. One struck Somoza in the right forearm, and broke it. Two others lodged in his right shoulder and right thigh, driving him to the ground. The fourth was the most serious: It entered the upper right thigh and stopped at the base of his spine.

HE WAS in great pain, but breathing normally. A doctor was sent for, and an ambulance took him to León, where he was transferred to the central hospital. Thomas Whelan, the U.S. ambassador to Nicaragua, and a poker-playing buddy of Somoza's, was immediately notified by Somoza staff members. He phoned Washington, and the White House alerted doctors in the Panama Canal Zone, ordering them to fly to Nicaragua.

Simultaneously, President Eisenhower sent off a plane bearing Major General Leonard D. Heaton, commanding officer at Walter Reed Army Hospital, and the chief surgeon at Eisenhower's recent ileitis operation. A U. S. helicopter flew to León, and it took the ailing Somoza to Managua.

Four hours later, the Constellation that brought Heaton to Managua was flying to Panama, with Somoza, his wife, and the task force of doctors. At Gorgas, four surgeons, headed by Heaton, worked for four hours and 20 minutes, removing the bullet from Somoza's spine.

But it failed to save his life. He died of his injuries on September 29, 1956.

EVEN BEFORE his death, Somoza's two sons assumed the running of the country. Luis, who was already vice president, took over as President, and Anastasio Jr. ("Tachito") the commander of the 4,100-man *Guardia Nacional*, jailed 3,000 suspec-

After the Somozas, The United States backed the Contras, here being hunted by Sandanista soldiers on patrol in Jinotega province in July 1985.

ted enemies of the regime. He released all but 300 of them, and unearthed no plot. Apparently harboring a desire for martyrdom, Perez had acted entirely on his own. Or, if there had been a conspiracy, it was frightened into silence and inaction by the *Guardia Nacional*'s swift roundup.

And so, on the surface, nothing seemed to change in Nicaragua, not even the past names of its presidents. Luis and Anastasio succeeded each other.

But the brutality of the Somoza family, begun by Anastasio Sr. and carried forth by his sons, plus the subterranean forces of social unrest brought on by generations of repression and poverty, eventually erupted, dramatically enough, at the same time that a powerful earthquake split the streets of Managua asunder.

It was December 23, 1972, and, while a combination of Luis Somoza and John Kennedy's Alliance for Progress had kept revolution at bay in the 1960s, the excesses of Anastasio Jr., very much like those of his father, finally toppled the Somozas, and replaced them with the Sandinistas.

And this led to an endless deterioration of U.S.–Nicaraguan relations, as successive conservative U.S. administrations financed 200,000 Contras, in a losing guerrilla war against the Sandinista government. And this in turn led to the scandal of the Iran-Contra Affair, an international quagmire that has yet to be drained.

GG 300

JOHN F. KENNEDY

POSITION: *President of the U.S.A.*
DATE: *November 22, 1963*
PLACE: *Dallas, Texas*
HOW: *Gunshot*
WHO: *Lee Harvey Oswald (Conspiracy?)*
CONVICTED: *No. Murdered*
MOTIVE: *Never determined*
DIRECT CONSEQUENCE: *Escalation of U.S. involvement in Vietnam War*

THERE ARE still thousands of Americans who ask each other, "Where were you on November 22, 1963, when they shot President Kennedy?" The answer is usually crystal clear, as if the clouded glass of memory has been, for an instant, wiped clean.

And usually, even now, the recitation of where one was and what one was doing is delivered in a hushed, choked voice, for there seem to have been few rejoicers at this horrible event. The 43-year-old, articulate, personable, intelligent, and ambitious young President, though gaining his presidency by one of the slimmest majorities in American history, had added a measure of dignity and world respect to the office that had not been in evidence within the memory of most voters, and which would disappear after his death.

NOT THAT he didn't have enemies. There were those who were distrustful of his wealth, his family, his life style, and his Catholic religion.

Big business was more than unhappy about the reforms he proposed to curtail their activities and profits.

His civil rights stand angered the South, and some blacks felt that he was too moderate. Communists blamed him for the CIA-directed, woefully bungled Bay of Pigs invasion of Cuba in 1961.

His confrontation with Russia over the building of missile launch sites in Cuba offended some as brinkmanship of the most irresponsible order, while his improvement of relations with Russia was viewed as Communist sympathizing by right-wing politicians.

And yet, the people of America and the world seemed to love him. To them, he represented the hope of youth, the efficacy of intelligence, the possibility that a sensitivity to the arts could exist in high places, and a belief that the rights of individuals, no matter what their income or situation or race or aspirations should, as the framers of the Constitution desired, be protected by the nation's laws and institutions.

Most of America breathed freely and easily in 1963. Kennedy's "New Frontier" programs, de-signed to reduce poverty and racial discrimination, and to provide meaningful jobs in such idealistic pursuits as the Job Corps, endeared him to the young, who wanted a chance to put their idealism to work.

But he was also a consummate politician. His father, Joseph Kennedy, had raised all of the males in the Kennedy clan to practice that art well and constantly; and so with politics the agenda, in 1963, in November of his third year in office, John F. Kennedy determined to depart Washington for a foray into Texas.

TEXAS in 1963 was a rebellious state. In the supposedly solid Southern front of the Democratic Party, its voters were in fact deeply split into liberal, conservative, and ultra-rightist factions. John Kennedy knew that he needed Texas to be reelected in 1964. So, he planned a two-day tour of the Lone Star State that would include stops in San Antonio, Houston, Fort Worth, and Dallas.

Death threats apparently flowed in before he left, and some of his advisers urged him not to go. But John Kennedy believed he had a charmed life.

When visitors entered the Oval Office for the first time, he would frequently display to them a coconut shell laminated in plastic. It was the shell that contained the note that he had set adrift after PT-109, the torpedo boat he had commanded in World War II, had blown up, flinging him into the water. He had swum from Japanese-held island to Japanese-held island then, and survived.

Johnson Takes Nation's Helm, Pages 4 and 5

The Dallas Morning News

John F. Kennedy Life History, Pages 16 and 17

VOL. 115—NO. 54 TELEPHONE: Riverside 7-4111 DALLAS, TEXAS, SATURDAY, NOVEMBER 23, 1963—50 PAGES IN 4 SECTIONS ★★★★ PRICE 5 CENTS

KENNEDY SLAIN ON DALLAS STREET

★ ★ ★ ★ ★ ★ ★ ★ ★ ★ ★ ★ ★ ★ ★ ★

JOHNSON BECOMES PRESIDENT

Receives Oath on Aircraft

By ROBERT E. BASKIN
Washington Bureau of The News

In a solemn and sorrowful hour, with a nation mourning its dead President, Lyndon B. Johnson Friday took the oath of office as the 36th chief executive of the United States.

Following custom, the oath-taking took place quickly—only an hour and a half after the assassination of President Kennedy.

Federal Judge Sarah T. Hughes of Dallas administered the oath in a hurriedly arranged ceremony at 2:39 p.m. aboard Air Force 1, the presidential plane that brought Kennedy on his ill-fated Texas trip and on which his body was taken back to Washington.

Mrs. Johnson and Mrs. Kennedy, her stocking still flecked with blood from the assassination, flanked the vice-president as he raised his right hand in the forward compartment of the presidential jetliner at Love Field. About 25 White House staff members and friends were present as Johnson intoned the familiar oath:

"I do solemnly swear that I will perform the duties of President of the United States to the best of my ability, and defend, protect and preserve the Constitution of the United States."

The 55-year-old Johnson, the first Texan ever to become President, turned and kissed his wife on the cheek, giving her shoulders a squeeze. Then he put his arm around Mrs. Kennedy, kissing her gently on her right cheek.

Mrs. Kennedy, in tears, was wearing the same bright pink suit she wore on the fatal ride, a ride in which she had been wildly acclaimed by friendly, cheering crowds in Dallas before rifle shots rang out and the President collapsed in the seat of the car beside her.

Johnson had deliberately delayed the ceremony to give Kennedy's widow time to compose herself for one of the gruelling aspects of her husband's assassination.

CONTINUED ON PAGE 15

Lyndon B. Johnson

Gov. Connally Resting Well

By MIKE QUINN

Gov. John Connally — felled Friday by a sniper's bullet in the back—rested in "quite satisfactory" condition late Friday night at Parkland Hospital following nearly four hours of surgery in the afternoon.

An aide for the governor reported at 10:30 p.m. that the governor was asleep and resting comfortably following the incident which claimed President Kennedy's life.

Meanwhile, Dr. Tom Shires, chief of surgeons at University of Texas Southwestern Medical School, said Connally barely missed a fatal wound:

"After consulting with Mrs. Connally and others on the scene, the consensus is that the governor was quite fortunate that he turned to see what happened to the President. If he had not turned to his right, there is a good chance he probably would have been shot through the heart—as it was, the bullet caused a tangential wound."

Dr. Shires rushed to Dallas by Air Force jet after word of the shooting was flashed.

Connally was operated on by Dr. Robert R. Shaw, thoracic

CONTINUED ON PAGE 2.

Impact Shattering To World Capitals

By the Associated Press

Word of President Kennedy's assassination struck the world's capitals with shattering impact, leaving heads of state and the man in the street stunned and grief-stricken.

While messages of condolence poured into the White House from presidents, premiers and crowned heads, the little people of many lands reacted with numbed disbelief.

Pubs in London and cafes in Paris fell silent, as the news came over radio and television.

IN MOSCOW, a Russian girl walked weeping along the street.

At U.N. headquarters in New York, delegates of 11 nations bowed their heads in a moment of silence.

In Buenos Aires, newspapers sounded sirens reserved for news of the utmost gravity.

Britain's Prime Minister Douglas-Home sent condolences, and Sir Winston Churchill branded the slaying a monstrous act.

"The loss to the United States and to the world is incalculable," Sir Winston declared. "Those who come after Mr. Kennedy must strive the more to achieve the ideals of world peace and human happiness and dignity to which his presidency was dedicated."

Douglas-Home issued this terse statement:

"The Prime Minister has learned with the most profound shock and horror of the death

CONTINUED ON PAGE 2.

Pro-Communist Charged With Act

A sniper shot and killed President John F. Kennedy on the streets of Dallas Friday. A 24-year-old pro-Communist who once tried to defect to Russia was charged with the murder shortly before midnight.

Kennedy was shot about 12:20 p.m. Friday at the foot of Elm Street as the Presidential car entered the approach to the Triple Underpass. The President died in a sixth-floor surgery room at Parkland Hospital about 1 p.m., though doctors said there was no chance for him to live when he reached the hospital.

Within two hours, Vice-President Lyndon Johnson was sworn in as the nation's 36th President inside the presidential plane before departing for Washington.

The gunman also seriously wounded Texas Gov. John Connally, who was riding with the President.

Four Hours in Surgery

Connally spent four hours on an operating table, but his condition was reported as "quite satisfactory" at midnight.

The assassin, firing from the sixth floor of the Texas School Book Depository Building near the Triple Underpass sent a Mauser 6.5 rifle bullet smashing into the President's head.

An hour after the President died, police hauled the 24-year-old suspect, Lee Harvey Oswald, out of an Oak Cliff movie house.

He had worked for a short time at the depository, and police had encountered him while searching the building shortly after the assassination. They turned him loose when he was identified as an employe but put out a pickup order on him when he failed to report for a work roll call.

He also was accused of killing a Dallas policeman, J. D. Tippit, whose body was found during the vast manhunt for the President's assassin.

Oswald, who has an extensive pro-Communist background, four years ago renounced his American citizenship in Russia and tried to become a Russian citizen. Later, he returned to this country.

Friendly Crowd Cheered Kennedy

Shockingly, the President was shot after driving the length of Main Street through a crowd termed the largest and friendliest of his 2-day Texas visit. It was a good-natured crowd that surged out from the curbs almost against the swiftly moving presidential car. The protective bubble had been removed from the official convertible.

Mrs. Connally, who occupied one of the two jump seats in the car, turned to the President a few moments before and remarked, "You can't say Dallas wasn't friendly to you."

At Fort Worth, Kennedy had just delivered one of the most well-received speeches of his ca-

CONTINUED ON PAGE 2.

FUNERAL FOR PRESIDENT WILL BE HELD ON MONDAY

WASHINGTON (AP)—President Kennedy's funeral will be held Monday at St. Matthews Roman Catholic Cathedral, the White House announced Friday night.

The body of the slain President will lie in repose at the White House Saturday and will lie in state in the rotunda of the Capitol on Sunday and Monday.

The President's body will be taken a couple of miles to the cathedral at 11 a.m. (EST) Monday. There, Richard Cardinal Cushing, Archbishop of Boston and close friend of the Kennedy family, will celebrate a pontifical requiem Mass at noon.

Acting White House Press Secretary Andrew T. Hatcher said he did not know where Kennedy will be buried. There has been one report, still unconfirmed, that burial would be in the family plot in Brookline, Mass.

The President's body will be moved from the White House in an official cortege to the Capitol rotunda at 1 p.m. Sunday. This ceremony will be attended by members of the

CONTINUED ON PAGE 12.

John F. Kennedy

GRAY CLOUDS WENT AWAY

Day Began as Auspiciously As Any in Kennedy's Career

(Robert E. Baskin, chief of the Washington Bureau of The News, was one of four persons representing the world press in the motorcade which resulted in the President's assassination. This is his account of what happened.)

By ROBERT E. BASKIN
Washington Bureau of The News

It was a day that started as auspiciously as any in the career of John F. Kennedy.

When we boarded the Presidential jetliner, Air Force One, at Fort Worth at midmorning, the White House party was in high spirits. The Fort Worth welcome had been a tremendous one. Shortly before the 15-minute flight to Love Field, ugly gray clouds were swept away by a brisk breeze. The sun was out, and the Texas sky was a vivid blue.

President and Mrs. Kennedy, she strikingly attired in a pink suit with a pert matching hat, made an instant hit at Love Field as they shook hands with hundreds of persons along the fence line.

Then the last journey began. The big open Lincoln car moved out smoothly, carrying Mr. and Mrs. Kennedy and Gov. John Connally and his wife, Nellie.

Three cars back was the press pool car, in which three other newspapermen and I rode. Just ahead of us were Dallas Mayor and Mrs. Earle Cabell and Rep. Ray Roberts of McKinney.

Malcolm Kilduff, assistant presidential press secretary, was with us, and as we moved into the heart of the city Kilduff expressed elation over the friendly nature of the welcome and the great outpouring of people.

Everyone in the press car agreed it was one of the most cordial receptions the President had received in quite a while.

Buoyed by the cheers of the multitudes on Main Street, our motorcade moved on past the courthouse. Then came the approach to the Triple Underpass, with the leading cars picking up speed as the crowd thinned out somewhat. Over to our right loomed the gaunt structure labeled the Texas State School Book Depositary.

It was 12:30 p.m.

The sharp crack of a rifle rang out. But at that moment we couldn't believe it was just that. "What the hell was that?" someone in our car asked.

Then there were two more shots—measured carefully.

We saw people along the street diving for the ground.

CONTINUED ON PAGE 2.

And from that point forward, despite the tragic cloud that seemed to hover over the Kennedy clan, nibbling at the edges of its well-being, he sincerely believed that he was destined to live long and brilliantly. And so far, he had been right. It was that feeling of endless good luck, bolstered by enthusiastic welcomes in San Antonio, Houston, and Fort Worth, and a sudden change in the weather from rain to bright sunshine that prompted President Kennedy to leave off the bullet-proof bubble top of his open limousine when he began the midday motorcade through the streets of Dallas.

The themes of the luncheon speech he was to deliver that day at the Trade Mart were peace, equal rights, and social justice, the hallmarks of the first thousand days of his administration.

AT THE same time that Air Force One, the President's plane, was flying from Fort Worth to Dallas, Lee Harvey Oswald, a 24-year-old, slightly balding filing clerk at the Texas School Book Depository, was, according to later news reports and testimony before the Warren Assassination Commission, fitting together the gun that would eventually be used to kill John F. Kennedy.

Oswald was apparently one youth in America who did not see a century of hope in the young President's policies. Perhaps no one will ever know exactly what his motives were for assassinating the President, or, in fact, if he *was* the one, and the *only* one who assassinated the President; he would be killed himself before he could speak to either the public or a court of law.

Oswald was a withdrawn, hostile loner who, at the age of 15, had read Karl Marx's *Das Kapital*, and was, according to acquaintances, profoundly affected by it. He was an ex-Marine Corps radar technician.

He had defected to Moscow, after leaving the Marine Corps, with the idea of passing on military secrets. He was rebuffed, married a Russian girl, and returned to the U.S.

The marriage fell apart and Oswald drifted from place to place and job to job. His mental state might have been reflected in the fact that he became involved, in New Orleans, with both pro- and anti-Castro Cubans, in Mexico with Soviet intelligence, and in Dallas with White Russians.

It was quite an odyssey for a man of Oswald's apparently limited capabilities, and so the inevitable question has arisen: Did he act on his own, or was he part of a conspiracy? Nobody who is speaking truly knows, to this day, though there have been numerous books and films and articles and testimony that have tried to prove that Oswald was a pawn in a coming together of the Mafia, a fanatical right-wing group, the CIA, the war party, and the military-industrial complex.

The conspiracy theories all agree that Oswald could not possibly have killed President Kennedy himself, for the following reasons, among many others that have been given:

- His view from his supposed assassination niche on the sixth floor of the Texas School Book Depository was partially obscured.
- Two men were observed by witnesses in that window in the Texas School Book Depository.
- At least six shots were heard, and no one person could have shot, reloaded, reaimed and fired that quickly.
- The shot that killed the President came, according to witnesses, not from the direction of Oswald's perch, but from the grassy knoll in front of the motorcade.

According to nonconspiracy advocates and the Warren Commission Report, the assassination was far more simple: Oswald arrived for his job at the Texas School Book Depository in Dallas at 8 a.m. that morning with the disassembled murder weapon wrapped in anonymous brown paper. At noon, when his fellow workers dispersed for lunch, he ascended to the sixth floor of the Book Depository.

No one worked here; its flooring was being replaced, and cartons of books were piled on one side to accommodate the work. Oswald carved out his sniper's nest and assembled his rifle with its telescopic sight, and waited.

THE PRESIDENTIAL motorcade moved off from the airport at 11:55 a.m. The first car was packed with police. Three motorcycle escorts followed it. Five lengths behind them traveled the open presidential car.

The front seat contained the chauffeur and a secret service agent. In the two jump seats behind the agent and the driver were Texas Governor John B. Connally and his wife Nellie. The President and his wife were seated in the rear.

Following the presidential limousine were four motorcyclists, a convertible with 10 security agents

The window from which Lee Harvey Oswald is supposed to have shot President Kennedy.

(two stood on the running boards), and, two and a half lengths behind them, Vice President Lyndon Johnson and his wife, followed by another car bulging with security agents.

Behind them were cars containing politicians and journalists.

The convoy inched southward into the heart of Dallas. Twice, it halted, while President Kennedy, to the consternation of the Secret Service, alighted and shook hands with members of the cheering crowds that lined the streets.

At 12:21 p.m., the motorcade entered a festively decorated Main Street. The supposedly hostile Dallas crowds were ecstatic. The procession inched past Dealy Plaza, turned right into Houston Street, then left, into Elm Street.

"You surely can't say Dallas doesn't love you, Mr. President," said Nellie Connally.

"No, you can't," answered the President, waving as the presidential limousine inched, at 11 miles an hour, down Elm Street, in front of the Texas School Book Depository.

AT 12:30, the first round was squeezed off. Its 6.5 millimeter bullet dug into the back of John F. Kennedy's neck, traveled through his throat, and punctured his windpipe. Continuing on, it traveled through Governor Connally, breaking two ribs, puncturing a lung, smashing his left wrist and imbedding itself in his left thigh.

The long journey of this supposed "magic bullet" was to form the basis of the Warren

Commission's conclusion—when it was appointed by President Lyndon Johnson to investigate the assassination—that only three shots were fired at President Kennedy.

The President gasped and grabbed at his throat. A few seconds later, the second, fatal bullet arrived, tearing off the right rear part of his skull and splattering the car and Jacqueline Kennedy with blood and brain matter. He raised his hand once to his forehead and then he collapsed into her lap.

"My God, they've shot him!" screamed Mrs. Kennedy, catapulting from her seat as a third bullet flew past her.

NOW THE contention begins. Anti-conspiracy advocates say that these were the second and third bullets from Lee Harvey Oswald's gun, and that they all came from behind the President.

Conspiracy advocates say that autopsy photographs (later altered) prove that the fatal shot came from *in front* of the motorcade, that the *rear* of the President's skull was blown off and that it can be seen flying backward, toward the rear fender of his car. Furthermore, they say, a fusillade of bullets hit the car and the ground around it, and the angle of some of them showed that they came, not from the Texas School Book Depository, but from the County Records Building.

Witnesses did see a puff of smoke coming from the grassy knoll across the Plaza and in front of the motorcade, and Dallas police ran to the spot, but were turned back by men flashing Secret Service credentials.

Other men were seen running away across railroad tracks below the scene. Later, a group of "bums" was rounded up and released without booking. The "bums" were clean-shaven, and wore clean clothing.

AFTER THE second shot smashed into the President, a security agent leaped on the back of the limousine and shoved Mrs. Kennedy back into her seat, then threw his body over her, shielding her from any further bullets.

The presidential limousine stood absolutely still, while the chauffeur apparently froze in his seat. Despite the fact that the car behind the limousine was filled with secret service agents, only one of them rushed forward, to protect Mrs. Kennedy. Meanwhile, in Vice President Lyndon Johnson's car, his entire complement of guards fell on him, forcing him to the floor.

Finally, after 10 terrible seconds of inaction, the presidential limousine lurched forward, past horrified, sobbing spectators.

The motorcade screeched into the emergency entrance to Parkland Memorial Hospital. Doctors did what they could, frantically slitting open the President's windpipe to let him breathe, and transfusing him.

But they knew from the beginning that the worst had happened. His brain had been shattered, and shortly before 1 p.m., his heart stopped. The charmed life and administration of John F. Kennedy ended.

But the horror continued. More odd occurrences unfolded at Parkland, as both the Warren Commission and the investigation in 1979 by the House Select Committee on Assassinations revealed.

The camera and film of a Navy enlisted man who was in the autopsy room, where the throat wound was marked as an entry wound and the wound at the back of the President's skull—or what was left of it—was marked as an exit wound, were both confiscated.

The body of the President was taken from the Parkland Hospital authorities—at gun point, according to certain witnesses—by the Secret Service.

At 1:15 p.m., a police officer saw a man fitting the description of Oswald walking along a street. He stopped his patrol car and approached Oswald, or the man who looked like him. The man drew a .38 caliber revolver and shot the policeman dead, then darted down the street and into a movie theatre.

Police followed him, and cornered him. He tried to fire at them, but when his revolver jammed, he was captured. It was Oswald.

THE WORLD went into shock. The trading markets closed; the UN adjourned; Broadway theatres canceled performances; ordinary and extraordinary citizens withdrew into their homes, feeling choked and hopeless and lost. Everyone, it seemed, needed badly to be with someone they loved.

On the following day, streets were deserted, as the Kennedy family brought the body back to Washington and put it on view beneath the capitol dome. Wordless families clung silently together, glued to their television sets, trying to preserve whatever was left of those bright moments of the Kennedy years.

But still the horror continued. On the Sunday following the assassination, millions watched as Oswald was taken through an underground garage from the Dallas police court to a County jail. Jack Ruby, who was the operator of a sleazy Dallas strip joint, shot Oswald dead. It was almost too much to bear, and as Oswald was silenced forever, the persistent and now incredulous questioning began: Who had hired Ruby? Was he the backup, to kill Oswald so he would not talk? To where did the conspiracy climb now?

Ruby would die in silence too–in jail, after a sudden and medically unprecedented onset of cancer. Before he died, he would tell Tom Johnson, a journalist and formerly an aide to Lyndon Johnson: "It is the most bizarre conspiracy in the history of the world. It'll come out at a future date . . ." However the Warren Commission, appointed by President Lyndon Johnson, and headed by Chief Justice Earl Warren, would now meet for nine months, conduct 25,000 F.B.I. interviews, fill 26 volumes with evidence, and conclude that Oswald acted alone.

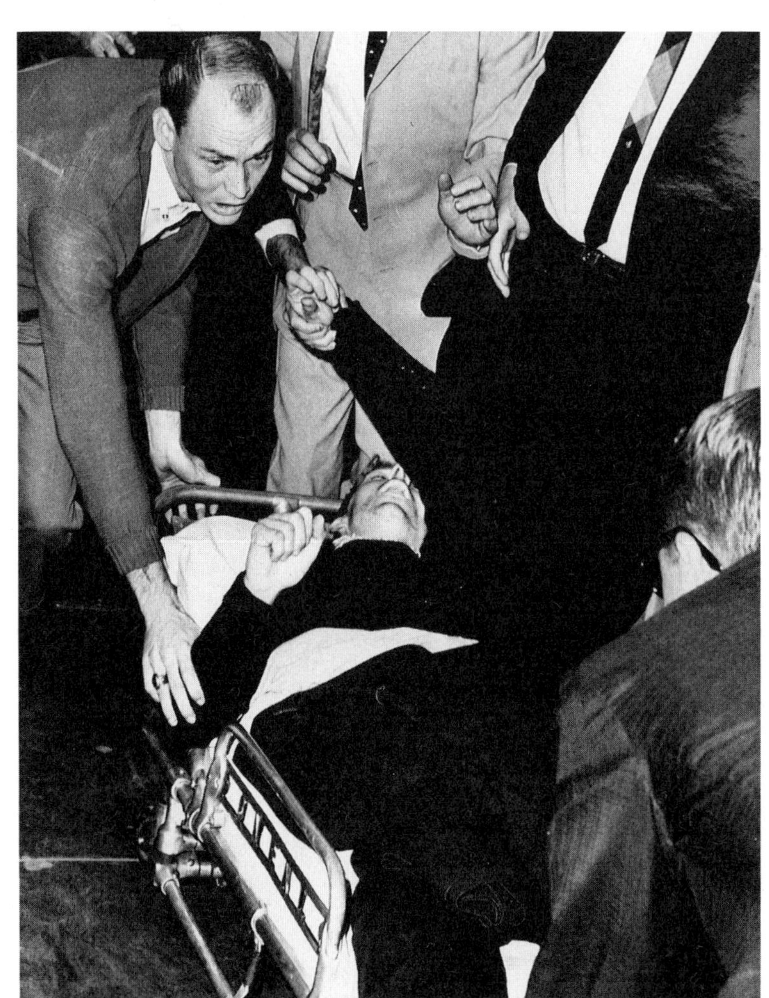

Lee Harvey Oswald, moments after he was shot by Jack Ruby.

Sixteen years later, in 1979, the House Select Committee on Assassinations would again review what conspiracy theorists insist was altered evidence (even the so-called "Zapruder" film—the amateur film that showed the moment of assassination, was, according to these theorists, doctored. Some of its frames were reversed to show the President's head lurching forward, when actually it was flung backward).

The 1979 House Committee would conclude that there was evidence of a conspiracy, which also included the assassination of the civil rights leader Dr. Martin Luther King (see page 98). But the evidence was never developed.

And so, more books, many very persuasive, were written and published, and a major motion picture flawed by inserting fictitious events was made, in an effort to reopen the investigation and answer some very disturbing questions: such as why important evidence continues to disappear from the National Archives, and why 21 witnesses scheduled to give testimony to the Warren Commission mysteriously died, a circumstance that the London *Times* has said had odds of 100,000 trillion to one against its ever happening. Chief Justice Warren's assertion that all of the facts would never be known "in our lifetime," left the door open to still more speculation and investigation, and both continue to this very moment.

As for the moments immediately following the assassination: Every leader of every country in the free world arrived in Washington for the immensely dignified and deeply moving funeral services, again witnessed by millions on television.

AND THE country survived. The machinery of government moved forward, and President Lyndon Johnson continued to press for the domestic reforms begun by President Kennedy, although he did not pursue the Kennedy vision in Vietnam.

But a part of everyone's heart was destroyed that November noontime in 1963. The world was a crueler and colder place for almost everybody who lived through those terrible hours.

The idealism that the Kennedy years had kindled in youth burned on for a time, until it was snuffed out by the Vietnam War, never to be entirely revived, at least in that open and innocent and visionary way.

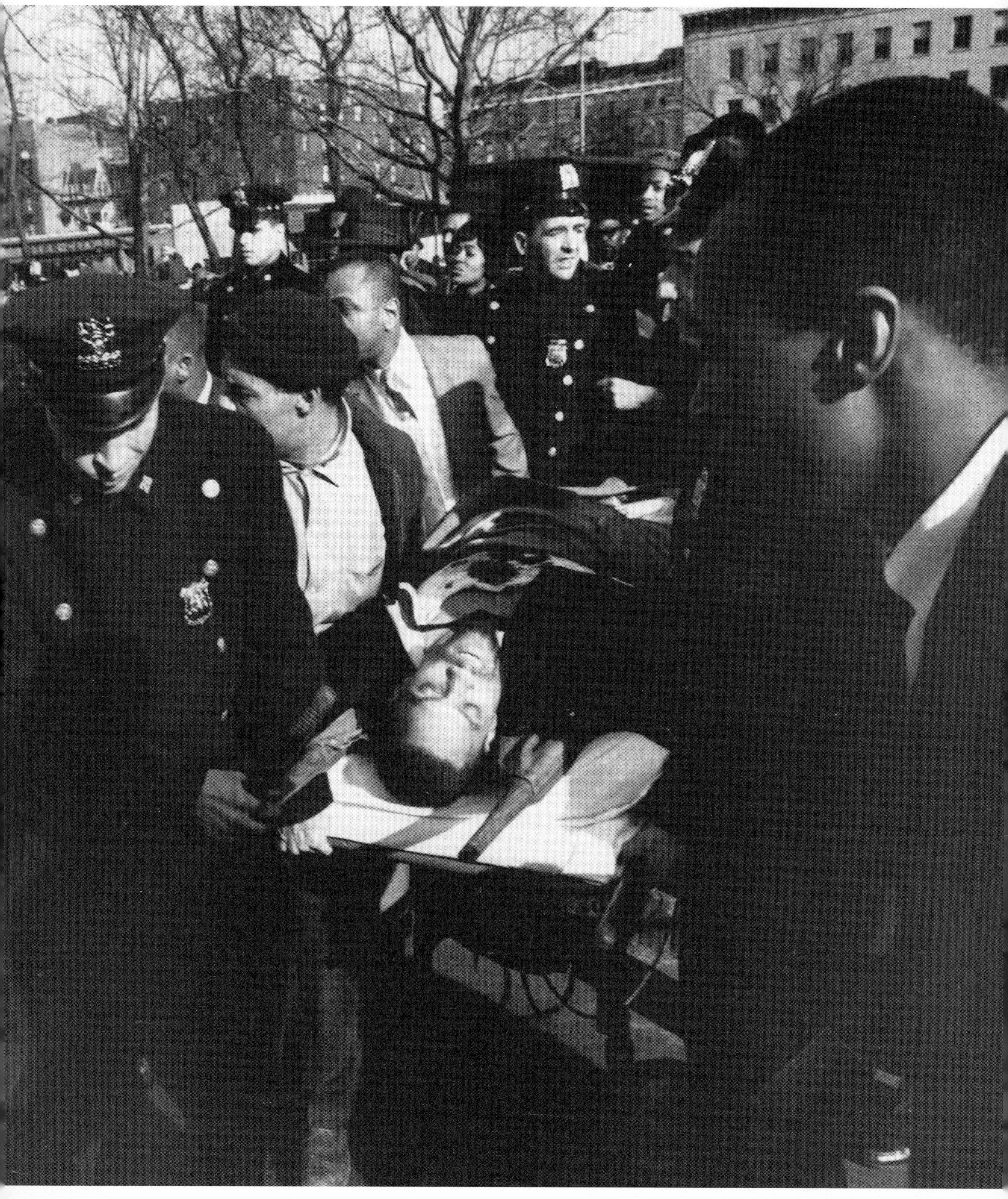

MALCOLM X

POSITION:	*Founder, Organization of Afro-American Unity*
DATE:	*February 21, 1965*
PLACE:	*New York City*
HOW:	*Gunshot*
WHO:	*Talmadge Hayer and accomplices*
CONVICTED:	*Yes. Sentenced to life imprisonment*
MOTIVE:	*Black Muslim revenge*
DIRECT CONSEQUENCE:	*Fierce war between black power factions*

"THERE IS a threat against my life, and there is no people in the U.S. able to carry out that threat better than the Black Muslims. I know. I taught them." And so, with the kind of clarity that borders on clairvoyance, Malcolm X predicted his own death—if the prosecutors and investigators of his assassination by shotgun blast on February 21, 1965 were accurate.

The problem is that, as in all of the assassinations of public figures in America in the 1960s, conclusions about the shooting of Malcolm X have been clouded by controversy, revisions, and reexaminations, on paper and in film. Each has raised multiple doubts and contradictory legends.

Maybe Malcolm X underwent a conversion; maybe he didn't. Maybe it was the Black Muslims who killed him; maybe it wasn't. Maybe it was an organized conspiracy; maybe it was the inspirational work of a few disgruntled followers of Elijah Muhammad. Maybe the entire truth will emerge; probably it won't.

THE FACTS of Malcolm X's life, from midwest boyhood to charismatic leadership of a small but powerful group of dedicated followers are documented in both his own autobiography and several bulging police dossiers.

He was born Malcolm Little on May 19, 1925 in Omaha, Nebraska, the son of a Baptist minister who was an enthusiastic adherent of Marcus Garvey's "Back to Africa" black nationalist movement. From infancy, his vision of whites was tinged by fire. His maternal grandmother had been raped by a white man, and Malcolm X's distinctive red hair was the result. In 1929, when he was four, his family moved to Lansing, Michigan. Shortly after their arrival, their home was torched by white racists. Two years later, when he was six, his father was run over by a streetcar. The body was covered with bruises and nearly cut in half. Malcolm swore that the police report of an accident was a cover-up. His father had actually been beaten by whites and thrown, unconscious, onto the streetcar tracks.

Malcolm Little's formal schooling ended at the eighth grade. As a terminally angry teenager, he made his way to New York City, where he worked for a while as a waiter at Small's Paradise, but was fired for pimping on the side. From there, he progressed to full-time hustling, drug-pushing, and burglary. In 1946, in Boston, he was arrested for the last, and received a 10-year jail sentence.

He only served six years, but they were apparently six of the most important years of his life. In prison, he began to educate himself, patiently copying every word and its meaning from an abridged dictionary. His goal was to establish the kind of vocabulary that would make him a riveting speaker, the sort who could draw multitudes of people to him. He discovered that he could speak and command those to whom he spoke.

MALCOLM'S SECOND breakthrough was equally important. In prison, he discovered, and became a convert to Elijah Muhammad's Black Muslim sect, as dedicated to the separation of the races as Marcus Garvey's Black Nation had been. Black Muslims were impatient with the early sit-ins and demonstrations of Dr. Martin Luther King and other black leaders who were fighting for equality and accommodation with whites. Black Muslims preached the sort of hatred that had energized Malcolm Little since childhood.

To Black Muslims, it was really a black world. Whites, orientals, Native Americans, Hispanics—any whose pigmentation was not black, had been bleached out at some point in history by a mad scientist named Yacub. What appealed even more to Malcolm Little was the Black Muslims' practice of discarding the names their slave owners had given them. In 1952, out on parole, he took the name of Malcolm X, which, as he later wrote, replaced "the white slave-master name which had been imposed upon my paternal forebears by some blue-eyed devil."

In addition, Black Muslims adopted the ascetic practices of world Muslims—the prohibition of the consumption of tobacco, alcohol, and pre-marital sex. In 1958, a considerably changed Malcolm X married a fellow Muslim, Betty Shabazz. They would have four daughters, and she would be pregnant with a fifth at the time of his death.

AS THE fifties gave way to the sixties, the growing civil rights movement lent publicity and credence to the Black Muslims and other more militant groups who regarded the work of Dr. King merely as modern Uncle Tomism. The dictionary study and determination to become a better preacher than his father paid off for the tall, thin, bespectacled and light-skinned Malcolm X. He became a riveting, savage spokesperson for the Nation of Islam, as the Black Muslims movement was now known.

Malcolm X progressed swiftly from the assistant pastorship of Detroit's Muslim Temple No. 1, becoming head of the New York Temple. By 1963, he was the first "national minister" of the Nation of Islam, and was appearing in public regularly enough to be considered the movement's second most powerful figure, next to Elijah Muhammad.

His speeches were fearsome, and, to non-blacks, corrosive. When an airliner containing 121 white members of the artistic community of Atlanta, Georgia, crashed in France, killing all of them, he told a Los Angeles audience of Black Muslims, "I would like to announce a very beautiful thing that has happened. I got a wire from God today. He really answered our prayers over in France. He dropped an airplane out of the sky with over 120 white people on it because the Muslims believe in an eye for an eye and a tooth for a tooth. We will continue to pray and we hope that every day another plane falls out of the sky."

Heartless, violent, advocating "bullets for ballots," in the fight for voting rights, Malcolm X orated himself to a position equal to and threatening to his mentor, Elijah Muhammad, and, perhaps more pointedly, to Muhammad's successor and son-in-law, Raymond Sharrief. It was no secret that Malcolm X had fallen out of favor with the leader of the Nation of Islam, and that that leader was merely waiting for Malcolm X to trip on his own excesses.

That opportunity arrived with the assassination of John F. Kennedy. The cold-blooded murder of this popular and charismatic young president horrified blacks and whites alike. Civil rights leaders particularly had much to lose, since the Kennedy administration was sympathetic toward and active in enforcing and establishing federal laws to protect all races.

But Malcolm X used the killing as a forum to sustain his hatred of whites. Commenting on the assassination, he told a gathering and the press, "Being an old farm boy myself, chickens coming home to roost never did make me sad; they've always made me glad." The outrage this caused was enough to enable Elijah Muhammad to suspend Malcolm X from the Nation of Islam.

SUSPENSION liberated the ascending young leader for a spiral to new heights of hatred. Forming his own activist army, the Organization of Afro-American Unity, he began to circulate stories designed to undermine the power of Elijah Muhammad, and draw disenchanted Black Muslims into his organization. In an open letter, he accused Elijah of fathering eight illegitimate babies by six teenage secretaries at Black Muslim headquarters in Chicago.

Other rumors of immorality followed, and disillusioned followers of Elijah began to defect to Malcolm X. Among the first defectors were two of Elijah Muhammad's sons, and this brought forth vitriol that could only be construed as unveiled threats. "Only those who wish to be led to hell or to their doom will follow Malcolm," said *Muhammad Speaks*, the biweekly newspaper of the Nation of Islam, adding, "the die is set, and Malcolm shall not escape."

Fatalistically, Malcolm X acknowledged, "No one can get out without trouble. This thing with me will be resolved by death and violence."

AND THEN, a miraculous transformation occurred. Malcolm X left his small band of followers for a five week trip to Africa and Mecca. The journey may have begun as an effort to achieve greater credibility than Elijah; it ended with a changed Malcolm X, a man whose savage hatred of whites

"All the News That's Fit to Print"

The New York Times.

LATE CITY EDITION

U.S. Weather Bureau Report (Page 66) forecasts: Fair, windy and cold today; clear and very cold tonight. Sunny tomorrow. Temp. range: 38—24; yesterday: 50—28.

VOL. CXIV. No. 39,111. © 1965 by The New York Times Company. Times Square, New York, N.Y. 10036 NEW YORK, MONDAY, FEBRUARY 22, 1965. TEN CENTS

Malcolm X Shot to Death at Rally Here

United Press International

Malcolm X being taken to hospital from Audubon Ballroom yesterday after he was shot while addressing a meeting

Three Other Negroes Wounded—One Is Held in Killing

By PETER KIHSS

Malcolm X, the 39-year-old leader of a militant black nationalist movement, was shot to death yesterday afternoon at a rally of his followers in a ballroom in Washington Heights.

Shortly before midnight, a 22-year-old Negro, Thomas Hagan, was charged with the killing. The police rescued him from the ballroom crowd after he had been shot and beaten.

Malcolm, a bearded extremist, had said only a few words of greeting when a fusillade rang out. The bullets knocked him over backward.

Pandemonium broke out among the 400 Negroes in the Audubon Ballroom at 166th Street and Broadway. As men, women and children ducked under tables and flattened themselves on the floor, more shots were fired. Some witnesses said 30 shots had been fired.

3 Weapons Fired

The police said seven bullets had struck Malcolm. Three other Negroes were shot.

About two hours later the police said the shooting had apparently been a result of a feud between followers of Malcolm and members of the extremist group he broke with last year, the Black Muslims. However, the police declined to say whether Hagan is a Muslim.

The Medical Examiner's office said early this morning that a preliminary autopsy showed Malcolm had died of "multiple gunshot wounds." The office said that bullets of two different calibers as well as shotgun pellets had been removed from his body.

One police theory was that as many as five conspirators might have been involved, two creating a diversionary disturbance.

Hagan was shot in the left thigh and his left leg was broken, apparently by kicks. He was under treatment in the Bellevue Hospital prison ward last night; perhaps a dozen policemen were guarding him, according to the hospital's night superintendent. The police said

Continued on Page 10, Column 1

Malcolm Knew He Was a 'Marked Man'

By THEODORE JONES

"I live like a man who's already dead," Malcolm X said last Thursday in a two-hour interview in the Harlem office of his Organization for Afro-American Unity.

"I'm a marked man," he said slowly as he fingered the horn-rimmed glasses he wore and leaned forward to give emphasis to his words. "It doesn't frighten me for myself as long as I felt they would not hurt my family."

Asked about "they," Malcolm smiled, shook his head, and said, "those folks down at 116th Street and that man in Chicago."

The references, Malcolm quickly confirmed, were to his former associates in the Black Muslim movement and to Elijah Muhammad, the organizer and head of the movement. Before Malcolm X left the movement 18 months ago, he was the minister of the Black Muslims' Harlem mosque at 116th Street and Lenox Avenue.

"No one can get out without trouble," Malcolm continued, "and this thing with me will be resolved by death and violence."

Why were they after him? "Because I'm me," he replied.

But realizing that was not enough to say, he pushed into an almost endless flow of sentences.

"I was the spokesman for the Black Muslims," he said. "I believed in Elijah Muhammad more strongly than Christians do in Jesus. I believed in him so strongly that my mind, my body, my voice functioned 100 per cent for him and the movement. My belief led others to believe.

"Now I'm out. And there's the fear if my image isn't shattered, the Muslims in the movement will leave. Then, they know I know a lot. As long as I was in the movement, anything he [Elijah Muhammad] did was to me by divine guidance."

Malcolm said that he knew many things that made him a

Continued on Page 11, Column 2

SCHOOL AID DELAY BRINGS A DEMAND FOR HOUSE ACTION

Administration Is Seeking to Get a Decision This Week From Powell Group

SHOWDOWN IS VOWED

Supporter Pledges Move if Measure Is Not Called Up at Thursday Session

By MARJORIE HUNTER
Special to The New York Times

WASHINGTON, Feb. 21 — The Administration is determined to get House committee action this week on the $1.25 billion school aid bill, a virtual legislative truant in the last few weeks.

This was to have been the week that the bill was to have come up for floor action in the House. Instead, the measure has not even been brought up before the full House Education and Labor Committee.

President Johnson and House leaders are "deeply concerned" over the failure of Representative Adam Clayton Powell, Democrat of Manhattan, to move the bill out of his committee, sources close to the President said today.

The bill, which has top priority on the President's legislative list, got off to a fast start early in the new Congress.

Met on Saturdays

Working day and night, a House subcommittee held 10 days of public hearings. The subcommittee even met on Saturdays, almost unheard of so early in a new session, in order to speed the bill.

The measure was approved Feb. 5 by the six subcommittee Democrats. The three Republicans boycotted the voting session in protest against failure to hold longer hearings.

"We were in good shape to move the bill right along," Representative Frank Thompson Jr., Democrat of New Jersey, a member of the subcommittee, said today. "But nothing happened."

Representative Powell failed to call the full committee into session the following week. And he did not call a meeting after the long Lincoln birthday holiday recess.

The committee is required under its own rules to meet next Thursday.

"If the chairman doesn't bring up the bill then, we'll have a showdown," Representative Thompson promised.

Linked to Travel Funds

Representative Powell could not be reached today to comment on whether he intended to call up the bill at the Thursday meeting.

Administration sources say that the delay over the education bill appeared to be tied in with Representative Powell's effort to win favorable House action on a resolution determining how much money will be authorized for his committee's travel and investigation this year.

The House is expected to vote this week on a number of such authorization measures, including one for the Powell committee.

Meanwhile, Republicans have used the more than two-week breather to draft proposed

Continued on Page 18, Column 1

POWELL OPPOSING NEW MOTLEY POST

Says Senator Can Be More Effective in Albany Than in Borough Presidency

By MARTIN GANSBERG

Representative Adam Clayton Powell asserted yesterday that the elected leaders of Harlem were opposed to the selection of State Senator Constance Baker Motley as Manhattan Borough President.

In a sharply worded telegram to Mayor Wagner, Mr. Powell, who heads the 12th District South, said that he also was speaking for Hulan Jack, Mark T. Southall and Percy Sutton in insisting that Mrs. Motley would "be much more effective as a Senator than as Borough President."

"Not one of the elected leaders representing the Harlem community has sponsored her," Mr. Powell asserted. "Unfortunately, and once again, the selection of a Negro is apparently being made by the white man."

Mr. Jack is leader of the 14th District North, Mr. Southall of the 12th District North and Mr. Sutton is a State Assemblyman from the 11th District. The other Harlem leaders are George Miller of the 11th District and J. Raymond Jones of the 13th District.

Mr. Powell's statement, released here by a spokesman for him, was issued at 1:30 yesterday morning after he had completed telephone conversations from Puerto Rico, where

Continued on Page 17, Column 7

Rise of 24 Million In U.S. Labor Force Is Forecast by 1980

By JOHN D. POMFRET
Special to The New York Times

WASHINGTON, Feb. 21 — The Labor Department issued new projections today indicating that the nation's labor force would grow to 86 million in 1970 and 101.4 million in 1980.

It was 77 million in 1964 and 73 million in 1960.

Although the projected increase between 1970 and 1980 —15.4 million—is 2.4 million higher than the projected increase between 1960 and 1970, the rate of gain would be about the same, 17.7 per cent from 1960 to 1970 and 17.9 per cent from 1970 to 1980.

An increase of 24 million workers between 1964 and 1980 would mean that 1.5 million new jobs would have to be created each year, on the average, merely to absorb the growth in the labor force. Still more jobs would be needed to offset gains in output per man-hour and to reduce the level of unemployment.

The projections were compiled by Miss Sophia Cooper and Denis F. Johnston of the Bureau of Labor Statistics.

According to their study, the rest of this decade will show

Continued on Page 19, Column 1

AGE IS A PROBLEM IN LABOR COUNCIL

Some in A.F.L.-C.I.O. Feel Older Chiefs Should Quit —Most Are Over 65

By DAMON STETSON
Special to The New York Times

BAL HARBOUR, Fla., Feb. 21—Some leaders of the American Federation of Labor and Congress of Industrial Organizations are beginning to worry about the superannuated character of the organization's executive council.

The 29-member council, which opens its winter meeting here tomorrow in the plush surroundings of an alabaster-white beachfront hotel, is getting along in years. Fifteen members—more than half—of the labor organization's top policy-making body are 65 years old or over, nine are 70 or over, and one is 82.

One of these elder statesmen of the labor movement, who is still playing an energetic role as leader of his own union, said that he did not feel age alone was any criterion of a labor leader's effectiveness. But he said that he was disturbed that some former union presidents were continuing as members of the council long after having given up active direction of their unions and going into retirement.

If the labor movement isn't careful, he said, the council will become little more than a fraternal organization of old men who like to come to Florida in the winter to play gin rummy.

Although some labor leaders here are willing to talk privately about the need for an infusion of new blood in the council, no one is saying much publicly about it at this time.

Among some of the younger council members, there is a feeling that the council and the merged labor organization ought to become more dynamic and aggressive. But there is a reluctance, at the same time, to push out old war horses of an earlier era.

George Meany, president of the A.F.L.-C.I.O., who is 70, is one member who has shown no

Continued on Page 19, Column 1

Democrats in Legislature to End Duplicate Bill-Filing as Waste

By SYDNEY H. SCHANBERG
Special to The New York Times

ALBANY, Feb. 21—Democratic leaders disclosed today that they had decided to abolish the wasteful practice of duplicate bill-filing in the Legislature.

Senate Majority Leader Joseph Zaretzki said he and Assembly Speaker Anthony J. Travia reached the decision at a meeting last week.

Under present practice, sanctioned by existing rules, hundreds of times every year several different legislators—sometimes dozens—file the same bill.

The bills are printed separately, but the wording is identical. It costs the state $12.32 a page to print legislative bills, and the cost of the duplication runs into tens of thousands of dollars.

Senator Zaretzki said that from now on, if more than one legislator wanted to introduce the same bill they would have to sponsor it cooperatively. That is, instead of many bills on one subject there would be only one, with the names of the sponsors affixed, whether Republican or Democratic.

Mr. Zaretzki said that although the change was based so far solely on a leadership decision, a formal change would be proposed this week in the Legislature's rules. The Senate leader said he was assured of enough votes in both houses to carry the proposal.

The Manhattan Democrat said he had already asked Earl W. Brydges, the Republican minority leader in the Senate, not to introduce any bills on Governor Rockefeller's program without

Continued on Page 17, Column 5

Washington's Birthday

Today is Washington's Birthday, a Federal and state holiday, and following is a list of services and facilities that are or are not affected:

Public and parochial schools, banks, stock and commodity exchanges—Closed.

Department stores and retail business in the city and suburban areas—Some open, some closed.

Post offices—Special delivery only, no business transacted.

Parking—Alternate-side rules suspended, all others, including parking meter rules, in effect.

Sanitation—No refuse collection.

Congo Seeks Return Of Ousted Teachers

By JOSEPH LELYVELD
Special to The New York Times

LEOPOLDVILLE, the Congo, Feb. 21—The Congolese Government sent an urgent message to Athens today inviting the UNESCO teachers it expelled yesterday as subversives to return to their classes here as soon as possible.

Actually, a decision not to expel the teachers was taken last night before their plane departed from Leopoldville for Athens. But something went wrong with official communications and the security police at the airport insisted that the teachers and their dependents, a total of 35 persons, board the plane.

The snag in communications was eventually straightened out to the satisfaction of the security police, but not before the plane was airborne. Leopoldville

Continued on Page 6, Column 1

PANEL OF 7 NAMED TO TRY TO IMPROVE TRANSIT FINANCES

Governor and Mayor Join In Attempt to Avert a Rise in the 15-Cent Fare

By EMANUEL PERLMUTTER

The appointment of a seven-man citizens' committee to try to solve the financial problems of the city's transit system was announced yesterday by Governor Rockefeller and Mayor Wagner.

The naming of the committee followed a recent announcement by Joseph E. O'Grady, chairman of the Transit Authority, that the 15-cent fare might have to be increased in view of the system's growing deficit.

With the election of a Mayor coming up this fall, and that of a Governor next year, both Mr. Wagner and Mr. Rockefeller have been reported to be trying to avoid a fare rise. One has been avoided in the last few years by increases in financial assistance from the city, with the acquiescence of the Legislature.

Make-up of the Panel

The chairman of the citizens' study committee, named by Mr. Rockefeller and Mr. Wagner, will be J. Victor Herd, board chairman of the Continental Insurance Company.

Other members of the committee are John A. Coleman, former president of the New York Stock Exchange; J. Clarence Davies, former chairman of the city Housing and Redevelopment Board; Charles Garrahan, vice president of the Amalgamated Clothing Workers of America; George S. Moore, president of the First National City Bank of New York; Clifton W. Phalen, president of the New York Telephone Company, and Walter N. Rothschild Jr., president of Abraham & Straus.

The announcement said the committee had been appointed "to make recommendations for the immediate and long-term solution of the substantial financial problem presented by the city subway and surface lines."

Review Is Planned

It "will review the administration and economics of public mass transit in the city and its relationship with other forms of transportation serving New York City," the statement continued.

"The committee will report to the Governor and the Mayor as quickly as their recommendations can be developed."

Although no time limit was set within which the committee is to make its recommendations, it is virtually under obligation to make them before the end of the year. The authority would have to know where it could get additional revenues before it could make a contract offer to its union employes late this fall.

The committee was envisaged almost 14 months ago in the contract settlement between the Transit Authority and the Transport Workers Union.

Asked about the delay in its creation, a spokesman for Mayor Wagner said yesterday, "It was a question of getting the right men for the committee."

On Feb. 2, Mr. O'Grady said the authority expected a deficit of more than $33 million in the fiscal year starting July 1. He said this prospect made it doubtful that the 15-cent fare

Continued on Page 22, Column 7

MILITARY COUNCIL DISMISSES KHANH; HE BOWS TO EDICT

VOTE UNANIMOUS

Tran Van Minh Named Acting Commander of Armed Forces

By JACK LANGGUTH
Special to The New York Times

SAIGON, South Vietnam, Monday, Feb. 22—Lieut. Gen. Nguyen Khanh bowed today to a unanimous decision of the Armed Forces Council to replace him with Maj. Gen. Tran Van Minh as commander in chief.

After the council voted late yesterday to oust him, General Khanh spent the night telephoning military commanders throughout the country to rally support. Unsuccessful, he called the council's headquarters in Saigon early this morning from the resort of Dalat, northeast of the capital, to admit defeat.

Council members said they hoped to bring General Khanh into the capital later in the day for a news conference.

Earlier, Brig. Gen. Nguyen Chanh Thi, commander of the army's I Corps, said the South Vietnamese Air Force would bomb any troops or tanks that moved toward Saigon.

Saigon Wary About Firing

General Thi, who helped to keep General Khanh in power in the past, had become a leader in the movement to drop him.

Unusual troop movements and some mortar fire on the outskirts of the capital kept Saigon wary after the broadcast announcement of General Khanh's removal. But the mortar fire and flares dropped around Tansonnhut Airport were apparently connected with operations against the Vietcong.

The ouster came a day after General Khanh, aided by loyal paratroops and air units, defeated a brief and bloodless attempt at a military coup d'état. Some of the officers who backed him were among those who now voted for his dismissal.

Suu Agrees to Action

General Khanh did not attend the council meeting.

The council's announcement did not specify whether General Minh, who was named acting commander in chief, would also inherit General Khanh's second post, the chairmanship of the Armed Forces Council.

A council delegation called on the chief of state, Dr. Phan Khac Suu, to tell him about the vote. The new Premier, Dr. Phan Huy Quat, was present.

Dr. Suu readily agreed to sign an order to dismiss General Khanh and appoint General Minh.

In his order, Dr. Suu said General Khanh would be reassigned. The general's ambitions and his courting of Buddhist political support have long made him suspect among his colleagues.

Second Meeting Held

Council members met again near midnight to map a strategy that would keep General Khanh from regaining power.

Air Vice Marshal Nguyen Cao Ky first insisted that General Khanh be required to leave the country.

But General Khanh was not yet ready to give up. From his command post at the southeastern beach resort of Cap Saint-Jacques, he telephoned offers to junior officers, not on the council, who he thought might support him.

Brig. Gen. Nguyen Van Chuan, General Thi's deputy, was offered command of the I Corps if he would send troops to support General Khanh. General Thi countered the call with a message of his own, cautioning the deputy that General

Continued on Page 3, Column 1

French Official Asks Talks to Stop War

By JACK RAYMOND
Special to The New York Times

WASHINGTON, Feb. 21—Maurice Couve de Murville, the French Foreign Minister, urged before a nationwide American television audience today that negotiations for a settlement in Vietnam be attempted "as soon as possible."

His public advocacy of negotiations followed three days of private talks with President Johnson, Secretary of State Dean Rusk and other officials during which he was unable to win them over to the idea.

In reply to a question, Mr. Couve de Murville said: "We think that the negotiations [to end the fighting in Vietnam] should be engaged as soon as possible.

"A long time, in our

Continued on Page 3, Column 6

U.S. FINDS BACKING IN WORLD'S PRESS

Extent of Support for Action in Asia Surprises Capital, U.S.I.A. Director Says

By JOHN W. FINNEY
Special to The New York Times

WASHINGTON, Feb. 21 — Foreign editorial reaction to the United States air strikes in North Vietnam has been generally favorable—more so than some Administration officials expected, according to Carl T. Rowan, director of the United States Information Agency.

An analysis by the agency shows that the actions this month drew almost universal support in the South American press, strong support in Southeast Asia and guarded endorsement in some countries of the Middle East and South Asia.

The only strong opposition, except from the Communist press, came from Africa and some sections of the Middle East and South Asia.

World Reaction 'Good'

Summarizing the reaction, Mr. Rowan said in an interview: "The general world reaction to our actions in Vietnam has been good, and considerably better than I had expected."

Among newspapers supporting the United States air strikes they were viewed as a legitimate and necessary response to the Communist attacks on American installations in South Vietnam and as a demonstration of American firmness.

There was a nearly unanimous feeling that the United States should not widen the war in South Vietnam. But a majority of the newspapers accepted the repeated policy statements of the Johnson Administration that it was seeking only to press the Communists into ceasing aggressive activities in South Vietnam.

A majority of the editorial

Continued on Page 3, Column 5

Moscow Announces a Relaxation Of Attitude Toward Intellectuals

By THEODORE SHABAD
Special to The New York Times

MOSCOW, Feb. 21—The Communist party proclaimed today a relaxed attitude toward the Soviet Union's intellectuals.

An article that appeared in Pravda, the principal party newspaper, assailed what was described as a trend toward anti-intellectualism under the Khrushchev era and asserted that "genuine creativeness is possible only through search, experimentation, free expression and clashes of viewpoints."

The article, viewed here as a policy statement of Premier Khrushchev's successors on the party's attitude toward intellectuals, was signed by Aleksei M. Rumyantsev, who was named the paper's editor-in-chief after Mr. Khrushchev's downfall in October.

In an evident allusion to the former Premier, Mr. Rumyantsev condemned "attempts to impose one's subjective evaluations and personal tastes as the yardstick of artistic creation, especially when they are expressed in the name of the party."

The Pravda editor, a leading ideological spokesman of the administration, said party criticism of literature would be guided by a policy statement made in 1925, long before Stalin imposed rigid controls over the arts.

The 40-year-old pronouncement, which he quoted, said:

"Communist criticism must rid itself of the tone of literary command. The party must in every way eradicate attempts at homebred and incompetent administrative interference in literary affairs." Mr. Rumyan-

Continued on Page 7, Column 2

NEWS INDEX

was transmuted into acceptance, then new knowledge that the two races could work side by side in the fight against racism. It was an astonishing epiphany, one that confounded some of his associates, and turned against him those who had been united with Malcolm in his fanatic militancy.

Returning to America, after writing his famous *Letter from Mecca*, in which he spelled out his new plans and point of view, Malcolm X began to talk in conciliatory tones about Dr. Martin Luther King and his associates. Gone was the Uncle Tomism with which he had heretofore painted Dr. King, his associates and his followers.

On the second week in February, 1965, he went to Selma, Alabama, during the voter registration drive in that city, and publicly told Coretta Scott King that his militancy had had one salutary effect upon the civil rights movement: it had scared whites into the King camp.

HE RETURNED to a hostile North, in which not only followers of the Nation of Islam were arrayed against him, but the most militant of his own followers—those with whom he had most closely identified before his trip to Mecca—were equally distrustful.

A few days after his return, in the darkest middle of the night, fire bombs were thrown at Malcolm X's home in East Elmhurst, Queens, a house he had "borrowed" from the Nation of Islam when he was in their best graces, and from which they were now attempting to evict him. The bombs ignited the house, engulfing it in fire and gutting it, but Malcolm and his family escaped, unhurt.

They moved in with friends, and Malcolm blamed the bombing on the Nation of Islam; the Nation of Islam blamed him, stating that he had set it himself for publicity purposes and to escape the humiliation of eviction. It was a time of personal and public crisis for Malcolm X. His philosophy now excluded the old rage and violence, and focused on ballots rather than bullets. But as the inner world softened, the outer one grew more menacing.

ON SUNDAY, February 21, he was scheduled to address 400 of his followers in the Audubon Ballroom, a not-very-elegant two-storey structure in New York's Harlem. On Saturday, he and his family moved to the New York Hilton. A few hours after they checked in, three black men entered the lobby, singled out a bellhop, and began to question him about the whereabouts of the Malcolm X family. The bellhop refused to reveal the room number and signaled a house detective. The detective approached, the three looked up, spotted him, and fled. Guarded by his own effective sentinels, Malcolm X spent a peaceful night.

Sunday was crisp and sunny. Malcolm X journeyed up Broadway to Harlem a half hour before his speech was scheduled to begin. But once there, he lingered for nearly an hour, drinking tea and eating a banana split and joking with his guards and associates.

Finally, he entered the ballroom, to high acclaim. "*As-salaam alaikam!*" he intoned. Peace be unto you, it meant, and the congregation responded, "*Wa-alaikum salaam*!" And unto you, peace. Malcolm then mounted the podium and arranged the sparse notes he would use for his speech on the plywood lectern. His bodyguards arrayed themselves in a phalanx before him.

He hadn't achieved two sentences when two men rose from the wooden folding chairs in the front of the room. They were scuffling. "Get your hands off my pockets!" shouted one of them. "Don't be messin' with my pockets!"

"Now brothers, be cool," Malcolm said, in a soothing voice. Four of his bodyguards moved forward, to break up the argument.

Instantly, another distraction erupted at the back of the auditorium. A man's sock, soaked in lighter fluid, was set ablaze. It flared up, sending off an acrid odor and a cloud of black smoke. Heads swiveled; the bodyguards strained to pick out the location of the commotion.

SEIZING on the distraction, a lone gunman rushed up the middle aisle, dragging a double barreled shotgun out of his overcoat. At point blank range, he pulled both triggers. The charge splintered the lectern, then drove into Malcolm's chest, flinging him backward over a collapsed chair. Two men rushed forward from the vicinity of the first squabble and pumped bullets from drawn pistols into Malcolm X's prostate body, then dashed for exits at the sides of the auditorium.

Malcolm's bodyguards had converged on the center aisle, chasing the gunman with the shotgun. He too, dashed for a side door, and had reached the first landing when one of the bodyguards drew his revolver and fired. The .45 bullet hit the gunman in his left thigh, but he continued to limp down the stairs, toward the street.

The crowd caught up with him, and flung him to the sidewalk, setting on him with fists and feet. By the time the police pulled the crowd away and rescued the assassin, they had bloodied him and broken his ankle.

Meanwhile, Malcolm X's pregnant wife, screaming, "They're killing my husband!" climbed onto the podium and kneeled over the mortally wounded black leader. His bodyguards lifted the prostrate, bleeding, but still breathing Malcolm X onto a rolling bed, which had been wheeled from nearby Columbia Presbyterian Medical Center.

Brought to the hospital, he was taken immediately to an operating room where a team of doctors laid open his chest, trying to mend him back to life. He stopped breathing. They attempted open heart massage, with no result, and he died in the operating room, at the age of 39.

THE ASSASSIN was identified as 22-year-old Talmadge Hayer of Paterson, New Jersey. Despite the fact that Hayer was not a Black Muslim, it was the assumption of the police, the press, and Malcolm X's supporters that Elijah Muhammad was behind the killing.

"He will be avenged," vowed Malcolm's half-sister, Ella Mae Collins. "We are going to repay them for what they did to Malcolm." Leon 4X Ameer added, "I don't know if Elijah will live out the month."

Within 36 hours, a fire bomb was tossed from an adjacent rooftop through an open window of Mosque Number 7 in New York. The mosque flared into flame and was left a gutted shell, exactly like Malcolm X's Elmhurst home. In San Francisco, the door of a Muslim temple was splashed with kerosene and set ablaze, but firemen doused the fire quickly. In Rochester, New York, police were tipped off to another mosque bombing, and confiscated five sticks of dynamite from a car parked nearby.

Armies of police surrounded the red brick mansion of Elijah Muhammad, on Chicago's South Side. From the safety of its interior, Muhammad issued a statement. "We are innocent of Malcolm's death," he said. "Malcolm died of his own preaching. He preached violence and violence took him away."

MORE THAN 20,000 people, under careful and abundant police guard, filed past Malcolm X's body, displayed in a glass-topped, wrought-copper casket in a Harlem funeral home. Five days after the assassination, police arrested Norman 3X Butler and Thomas 15X Johnson, both of them Black Muslim enforcers. All three were convicted and sentenced to life in prison.

To the end, Hayer vowed that the other two were not his accomplices; they were three other men whom he refused to name. And, as time passed, opinion grew that the police conducted a cursory investigation at best, and that the trial was decidedly hasty. Although Hayer was obviously guilty, it seemed nearly impossible to think that two such high visibility Black Muslims as Butler and Thomas could have penetrated the tight security around the Audubon Ballroom on February 21. The real accomplices, it seemed, escaped.

And that was given further credence when, in the winter of 1977–78, Hayer signed two affidavits, describing in great detail the casing of the Audubon Ballroom, the exact positioning of the gunmen in it, and the strategy sessions held. The conspirators he named were four, and none of them was Norman 3X Butler or Thomas 15X Johnson.

Unsuccessful attempts were made to vacate the charges against the two men, who have since been paroled. Their innocence is further advocated by film-maker Spike Lee, who contends that Captain Joseph, who now takes the name Yusuf Shah, and who was a high official in the Nation of Islam at the time of the killing, has confirmed that it and the bombing of Malcolm X's home in Queens were planned at the highest levels of that organization. But no further arrests have been made.

MALCOLM X was buried in Fercliff Cemetery, in suburban Westchester, attired in the white robe of a Muslim, his head pointed toward the east and Mecca, the name on the gravestone Al Hajj Malik Shabazz, a title he had earned by his pilgrimage to Mecca. Had he lived, he might have joined Dr. Martin Luther King's crusade for equal rights as an effective, young spokesperson for peaceful resolution of racial inequalities in America. He might even have inherited Dr. King's mantle after the civil rights leader's murder at the hands of James Earl Ray. But it didn't happen. Assassination claimed the two most charismatic black leaders of the 1960s, and no one rose to take their places.

Martin Luther King

POSITION:	*Leader of the civil rights movement in the U.S.A.*
DATE:	*April 4, 1968*
PLACE:	*Memphis, Tennessee, U.S.A.*
HOW:	*Gunshot*
WHO:	*James Earl Ray*
CONVICTED:	*Yes. Sentenced to 99 years in prison*
MOTIVE:	*Unclear*
DIRECT CONSEQUENCE:	*The civil rights movement lost its charismatic leader*

"I HAVE a dream," Martin Luther King proclaimed, at the climax of a massive march of 250,000 people, gathered in Washington in the summer of 1963 to affirm the necessity of civil rights for all in America.

Utilizing the nonviolent, civil disobedience principles of American poet David Thoreau and Indian leader Mohandas Gandhi, King became, like Gandhi, the conscience and spiritual force of a nation. And, like Gandhi, he met his death violently, at the hands of an assassin.

BORN IN 1929 in Atlanta, Georgia, the son of Martin Luther King, Sr., minister of the Ebenezer Baptist Church, King asserted his uniqueness very early. At the age of five, he could recite biblical passages and sing entire hymns from memory. His public schooling was briefer than most; an exceptional student, he skipped his senior year in high school and, at the age of 15, was admitted to Morehouse College in Atlanta. His early ambitions tended toward medicine or law, but Benjamin Mays, president of Morehouse, redirected the young scholar into the ministry.

In 1947, before graduating from Morehouse with a degree in sociology, Dr. King was ordained, and became assistant pastor of his father's church—a largely honorary ordainment, since he hadn't yet finished his religious schooling.

He attended Crozer Theological Seminary in Pennsylvania from 1948 to 1951, graduating at the top of his class with a B.A. in divinity. From here, on a scholarship, he spent two years at Boston University, graduating in 1955 with a Ph.D. in systematic theology.

In 1953, he married Coretta Scott, a student at Boston's New England Conservatory of Music. She would give him four children and be his most eloquent spokesperson, particularly after his death.

Of medium height, with almond shaped eyes, a mobile, full face and expressive hands, King described himself as an "ambivert"—i.e., part extrovert and part introvert, with a tender heart and a tough mind. Throughout his life, Martin Luther King's strong impulses and talents would often be at variance with each other.

As a boy, he was extraordinarily private and sensitive, and twice tried to commit suicide, once when he thought his grandmother had been killed; once after she actually died. As a boy, growing up black in Atlanta, he hated whites and the cruel advantages they enjoyed and misused unremittingly. But as a college student, he modified his anger against whites, and intensified his hatred of segregation and injustice. He was an angry young crusader, until he entered Crozer seminary.

It was there that he encountered the teachings of Thoreau, social gospeler Walter Rauschenbusch and spiritual leader Mohandas Gandhi. Thoreau taught him civil disobedience as a weapon for change. Rauschenbusch's writings informed him that faith must be socially relevant to be meaningful. Gandhi's teachings imbued him with the conviction that nonviolent resistance and redemptive love can move multitudes and give inner strength to a single believer's path through this world and beyond it. In fact, Gandhi's life and the way he conducted it shook King to his very roots and harnessed his anger, without diminishing its energy.

Yet, although he became the western embodiment of the Mahatma's spiritual teachings, and the inheritor of Gandhi's charismatic social and spiritual power, Dr. King failed to inherit the Indian guru's asceticism. He was not above venal temptations, and this gave much aid and comfort to his later enemies, who would be numerous and plentiful.

"All the News That's Fit to Print"

The New York Times

LATE CITY EDITION

Weather: Clearing today, turning cold tonight. Fair, cool tomorrow. Temp. range: today 62-44; Thurs. 73-52. Full U.S. report on Page 92.

VOL. CXVII . No. 40,249 — NEW YORK, FRIDAY, APRIL 5, 1968 — 10 CENTS

MARTIN LUTHER KING IS SLAIN IN MEMPHIS; A WHITE IS SUSPECTED; JOHNSON URGES CALM

JOHNSON DELAYS TRIP TO HAWAII; MAY LEAVE TODAY

President Spends a Hectic Day Here and in Capital —Sees Thant at the U.N.

By MAX FRANKEL
Special to The New York Times

WASHINGTON, April 4 — President Johnson postponed his trip to Hawaii at least until tomorrow after he heard of the death of the Rev. Dr. Martin Luther King Jr. tonight.

The news, which visibly shocked the President, came at the end of one of the most extraordinary days in perhaps the most extraordinary week of his Administration.

Mr. Johnson was to have flown from Washington at about midnight for a weekend of strategy conferences with his military and diplomatic leaders stationed in South Vietnam. On the way, he had planned a breakfast meeting in California with former President Dwight D. Eisenhower.

Instead, the President telephoned Mrs. King in Atlanta, made a brief appeal for calm on television and went to his office to follow the reports of unrest and disturbance given him periodically by Attorney General Ramsey Clark.

Cancels Dinner Appearance

Mr. Johnson also canceled an appearance before a Democratic party fund-raising dinner here —the final event of a hectic schedule that became ever more hectic as the day unfolded.

The President began the day by making final arrangements for the Hawaii meeting. It had been tentatively planned before his order Sunday to curtail the bombing of North Vietnam and the news yesterday that Hanoi was interested in establishing direct contact.

[The new United States peace moves are producing a quiet but bitter reaction in the South Vietnamese Government that is causing increasing concern among United States officials in Saigon. Page 14.]

But the diplomatic development, though not the principal subject of the Honolulu meetings, added special weight to his conversations with Gen. William C. Westmoreland, the American commander in South Vietnam, and other officials.

Mr. Johnson was careful not to arouse false hopes of peace, but he appeared encouraged and in buoyant spirt as he decided before noon to fly first to New York to attend the investiture of the Most Rev. Terence J. Cooke as Archbishop of New York.

Then, while in New York,

Continued on Page 12, Column 1

Hanoi Charges U.S. Raid Far North of 20th Parallel

By EVERT CLARK
Special to The New York Times

WASHINGTON, April 4 — North Vietnam charged in a broadcast today that United States planes had bombed a "populated area" in northwestern Vietnam far north of the 20th parallel. The Defense Department said it knew of no such raid but was investigating.

President Johnson has ordered that there be no attacks on North Vietnam north of the 20th Parallel as a step toward de-escalating the war.

[In South Vietnam, United States marines beat off an attack by about 400 North Vietnamese soldiers charging up a hill near Khesanh, killing 93, The Associated Press reported. Meanwhile, an American relief column was nearing the besieged base. Page 15.]

The Hanoi radio, in a broadcast monitored and translated here, said three waves of United States planes dropped more than 50 bombs on a "populated area" about 30 miles west of Laichau, capital of Laichau Province, this morning.

The nearest village to that

Continued on Page 15, Column 1

The New York Times — April 5, 1968

Hanoi said that area near Laichau (cross) was target.

HUMPHREY HINTS HE'LL ENTER RACE

Tells Unionists in Pittsburgh He Will Act Soon—Abel and Wirtz Back Him

By ROY REED
Special to The New York Times

PITTSBURGH, April 4—Two thousand labor representatives, including the head of the United Steel Workers union, clamorously urged Vice President Humphrey today to run for President.

The Vice President left little doubt that he would oblige them, but he indicated that he would wait until President Johnson returned from his Hawaii conference before making an announcement.

"I know what your request is, and I know what your thoughts are," he told the delegates to the Pennsylvania A.F.L.-C.I.O. convention. "I am most grateful. I am not one to walk away from a decision, and a decision will come in due time."

But nothing he does should interfere with President Johnson's peace mission, he said.

Several other political leaders urged Mr. Humphrey today to enter the race for the Democratic Presidential nomination. The most prominent among them was Secretary of Labor W. Willard Wirtz, who was addressing a union convention at Miami Beach.

I. W. Abel, president of the steelworkers Union, rose as Mr.

Continued on Page 32, Column 1

Johnson Shuns Role Of '68 'Lame Duck,' Kennedy Was Told

By JOHN HERBERS
Special to The New York Times

WASHINGTON, April 4—In his meeting with Senator Robert F. Kennedy yesterday President Johnson said he would remain out of the political fight this year because he did not believe it was appropriate for a "lame duck" President to try to pick his successor.

This and other details of the Johnson-Kennedy meeting were learned today from knowledgeable sources.

The meeting, which Senator Kennedy had requested in the interest of "national unity," was described as an extraordinarily friendly one, with both the Senator and the President speaking in a conciliatory manner.

President Johnson was pictured as the "elder statesman" of the party who had decided to remain aloof from this year's scramble for the Presidency in an effort to keep the party as strong as possible and retain his own dignity and effectiveness as President.

At one point, it was reported, the President said he did not want to make a spectacle of himself as a lame duck President attempting to dictate to the party who should be nominated at the national convention.

In this regard, he pointed out that in 1956 former President Harry S. Truman went to the

Continued on Page 31, Column 4

DISMAY IN NATION

Negroes Urge Others to Carry on Spirit of Nonviolence

By LAWRENCE VAN GELDER

Dismay, shame, anger and foreboding marked the nation's reaction last night to the Rev. Dr. Martin Luther King Jr.'s murder.

From the high offices of state to the man in the street, news of the moderate civil rights leader's violent death in Memphis yesterday drew, for the most part, stunned and sober statements.

Most major Negro organizations and Negro leaders, lamenting Dr. King's death, expressed hope that it serve as a spur to others to carry on in his spirit of nonviolence. But some Negro militants responded with bitterness and anger.

Roy Wilkins, executive director of the National Association for the Advancement of Colored People, said his organization was "shocked and deeply grieved by the dastardly murder of Dr. Martin Luther King."

"His murderer or murderers must be promptly apprehended and brought to justice," Mr. Wilkins said.

'A Man of Peace'

"Dr. King was a symbol of the nonviolent civil rights protest movement. He was a man of peace, of dedication, of great courage. His senseless assassination solves nothing. It will not stay the civil rights movement; it will instead spur it to greater activity."

Whitney M. Young Jr., executive director of the National Urban League, said:

"We are unspeakably shocked by the murder of Martin Luther King, one of the greatest leaders of our time. This is a bitter reflection on America. We fear for our country.

"The only possible answer now is for the nation to act immediately on what Dr. King has been fighting for—passage of the civil rights and antipoverty bills and a true and just equality for all men. Those of us who have remained loyal to his concept of nonviolence have been dealt a mortal blow."

Mayor Richard G. Hatcher of Gary, Ind., a Negro, termed the death of Dr. King "every man's loss."

"Men who care for humankind and struggle for its salvation through reason and faith have lost a leader of monumental stature," he said. "A man of his magnitude will not soon pass this way again."

At his home in Stamford, Conn., the former baseball star Jackie Robinson called the

Continued on Page 28, Column 1

PRESIDENT'S PLEA

On TV, He Deplores 'Brutal' Murder of Negro Leader

Statements by Johnson and Humphrey are on Page 24.

Special to The New York Times

WASHINGTON, April 4— President Johnson deplored tonight in a brief television address to the nation the "brutal slaying" of the Rev. Dr. Martin Luther King Jr.

He asked "every citizen to reject the blind violence that has struck Dr. King, who lived by nonviolence."

Mr. Johnson said he was postponing his scheduled departure tonight for a Honolulu conference on Vietnam and that instead he would leave tomorrow.

The President spoke from the White House. At the Washington Hilton Hotel, where Democratic members of Congress had gathered to honor the President and the Vice President, Mr. Humphrey, his voice strained with emotion, said:

"Martin Luther King stands with our other American martyrs in the cause of freedom and justice. His death is a terrible tragedy."

The dinner was canceled 10 to 15 minutes after the Vice President spoke. Mr. Johnson, who was scheduled to appear at the dinner, canceled his plans to attend.

F.B.I. Inquiry Ordered

Attorney General Ramsey Clark ordered an immediate inquiry by the Federal Bureau of Investigation into the shooting of Dr. King in Memphis.

He said the purpose of the investigation would be to determine whether any Federal law had been violated.

One provision of the law that could be invoked makes it a crime to engage in a conspiracy to deprive a person of his civil rights.

In addition to F.B.I. agents, Department of Justice civil rights representatives were on the scene in Memphis and were in touch with the Attorney General.

Military sources said that no National Guard units had yet been Federalized and no Regular Army troops had been alerted yet for possible movement to cities where violence had broken out.

National Guard troops, such as the 4,000 men who have been called into Memphis, remain under state control until the responsible Governor requests help and the President

Continued on Page 24, Column 1

Associated Press

THE REV. DR. MARTIN LUTHER KING Jr.

Scattered Violence Occurs In Harlem and Brooklyn

12 Are Arrested Here

By THOMAS A. JOHNSON

Sporadic violence erupted in Harlem and Brooklyn's Bedford-Stuyvesant section last night after news of Dr. Martin Luther King's assassination spread in the two predominantly Negro communities.

Mayor Lindsay, who went to Harlem in an effort to quiet the outbreaks, was caught in the midst of an unruly crowd and had to be hustled into a limousine by bodyguards.

Police reinforcements, including elements of the riot-trained Tactical Patrol Force, were rushed into both communities.

Two arrests were reported in Brooklyn and 10 in Harlem. A television crewman was said to have been injured by flying glass.

There were numerous instances of rock-throwing, looting and arson reported both in Brooklyn and in Harlem, starting around 11 P.M. and continuing early today.

Gangs of youth in both areas were reported roaming through the streets, now and then taunting policemen and firemen on duty.

The police fired several volleys of shots in the air to disperse crowds along Brooklyn's Fulton Street and Harlem's

Continued on Page 28, Column 2

Widespread Disorders

Disorders broke out in scattered parts of the nation last night after the slaying of the Rev. Dr. Martin Luther King Jr. The National Guard was called out or alerted in several cities.

In Washington, scattered but persistent looting and vandalism erupted, led for a time by Stokely Carmichael, former head of the Student Nonviolent Coordinating Commitee. All available policemen were being called to duty.

About 4,000 Tennessee National Guardsmen were ordered to duty in Nashville because of disorders.

In North Carolina, Gov. Dan K. Moore alerted the Guard in Greensboro at the request of Mayor Carson Bain. State Highway patrolmen were dispatched to Raleigh.

There were riotous outbursts

Continued on Page 26, Column 5

NEWS INDEX

GUARD CALLED OUT

Curfew Is Ordered in Memphis, but Fires and Looting Erupt

By EARL CALDWELL
Special to The New York Times

MEMPHIS, Friday, April 5— The Rev. Dr. Martin Luther King Jr., who preached nonviolence and racial brotherhood, was fatally shot here last night by a distant gunman who then raced away and escaped.

Four thousand National Guard troops were ordered into Memphis by Gov. Buford Ellington after the 39-year-old Nobel Prize-winning civil rights leader died.

A curfew was imposed on the shocked city of 550,000 inhabitants, 40 per cent of whom are Negro.

But the police said the tragedy had been followed by incidents that included sporadic shooting, fires, bricks and bottles thrown at policemen, and looting that started in Negro districts and then spread over the city.

White Car Sought

Police Director Frank Holloman said the assassin might have been a white man who was "50 to 100 yards away in a flophouse."

Chief of Detectives W. P. Huston said a late model white Mustang was believed to have been the killer's getaway car. Its occupant was described as a bareheaded white man in his 30's, wearing a black suit and black tie.

The detective chief said the police had chased two cars near the motel where Dr. King was shot and had halted one that had two out-of-town men as occupants. The men were questioned but seemed to have nothing to do with the killing, he said.

Rifle Found Nearby

A high-powered 30.06-caliber rifle was found about a block from the scene of the shooting, on South Main Street. "We think it's the gun," Chief Huston said, reporting it would be turned over to the Federal Bureau of Investigation.

Dr. King was shot while he leaned over a second-floor railing outside his room at the Lorraine Motel. He was chatting with two friends just before starting for dinner.

One of the friends was a musician, and Dr. King had just asked him to play a Negro spiritual, "Precious Lord, Take My Hand," at a rally that was to have been held two hours later in support of striking Memphis sanitationmen.

Paul Hess, assistant adminis-

Continued on Page 24, Column 1

Archbishop Cooke Installed; President Looks On

By EDWARD B. FISKE

The Most Rev. Terence J. Cooke was installed as the seventh Roman Catholic Archbishop of New York yesterday in a historic pageant attended by the President of the United States and highlighted by prayers for the success of his peace efforts in Vietnam.

"Let us pray with all our hearts that God will inspire our President," the 47-year-old Archbishop said in his homily at St. Patrick's Cathedral.

"In the last few days, we have all admired his heroic efforts in the search for peace in Vietnam. We ask God to bless his efforts with success. May God inspire not only our President, but also other leaders and the leaders of all nations of the world to find a way to peace."

Then the Archbishop, speaking from a white marble pulpit and surrounded by a blaze of purple, gold and scarlet robes, addressed himself directly to Mr. Johnson, who sat below him in a front pew.

The President, sitting with his hands clasped and his legs crossed, listened with obvious intensity to the Archbishop's words.

"Mr. President," he said, "our hearts, our hopes, our continued prayers go with you."

Mr. Johnson, accompanied by his daughter, Mrs. Patrick J. Nugent, led a festive congregation of about 5,000 cardinals, bishops, priests, laymen, nuns, civic leaders

Continued on Page 38, Column 1

The New York Times (by Neal Boenzi)

President Johnson and his daughter, Mrs. Patrick J. Nugent, right, listening during yesterday's ceremonies. At left are Mrs. John F. Kennedy and Lieut. Gov. Malcolm Wilson. Security personnel are in the row between them.

Archbishop Luigi Raimondi, Apostolic Delegate to the U.S., speaking after Archbishop Terence J. Cooke was enthroned

His first congregation was that of the Dexter Avenue Baptist Church in Montgomery, Alabama, an assignment he regarded as a stopping off place to a professorship at a seminary or a university. But fate in the form of a boycott of segregated city buses in December of 1955 by Montgomery blacks changed those plans forever.

Mass meetings took place in the churches of Montgomery then, and here the rich and resonant baritone of Dr. Martin Luther King Jr. first began to stir multitudes of people. Journalist Almena Lomax described it as a "narrative poem" which could "charm your heart right out of your body." "I don't know what that boy talkin' about," one black woman said at one meeting, "but I sure like the way he sounds." The personal power that would propell him to the top of the civil rights movement in America in a few short years was making itself heard for the first time.

On November 13, 1956, the Montgomery boycott ended in victory. The U.S. Supreme Court nullified the Alabama laws that legalized segregated buses. Two months later, King's home was dynamited by white supremacists. No one was hurt, and within a few months, Dr. King and 115 other black leaders, meeting in Montgomery, formed the Southern Christian Leadership Conference. With him as their leader, blacks were about to spread the "Montgomery way" throughout the South.

IN THE EARLY 1960s, like his mentor Gandhi, Dr. Martin Luther King Jr. was arrested and jailed, over and over, for conducting nonviolent protests against segregation. And, like Gandhi, he now turned his attention toward the Federal government, pressuring it into action against the injustice within its jurisdiction.

In 1962, Dr. King led his marchers through the streets of Birmingham, Alabama, and met with such savagery at the hands of Police Commissioner Eugene ("Bull") Connor, his men, his fire hoses, and his savage police dogs—and all in front of world reporters and television cameras—that the federal government could no longer fail to heed his message. By 1963, Dr. King was delivering his famous "I have a dream" speech before 250,000 mesmerized followers at the Lincoln Memorial in Washington, D.C. By 1964, the nation possessed a Civil Rights Act, and Martin Luther King Jr. possessed the Nobel Peace Prize.

But the fight was far from over. Blacks still didn't have the vote in the South, and in 1965, in Selma, Alabama, one of Dr. King's marches ended in wholesale beatings of blacks by state troopers and deputies, and the killing of a young black deacon and a white Unitarian minister. He issued a call for solidarity among all races, and a march from Selma to the state capital in Montgomery–25,000 people joined him.

There was a certain nobility about what was happening, and not the least of its effects was the growing sense among blacks that, at long last, they were able to matter not only to the world but to themselves. In 1965, the Federal Voting Rights Act became law.

As the 1960s progressed, and the Civil Rights Act failed to gain the force of federal law, other more militant black leaders rose, among them Huey Newton, Malcolm X, and Eldridge Cleaver. But Dr. King refused to embrace their less peaceful approach to righting civil wrongs. Instead, he broadened his fight to include opposition to the Vietnam War and the plight of the poor. These concerns brought down on Dr. King the wrath of the right wing, and particularly that of F.B.I. chief J. Edgar Hoover, who developed a full-blooded, raging hatred against Martin Luther King. From then until the end of Dr. King's life, Hoover hounded the man, tapping his phones, sending undercover agents to infiltrate the Southern Christian Leadership Conference, publishing vicious and anonymous cartoons and tracts. An entire task force within the F.B.I. was formed to discredit King and his followers, prove that they were led by a venal womanizer and influenced—perhaps financed—by Communists. In one internal memo, Hoover instructed this task force to "remove [King] from the national scene."

IN 1968, Dr. King planned a massive poor people's march on Washington, but, at the end of March, he interrupted the strategy sessions for a trip to Memphis, Tennessee, to support a strike of 1,300 sanitation workers in that city. On the 28th of the month, he led a march in the strikers' cause through the streets of Memphis. The head of the line of march remained peaceful; the end did not. Violence—some said from militant blacks, others said from the white police—erupted, then escalated. A 16-year-old black was killed; 62 peoples were injured, and 200 were arrested.

But Dr. King was far from deterred, even though he received death threats after the march. On April 3, he decided to return to Memphis. His plane was delayed at the Atlanta airport when reports were received that a bomb had been placed aboard. Security agents searched the aircraft, but found no bomb.

That night, at a rally for 2,000 supporters in Memphis, he alluded to the death threats. ". . . there have been some threats around here," he said, "We've got some difficult days ahead, but it really doesn't matter now, because I've been to the mountaintop . . . Longevity has its place. But I'm not concerned about that now. I just want to do God's will. And He's allowed me to go up to the mountain."

Dr. King took up residence in room 305 of the Lorraine Motel in Memphis. Across the way from it, at 422½ South Main Street, was a semi-flophouse, in which James Earl Ray, an ex-convict and drifter, had rented room 5, under the name of John Willard. Before that, as Eric Starvo Galt, Ray had stayed at various rooming houses in Montreal, Birmingham, Los Angeles, New Orleans, and Atlanta.

BORN IN Alton, Illinois to a poverty-stricken family, James Earl Ray had become a petty criminal early in life, spending time in various reform schools and jails. In 1959, he was given a 20-year term in the Missouri state prison for a grocery store holdup. During the seven years he spent there, he repeatedly attempted to escape, and, finally, on April 23, 1967, he hid under a shipment of bread that was being taken from the prison kitchen, and got away.

After this, he did odd jobs, took a bartending course, drank heavily and left a bewildering and contradictory trail from Missouri to Memphis. In some places he was known as a quiet, conservative, nondrinking person. In others, he was known as a hard-drinking, loud-mouthed racist.

On April 1, he drove to Memphis in a white Mustang. In Birmingham, he stopped at the Arrow Marine Supply store and bought a rifle and ammunition. The next day, he came back and exchanged the original gun for a 30.06 Remington pump rifle and a telescopic sight.

Late on the afternoon of April 4, 1968, according to eventual police and F.B.I. investigation, Ray positioned himself in the community bathroom one flight up from his room. Here, he had a clear view of the balcony that fronted rooms 305 and 306 of the Lorraine Motel.

He had a long wait. Dr. King spent all afternoon in room 306, which was occupied by his associate, Dr. Ralph Abernathy. Finally, at 6 p.m., dressed in a black suit, the Civil RIghts leader emerged, ready to appearing at a rally that night. He leaned over the green iron railing of the motel balcony to chat with his aid, Jesse Jackson, who was standing in the courtyard below.

Dr. King chided Jackson for wearing informal clothes, and advised the younger man to go in and dress for dinner. Jackson, momentarily placing in abeyance the advice of his mentor, introduced Ben Branch, of Chicago, a musician who was to play at that night's rally. "Do you know Ben?" he asked Dr. King.

"Yes, that's my man!" he answered, then requested that Branch play the spiritual "Precious Lord, Take My Hand" at the rally. "I really want you to play that tonight," he emphasized, enthusiastically.

Dr. Abernathy had finished his work in the room and was about to come out onto the balcony, when a tremendous explosion stopped him in his tracks. Dr. King clutched at his throat, then sank to the floor of the concrete balcony. Blood poured from the right of his jaw and neck. His tie had been ripped off by the blast.

Within moments, police, who had been stationed around the motel to protect those in it from just such a happening, appeared. Dr. King had only been in the open for three minutes, but they had been fatal ones, long enough for Ray to get off the one shot that would kill the charismatic leader.

Dr. King's aides rushed to him. One pressed a towel to the wound to stop the flow of blood; one spread a blanket over him. It would be 10 minutes before a fire department ambulance would arrive to take the mortally wounded man to St. Joseph's Hospital, where emergency surgery would fail to prevent him from slipping into death at 7:05 p.m. The single bullet had exploded through the right side of Dr. King's jaw and neck, severing his spinal cord in the region of the second thoracic vertebra.

James Earl Ray had already escaped, after depositing a neatly wrapped bundle in the doorway of an amusement arcade next door to the rooming house. The bundle contained the gun, a

The rooming house (left) from which James Earl Ray is supposed to have shot Martin Luther King.

box of bullets, shaving cream, binoculars, beer cans, a nail clipper, and a radio with Ray's prison ID on it. His finger prints were on every article.

That night, the nation erupted in a series of violent riots. Stores were looted, buildings were set afire in black sections of Chicago, Detroit, Boston, Washington D.C., and New York.

In Chicago, 6,000 National guard troops were called up. Seven blacks were killed and 350 arrested on the two nights immediately following Dr. King's murder. Washington D.C. was brought to a standstill, as buildings were set afire and rioters ran rampant through the streets. Thousands of office workers left their places of business early on the afternoon of April 5 to escape roving bands of looters.

Trying to stem the violence, Dr. King's widow Coretta Scott King issued statements pleading with the demonstrators to stop and "join us in fulfilling his dream of a creative rather than a destructive way."

By Sunday, April 7, an uneasy peace had settled over the country's major urban centers. More than 9,000 troops patrolled Washington, and a 4 p.m. curfew was instituted; 3,263 arrests were made in the nation's capital alone; 620 fires were started there, 705 people were injured, including 23 policemen, 17 firemen and two soldiers. Eight blacks were killed.

Around the world, memorial services and silent marches were held, and on Tuesday, April 9, a massive funeral for Dr. King took place in Atlanta. To represent symbolically his identification with the poor of the country, his body, in a shining mahogany coffin, was placed on the green boards of a crude farm wagon pulled by two Georgia mules.

The march began at Ebenezer Baptist Church, then wound three and a half miles through the streets of Atlanta, concluding at an open air general service at Morehouse College. Behind the cortege walked some of the nation's most elevated

Mourners linking arms in King's funeral procession included (second from left) New York Governor Nelson Rockefeller, (fourth from left) New York Senator Jacob Javits, (eighth from left) New York's Mayor John Lindsay.

figures in finance, politics, religion, and government, plus 100,000 others who trudged through the blistering, eighty-degree heat of the afternoon.

Mrs. John F. Kennedy, the widow of the slain President, came to the Ebenezer Baptist Church, and spent five minutes with Dr. King's widow, comforting her, then paused briefly to talk to the four King children before taking her seat in the Ebenezer Baptist Church. Around the nation, many businesses closed, the opening game of the National League baseball season was postponed, and the nation in general mourned.

But the white sections of Atlanta, where Dr. King was born and buried, remained largely unmoved, and conducted business as usual. The Reverend John B. Morris of the Episcopal Society for Cultural and Racial Unity said to a *New York Times* reporter: "He was more famous to the world than to Atlanta. I would say sadly he was never a power in this city."

A week later, President Johnson signed the Civil Rights Act into law. It assured racial, sexual, and ethnic fairness throughout America, and established the federal machinery to enforce it. The law would be enforced for 14 years, until its federal machinery was, for all intents and purposes, dismantled by the administration of President Ronald Reagan.

MEANWHILE, the hunt for James Earl Ray went on. It would be four months before he would be captured, and then, a bizarre odyssey would be uncovered: Four days after allegedly shooting Dr. King, Ray, under the alias of Paul Bridgeman, checked into a boarding house in Toronto. Applying for a Canadian passport, he discovered that the real Paul Bridgeman already had one, so he changed his name to Ramon George Sneyd, obtained another passport, and, on May 5, flew to London. From there, he flew on to Lisbon, where he tried to enlist as a mercenary with Biafran forces, but was turned down.

On May 17, he returned to London, where he attempted to enlist with Angolan or Rhodesian forces as a mercenary, and was again turned down. On June 8, one day after the assassinated Robert Kennedy was buried, and on the same day that Kennedy's assassin, Sirhan Sirhan, was arraigned (see pg. 106), James Earl Ray was arrested by London police at Heathrow Airport. He was about to board a flight to Brussels. On him, the police found two Canadian passports and a loaded pistol.

Ray was eventually extradited to the United States, where, in Tennessee, he was convicted of murder and sentenced to 99 years in prison. He pleaded guilty and swore that there was a complex conspiracy behind the killing. He later recanted the plea, claiming that his third lawyer, Percy Foreman, pressured him into it. His revised plea stated that when the shooting took place, he was in another part of Memphis, having a flat tire fixed on his Mustang. He demanded a new trial. But the government refused it, and the conspiracy theorists immediately began to publish their conclusions. According to most of them, James Earl Ray, like Lee Harvey Oswald, President John F. Kennedy's killer (see page 84) was merely a patsy and not the assassin at all.

THE QUESTIONS persist: Why, for instance, were there no powder burns or fingerprints in the bathroom from which the gun was supposedly fired? Why did Ray take such care to leave a bundle of evidence, covered with his fingerprints, in the street, where it could be instantly found and identified by the police? Where did he get the money to travel to Europe after the murder?

Where did he get the knowledge to pick the aliases of men who resembled him in Toronto? Why did the F.B.I. neither inspect, test nor fire the murder weapon, to prove conclusively that it matched the bullet taken from King's body? Why did the F.B.I. refuse to question *New York Times* reporter Earl Caldwell and King's driver, Solomon Jones, who swore they saw a man in the bushes below the bathroom window of the boarding house? Why did prosecutors accept the testimony of Charles Stevens, the sole witness to Ray's flight from the scene, when they themselves thought it untrustworthy enough to deny him the reward he claimed for talking to them? And finally, why, when his reputation before the assassination was as a blowhard and a petty robber, did James Earl Ray turn into the assassin of a major world figure?

On the other hand, if he was just a patsy, why was he allowed to live?

The question of the money in Ray's pocket was possibly answered during the 1978 convening of the House Select Committee on Assassinations. The committee concluded that he was the lone killer, but was linked to John Kauffman and John Sutherland, two right wing residents of the St. Louis area.

Despite discovering this link and speculating that the King and John Kennedy assassinations were related, the congressmen refused to draw any further conclusions, or to suggest that the case be reopened.

Researcher Harold Weisberg and attorney Mark Lane have, however, under the Freedom of Information Act, pressed forward with the fight to prove the "complex conspiracy" to which Ray himself referred by attempting to open the files on the Martin Luther King assassination, which have been sealed until the year 2027.

IN 1978, investigator Walter Fauntroy concluded that J. Edgar Hoover, in his zealousness to destroy Dr. Martin Luther King's credibility as a civil rights leader, created an atmosphere that was conducive to assassination. That assassination not only destroyed Dr. King, but removed the charismatic leadership that might have united the violent and the nonviolent fighters for equal rights for the disenfranchised and poor of America. And so, the parallel between not only the lives but the deaths of Mohandas Gandhi and Dr. Martin Luther King was cast in the concrete of legend and fact. And this parallel becomes stronger as time progresses. No strong spiritual leader, no voice of the conscience of either India or America has risen to replace either Gandhi or King. And the divisions and the violence continue to intensify.

Robert F. Kennedy

POSITION:	*U.S. Attorney General; U.S. Senator*
DATE:	*June 5, 1968*
PLACE:	*Los Angeles, California*
HOW:	*Gunshot*
WHO:	*Sirhan Bishara Sirhan*
CONVICTED:	*Yes. Sentenced to life in prison*
MOTIVE:	*Anger over America's pro-Israel stand*
DIRECT CONSEQUENCE:	*Democrats lose their strongest presidential candidate*

FOUR AND a half years after the assassination of his brother, President John F. Kennedy, and just two months after the assassination of Martin Luther King, Jr., Robert F. Kennedy, at the age of 42, was shot to death in a kitchen corridor of the Ambassador Hotel in Los Angeles, California, just moments after he had won the California Democratic presidential primary.

A MEMBER of the Kennedy clan, that fiercely competitive family who had, under the tutelage of their patriarch, Joseph Kennedy, learned to achieve, and achieve again—sometimes at the sacrifice of their own personal safety—Robert, or "Bobby," as he was known to both friends and foes, was generally considered, by the time he had gained presidential ambitions, to be the most energetic and ambitious of all the Kennedys.

It hadn't always been so. Born in 1925 in Brookline, Massachusetts, he was the seventh child of nine, and the smallest of its boys. As a youth, he was also the least articulate and physically coordinated, and so was generally eclipsed by his older brothers Joe and John.

It was perhaps because of this that he concentrated more on sports than academics at school in Riverdale, New York, the Gibbs School in London during his father's tenure as ambassador to Great Britain, Milton Academy in Massachusetts, Harvard University, and the University of Virginia law school.

He served in the naval reserve from 1943 to 1946, and somewhere along the way, this retiring member of the Kennedy clan acquired a scrappiness, a censoriousness, an aggressiveness, and a rigid morality. The kindness and vulnerability he had always possessed remained underneath, and they would burst wholeheartedly to the surface after his 1950 marriage to Ethel Skakel. At their sprawling mansion and grounds in McLean, Virginia, their 11 children, accompanied by armies of dogs, horses, and other more anonymous pets were kept in constant motion by an unflaggingly energetic Bobby Kennedy.

BUT IT was his bristling exterior that informed Kennedy's political activity, which began with a brief tenure in the U.S. Department of Justice's criminal division and truly became public with his management of his brother John's successful 1952 Senate campaign. From here, Robert Kennedy served as a special counsel for Senator Joseph R. McCarthy, the not altogether principled Communist hunter. Senator McCarthy's methods, both within his Senate Subcommittee on Investigations and outside of it, sickened the young attorney.

He carried out one assignment, an inquiry into the trade between NATO allies and the People's Republic of China during the Korean War, submitted a factual report, and resigned in July of 1953. In 1954, as counsel for the Senate Democratic minority, he wrote the minority report which condemned McCarthy's conduct of his investigation of the U.S. army, the witch hunt that eventually led to the Senator's censure by the Senate.

Later that year, Kennedy became chief counsel for the Senate Investigations Committee, which, because of that year's midterm elections, passed to Democratic control. Its inquiry into fraud and mismanagement in government snared secretary of the air force Harold Talbott, who resigned in 1955.

In 1957, Robert Kennedy became chief counsel for the Senate Select Committee on Improper Activities in the Labor or Management Field. It was here that he pressed hard to gain convictions of

Teamsters Union officials, including Jimmy Hoffa, and it was through these activities that one conspiracy theory of the assassination of both Kennedy brothers was grounded.

ALL OF this committee work was mere preparation, however, for what was to come. In 1960, John Kennedy drafted his younger brother to manage his campaign for the presidency of the United States. Bobby ran it brilliantly, J.F.K. was elected, and he convinced a reluctant Robert to take on the post of attorney general.

And here, an almost legendary closeness, a symbiotic identification grew between the two men. Their enemies despised it and their supporters regarded it with not a little wonder. It resulted in a more mature and effective persona for Robert Kennedy. In Washington, he visibly relaxed, and acquired an edge of humor and charm which did nothing to dim his agitated energy, frequent brusqueness, and emotional intensity. Played off against his older brother's urbaneness, control, and tendency to reason rather than rush to judgment, it made them a formidable combination. According to one historian, John Kennedy was a ". . . realist disguised as a romantic, and Robert, a romantic disguised as a realist."

For the first part of his tenure as attorney general, Robert Kennedy concentrated on purely interior matters. In his vigorous but precisely constitutional pursuit of civil and voter rights, he incurred the disapproval of some civil-rights activists, who felt that he could have brought more federal power to their cause. In his efforts to turn F.B.I. director J. Edgar Hoover from his role as Communist-chaser and goods-gatherer on the great to prosecutor of organized crime and racial injustice, he earned the F.B.I. director's lifelong enmity.

There were those in the President's circle who questioned the bringing of his brother into foreign policy considerations. But John Kennedy, who had conducted the Bay of Pigs fiasco without Robert, knew better. He needed that extra dimension of deliberation, and so, in 1962, Robert Kennedy played a large part in the peaceful defusing of the Cuban missile crisis. It was he who was generally credited with coming up with the compromise that assured the Russians that if they removed their missiles from Cuba, America would remove its missiles from Turkey.

AND THEN, John Kennedy was assassinated. It was a crushing, impossible nightmare. Robert Kennedy was inconsolable. His role in his brother's administration had been more than a partnership; it had been his proof to himself that he had risen above seventh place in the Kennedy clan. Now, suddenly, he was the oldest and the one upon whom everyone was depending. The weight seemed stupendous.

For a while, he remained on in the cabinet of Lyndon Johnson, but he and the new President didn't get along. Each distrusted the other, and when Johnson decided to seek reelection in 1964, he rejected Robert Kennedy as a running mate.

It freed him to run for the Senate, which he did in 1964, defeating Republican incumbent Kenneth Keating for the seat from New York, a state he adopted abruptly enough to raise cries of "carpetbagger" from friend and foe alike.

Kennedy was, by and large, a champion of Lyndon Johnson's domestic policies, but he opposed Johnson's foreign policies with increasing intensity and vigor. He was opposed to U.S. intervention in the Dominican Republic in 1965, and was dissatisfied with Johnson's carrying out of the reforms begun by his brother's Alliance for Progress in Latin America.

But the greatest parting of the ways between Robert Kennedy and Lyndon Johnson was over Johnson's Vietnam policy. Conspiracy theorists call this reversal of J.F.K.'s plan to gradually withdraw from Vietnam one of the reasons for the President's assassination (see page 91), and there's no doubt that Johnson's escalation of involvement was contrary to the foreign policy of his predecessor. Robert Kennedy was constantly on the floor of the Senate to remind him of it.

"Are we," he entreated in 1968, "like the God of the Old Testament that we can decide in Washington, D.C. what cities, what towns, what hamlets in Vietnam are going to be destroyed?"

As the war escalated, and America began to divide along political, racial, economic, religious, philosophical, and age lines, Robert Kennedy became identified with the disenfranchised, the racial and economic minorities for whom he and his brother had provided a voice.

NOW, SENSING that he could bring order out of the maelstrom of an America in 1968 that he described as "two worlds," and also sensing that the majority

Los Angeles Times

LARGEST CIRCULATION IN THE WEST, MORE THAN 950,000 DAILY; MORE THAN 1,250,000 SUNDAY.

VOL. LXXXVII 5† FIVE PARTS—PART ONE CC WEDNESDAY MORNING, JUNE 5, 1968 104 PAGES DAILY 10c

KENNEDY SHOT; CONDITION IS CRITICAL

Wounded in Head, Leg at Victory Fete; Suspect Arrested

Senator Attacked at Hotel; Bodyguard Captures Gunman

BY DARYL E. LEMBKE
Times Staff Writer

Sen. Robert F. Kennedy was shot in the right ear early this morning in a kitchen of the Ambassador only a few moments after he had made a victory statement after capturing the California Democratic presidential primary.

The New York senator's condition was listed as critical at Good Samaritan Hospital, where he was in the intensive care unit.

A suspect in the s hooting was arrested minutes after the shots were fired and was taken to the police administration building downtown under heavy guard. The suspect was not identified.

Inspector Robert Rock of the Los Angeles police said that only one suspect was involved. Rock said there was no reason to believe more than one person was involved.

The police also have the gun that fired the shots, Rock said.

Witnesses nearby said Kennedy's head was covered with blood and a woman standing nearby was also splattered with blood.

Also shot was Paul Schrade, UAW official. The extent of his injuries was not known.

The shooting occurred at 12:20 a.m.

Shouts, Screams Fill Hall

Shouts and screams filled the packed hall as the call went out over the public address system for a doctor. Three came to Kennedy's aid as his campaign assistants pleaded for his supporters to be calm and clear the hall.

The senator appeared to be in great pain, but conscious.

As he was lifted into the police ambulance, Kennedy was heard to say:

"Oh, no! No! Don't . . .!"

Mrs. Kennedy whispered to him, apparently trying to comfort and reassure her husband. Then she entered the ambulance, doors were closed behind them and the vehicle sped away.

Kennedy was taken first to Central Receiving Hospital, then was transferred to Good Samaritan, his head wrapped in bandages.

Eyewitness account on Page 23, Part 1.

Back in the hotel, shocked and silent members of the Kennedy party gathered in small groups around television sets, attempting to clarify their own memories of the event.

Others left in tears.

Leaving Ambassador

Kennedy was leaving the Ambassador to attend a party at the Factory in the aftermath of his victory in the Democratic primary.

His path through the kitchen was taken on the spur of the moment.

The assailant fired at the senator at close range and began spraying bullets around the kitchen, witnesses said.

William Barry, a former FBI agent, who is Kennedy's bodyguard, grabbed the gun from the man and wrestled him to the floor.

Roosevelt Grier, the football player, then sat on the assailant until police officers arrived.

Please Turn to Page 23, Col. 8

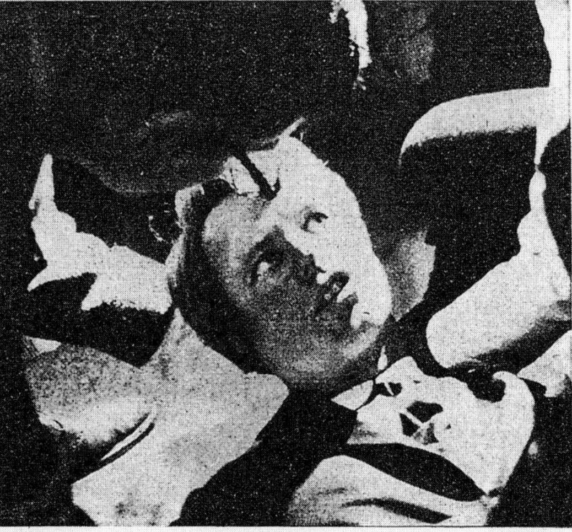

MOMENTS AFTER SHOOTING—Sen. Robert F. Kennedy on floor of Ambassador after he was struck down. Times photo by Boris Yaro

Kennedy Wins Race; Rafferty Apparent Victor Over Kuchel

BY RICHARD BERGHOLZ
Times Political Writer

A late surge of votes from Mexican-American and Negro precincts—particularly in Los Angeles County—made Sen. Robert F. Kennedy the winner in California's Democratic Presidential primary battle Tuesday.

Sen. Eugene McCarthy of Minnesota, Kennedy's major rival in the key primary contest, said he was "reconciled" to a Kennedy triumph. But he said he intended to keep fighting for the party nomination at the Chicago convention Aug. 26.

On the Republican ballot, Dr. Max Rafferty, state superintendent of public instruction, appeared to have ended the political reign of Sen. Thomas H. Kuchel of Anaheim.

The Senate GOP whip and a veteran of 15 years on Capitol Hill ran up leads in Northern and Central California.

But the late surge of votes from Southern California wiped out the Kuchel margin and, on the basis of vote projections, appeared to have swept the conservative Rafferty to an impressive victory.

Rafferty Vote Projection

NBC analysts said their projection of the vote showed Rafferty would get 52% of the Republican vote, and Kuchel would get 45% with the balance going to lesser-known candidates.

The Democratic race for the U.S. Senate nomination was never in doubt.

Former State Controller Alan Cranston easily outdistanced four lesser-known opponents from the very start of the vote-count. For Cranston, it was a political comeback after his defeat two years ago by the current state controller, Republican Houston I. Flournoy.

Cranston had tried for the Democratic nomination for U.S. senator in 1964 but was defeated by Pierre Salinger, who then lost to Republican George Murphy in the finals.

Returns were badly delayed in Los Angeles County, where the old-style paper ballot voting system was changed this year to the IBM-Votomatic punchcard system.

Delays in transporting the punchcard ballots from the precincts to the 93 collection centers and then to the computer counters were blamed for the breakdown in tabulations.

And in Fresno County, a programming error in computers was blamed for a breakdown that made

Please Turn to Page 23, Col. 3

Kennedy Shooting May Alter Nature of '68 Campaign

BY ROBERT J. DONOVAN
Times Washington Bureau Chief

The shooting of Sen. Robert F. Kennedy at the moment of his California primary victory could change the whole nature of the 1968 campaign.

If he should recover in time to continue his quest for the Democratic Presidential nomination, public sympathy could fan the fires of his support to a degree that would diminish Vice President Humphrey's current lead.

If Kennedy is disabled and cannot continue the race, the result would approach a national crisis.

Stability of Politics

If the United States has reached a point where candidates for the Presidency are retired by gunfire, the stability of the American political process is in jeopardy.

If Kennedy was not safe in the midst of his followers, what security would there be, say, for Richard M. Nixon in crowded streets or Humphrey in a typical mob scene in an airport?

In this new disorder in America, with its already grim landmarks in

Please Turn to Page 26, Col. 1

Israeli Jets Rip Jordan as New Fighting Erupts

Ambassadors of Nations Trade Charges at U.N.; Two Claims Vary Widely

By Associated Press

Israeli jet fighters attacked Jordanian positions Tuesday while Israeli and Jordanian artillery crews fired thunderous barrages across the Jordan River like those of the Mideast War that began a year ago today.

Ambassadors of the two countries traded charges at the United Nations.

Jordanian sources said fighting south of the Sea of Galilee lasted more than eight hours. They said the area was quiet at 9 p.m. and reported nearly 100 Jordanian and about 45 Israeli casualties.

Most Serious Since March

The outbreak was the most serious since March 29, when Israeli planes dive-bombed Jordanian gun emplacements that Israelis said were used to harass farmers across the cease-fire line.

Officials in Jordan said the Israelis fired first Tuesday in a "surprise attack." Israeli spokesman said the attack was in reply to the shelling of six Israeli cooperative settlements.

"We hope that this will teach Jordan the lesson once and for all that the shelling of settlements and army positions is taboo," Maj. Gen. Haim Bar-Lev, Israel's chief of staff, told a newsman.

Bar-Lev said Jordanian forces began by shelling an Israeli army position, then turned their guns on civilian targets. He said there were no attempts to negotiate a cease-fire because Jordanian units appeared to have been put out of action.

Widespread Fires in Fields

Ambassador Muhammad H. El-Farra of Jordan said at the United Nations the shooting set off raging forest fires around the Jordanian city of Irbid, focus of much of the battle. Associated Press correspondent Rodney Pinder reported from Israel that widespread fires were started in ripe wheatfields on both sides of the river.

Yosef Tekoah, Israel's U.N. Ambassador, said three farm people were killed and six wounded in "a large-scale Jordanian assault." He said it became necessary "to order Israeli aircraft to take action in self-defense to silence the sources of fire."

In Amman, a government communique reported casualties on both sides as 32 Jordanian civilians and three soldiers killed, 52 Jordanian civilians and 10 soldiers wounded and an estimated 45 Israeli soldiers killed or wounded.

Please Turn to Page 10, Col. 1

L.A. COUNTY RETURNS

PRESIDENTIAL DELEGATION

Democratic — 1,077 out of 6,924 Precincts

Candidate	Votes	%
Kennedy	88,891	51%
McCarthy	68,442	39
Lynch	18,193	10

Republican — 1,077 out of 6,924 Precincts

Candidate	Votes	%
Reagan	69,759	100%

U.S. SENATOR

Democratic — 1,077 out of 6,924 Precincts

Candidate	Votes	%
Cranston	84,097	53%
Beilenson	48,109	30
Buchanan	11,378	7
Bennett	9,508	6
Crail	4,839	3

Republican — 1,077 out of 6,924 Precincts

Candidate	Votes	%
Rafferty	62,181	58%
Kuchel	42,478	39
Ware	1,230	1
Jones	864	1
Cammack	787	1

CONGRESS

13th DISTRICT — Democratic — 4 out of 53 Precincts

Candidate	Votes	%
Sheinbaum	204	47%
Horwitz	154	35
Cole	80	18

13th DISTRICT — Republican — 4 out of 53 Precincts

Candidate	Votes	%
Teague (Inc.)	473	100%

17th DISTRICT — Democratic — 22 out of 394 Precincts

Candidate	Votes	%
Anderson	1,459	32%
Tucker	1,167	25
Gibson	860	19
Hayward	425	9
Frantz	377	8
Griffin	167	4
Pipersky	70	2
Van Petten	67	1

17th DISTRICT — Republican — 22 out of 394 Precincts

Candidate	Votes	%
Howard	443	34%
Blatchford	419	32
Sciarrotta	255	20
Hooper	100	8
Berry	84	6

Please Turn to Page 22, Col. 1

STATEWIDE RETURNS

PRESIDENTIAL DELEGATION

Democratic — 5,749 out of 21,301 Precincts

Candidate	Votes	%
Kennedy	303,965	44%
McCarthy	297,449	43
Lynch	89,401	13

Republican — 5,679 out of 21,301 Precincts

Candidate	Votes	%
Reagan	296,348	100%

U.S. SENATOR

Democratic — 5,613 out of 21,301 Precincts

Candidate	Votes	%
Cranston	360,066	61%
Beilenson	116,916	20
Bennett	55,306	9
Buchanan	43,536	7
Crail	17,246	3

Republican — 5,624 out of 21,301 Precincts

Candidate	Votes	%
Kuchel	244,446	55%
Rafferty	186,232	42
Jones	3,920	1
Ware	5,590	1
Cammack	5,452	1

KIDNAPING, ROBBERY ON SUBWAY

Reporter Indicts Himself and Passengers for Doing Nothing

BY BRIAN D. BOYER
Exclusive to The Times from the Chicago Sun-Times

CHICAGO — Two men who claimed they were police officers kidnaped the father of four children from a subway Monday while half a dozen persons watched without attempting to assist him.

The victim, Eddie Martin, 38, was then robbed of $300 in wages and savings in a station vestibule.

The kidnaping and the robbery should not have happened, if the train conductor and Martin's fellow passengers had done their duty—or police had been guarding the train.

I know, because I was one of the witnesses who lacked courage and resolve at the critical moment. I was one of the six passengers, confused and fearful of "getting involved," who rode with Eddie Martin and the two thugs.

Martin was not hurt but he could have been injured or killed.

What happened and what didn't happen is an indictment of myself and my fellow citizens, who found it all too easy to watch danger stalk and capture the other guy.

I boarded the mostly empty train at 2:07 a.m. on my way home from work.

Facing me in the seat across the

Please Turn to Page 34, Col. 1

THE WEATHER

Light smog today.

Heavy night and morning low cloudiness with partial afternoon clearing today and Thursday. High today and Thursday near 73. Low Thursday near 59. High Tuesday, 70; low, 63.

Complete weather information on Page 8, Part 2.

FEATURE INDEX

Southland elections on Page 9, Part 2.

TRANSPORTING OF CARDS DELAYED

Flow of Ballots to Computer Bogs Down

BY JOHN KENDALL
Times Staff Writer

Two major breakdowns in plans to use a new electronic voting and tabulating system disrupted Tuesday's primary election in Los Angeles County.

The initial vote count, in tabulating summaries for news media, ran more than an hour behind the old-fashioned manual counting system.

The reason: delays at polling precincts in verifying and certifying the punch card ballots before they were transported to 93 checking centers throughout the county.

The vaunted electronic devices, capable of tabulating 14,000 ballots a minute, virtually stood idle for more than two hours after the polls were closed.

A report that the computer equipment had broken down, causing the delay was denied by a spokesman for International Business Machines at a computer center on Wilshire Blvd.

Except for absentee ballots, the punch card ballots failed to arrive in bulk for processing until about 10:30 p.m., he said.

Earlier, hundreds of voters were confused by another breakdown — late delivery of sample ballots. Many said they never received their sample ballots at all.

It was the first time punch card ballots were used throughout Los Angeles County and tabulated on electronic data processing equipment.

An administrative analyst for the county said sheriff's officers moved on schedule in transporting ballots from the 93 checking centers to the computer centers.

"We just didn't get them for an hour or more because they were held up at the polling precincts," he said. "Precinct clerical workers had no prior experience in handling cards and probably spent more time than planned in verifying that the number of ballots corresponded with the number of voters who signed polling sheets at their precincts."

The delay in tabulating Los Angeles County's vote caused suspense to build up throughout the nation during the night, because the county's returns were expected to be decisive in the race between Sens. Eugene J. McCarthy and Robert F. Kennedy for the Democratic presidential nomination.

Please Turn to Page 28, Col. 3

of the populace had wearied of, as he put it, "[President Johnson's] disastrous, divisive policies in Vietnam," Robert Kennedy, on March 16, 1968, declared his candidacy for the Democratic nomination for President.

It placed him squarely in opposition not only to Lyndon Johnson, but to Eugene McCarthy, the representative of as many anti-Vietnam, anti-Washington activists as Kennedy. McCarthy adherents cried foul, and warned of further division of the Democratic Party. But Kennedy saw himself as a healer, and one who could, through his name, know-how and charisma, unite the fiercely warring segments of American society.

Then, in late March, Lyndon Johnson announced that he would not seek reelection, and the race turned three-sided, between vice president Hubert Humphrey, senator Eugene McCarhy, and senator Robert Kennedy.

Kennedy launched a vigorous, well-supported campaign. Dr. Martin Luther King Jr. voiced support for him on an informal basis, and was planning to officially endorse him. And then, on April 4, Dr. King was assassinated. It added further weight to the Kennedy presence and persona, and the primary battles in the West and Midwest took on a weighty significance.

McCarthy won in Oregon, but Kennedy won in Indiana and Nebraska. The June 4 primaries in California and South Dakota were particularly important, since California carried so many electoral votes and power in the convention, and since South Dakota was at the opposite end of the spectrum from the glitz and sophistication of California.

KENNEDY won both primaries, and in a spirited speech in the ballroom of the Ambassador Hotel in Los Angeles that night, he exulted over winning "the most urban of states and the most rural of states . . . We can work together in the last analysis," he said to a cheering crowd. He expressed gratitude to his wife Ethel, to Cesar Chavez, organizer of the grape pickers in California, to Roosevelt Grier, the huge defensive back for the Los Angeles Rams football team, and to Paul Schrade, an official of the United Automobile Workers Union. He concluded by saying that "We are a great country, an unselfish country and a compassionate country. And I intend to make that my basis for running . . ."

The Chicago Convention of the Democratic Party was his goal, and the momentum he had built in California made it clear that he was now the odds-on, hands-down favorite of the Democratic electorate. Now it was important to get this message to the people, nationwide.

Anxious to move on, to the small room that had been set up as a press headquarters and begin his scheduled press conference, Robert Kennedy, his aides and attendants rapidly left the ballroom, and entered a narrow kitchen passageway that led to the conclave of reporters. It was 12:13 a.m.

Waiting, pressed against a stained and aromatic wall, was a slightly built, 24-year-old Palestinian.

SIRHAN Bishara Sirhan, born in Jerusalem and describing himself as a Christian Arab and a Jordanian, had, in January of 1957, at the age of 12, entered the country as an immigrant.

His family had disintegrated soon after it reached America. His father had stayed in New York to work as a plumber, and then had gone back to their former home in Palestine. The mother had moved to California with their five children.

In 1968, Sirhan Sirhan lived in an apartment in Pasadena with two of his brothers, Adel and Munir, also known as Joe. Joe had bought a snub-nosed .22 caliber Iver Johnson Cadet pistol from an 18-year-old boy in Pasadena weeks before Robert Kennedy came to Los Angeles.

Apparently acting without the knowledge of either of his two brothers, Sirhan Sirhan planned to use his brother Joe's pistol to kill Robert Kennedy. A notebook later found in his apartment had, according to a statement later made by Los Angeles mayor Samuel W. Yorty. ". . . a direct reference to the necessity to assassinate Senator Kennedy before June 5, 1968." June 5 was the first anniversary of the Six-Day War, in which Israeli forces smashed those of the United Arab Republic, Syria, and Jordan, and Robert Kennedy apparently represented a convenient symbol of U.S. support for Israel. This was Sirhan Sirhan's reason for placing himself against the wall of the kitchen corridor in the Ambassador Hotel in Los Angeles California at 12:13 a.m. on June 5, 1968.

There is a conspiracy theory that disputes this and links the John F. Kennedy, Martin Luther King, and Robert F. Kennedy assassinations. According to the theory, Sirhan Sirhan was only one of a group of assassins waiting for Robert Kennedy that night.

None of this has been proved, however, and the official version of what unfolded in the first minutes of June 5, 1968, places a lone assassin in the kitchen corridor.

ROBERT KENNEDY and his group advanced 30 steps from the podium at which he had delivered his victory speech and were 15 steps away from the pressroom at 12:16. The Senator reached his hand out to shake the hand of a waiter. And at that precise instant, Sirhan Sirhan stepped away from the wall, drew out his pistol, and fired eight shots at point blank range.

Hysteria erupted. Five people were slightly wounded. Robert Kennedy—shot, as his brother had been, through the brain—was mortally wounded. The bullet penetrated the cerebellum, the portion of the brain that controls balance and coordination, tore the superior cerebellar artery, ripped through the occipital lobe on the right side of the brain and then lodged itself near the upper part of the brain stem. One other bullet went through Kennedy's shoulder and remained in his neck. The other creased his forehead.

He fell to the floor, bleeding terribly. One eye closed; the other remained open. He was obviously in horrible pain, and his wife Ethel, who was at his side, kneeled next to him, cradling his head in her lap.

Meanwhile, guards and aides, led by the massive Rosey Grier, leaped on Sirhan Sirhan. Grier pounded the hand holding the gun on a steel table top until the weapon spun away. Rafer Johnson and William Barry, a bodyguard, pounced upon it. A group of waiters grabbed the assassin and began to pummel him. Grier pulled them away, while eight bodyguards held the squirming and silent assassin. At 12:30, Los Angeles police arrived, picked Sirhan up by the arms and legs, and hauled him off to a police wagon.

Robert Kennedy was put on a stretcher and taken to the Good Samaritan Hospital, where surgeons performed multiple, unsuccessful operations. He clung to life for almost another 26 hours, and then died at 1:44 a.m. on June 6, 1968.

That day, his body was flown, on a presidential jet, from Los Angeles to New York, where, the following day, a funeral service was held at St. Patrick's Cathedral. More than 2,300 people attended the funeral mass, officiated over by Richard Cardinal Cushing of Boston. Kennedy's brother Edward delivered the intensely emotional and articulate eulogy.

A black-draped funeral train, containing 20 cars and more than a thousand people, transported Robert Kennedy's body from Pennsylvania Station in New York to Union Station in Washington, D.C., and even that trip was touched by tragedy.

In Elizabeth, New Jersey, a New York-bound express train rounded a curve and plowed into the fringe of a crowd that had gathered to watch the passing, slow-moving train. Two people were killed and five were injured.

Later, at Trenton, an 18-year-old boy was critically burned when he stood on a boxcar on a side track and touched a live wire while trying to get a better view of the Kennedy train.

Finally, the cortege arrived in Washington, and Robert Kennedy was taken to Arlington National Cemetery, where he was laid to rest alongside his brother John.

SIRHAN SIRHAN was arraigned before a Los Angeles court, where he pleaded guilty. On April 7, 1969, he was convicted of five counts of assault with a deadly weapon with intent to kill, and sentenced to death in the gas chamber.

It would be years before his appeals would be exhausted, and in the middle of them, on August 8, 1970, he was moved from death row at San Quentin prison when the California Supreme Court upheld a ban on the death penalty in the state.

His appeals finally exhausted, Sirhan Sirhan began a life sentence at San Quentin. Repeated parole hearings have returned him to his cell, despite the recanting of his confession and his guilty plea. Even those who support a conspiracy theory of three major assassinations of three public figures within five years of each other have concentrated more on the King and John Kennedy killings than the Robert Kennedy assassination. And so, unless dramatic new evidence is uncovered, the sentence and the story seem destined to remain as they are.

Lord Louis Mountbatten

POSITION:	*Retired military commander and senior statesman*
DATE:	*August 27, 1979*
PLACE:	*Mullaghmore, County Sligo, Ireland*
HOW:	*Bomb*
WHO:	*Thomas McMahon, Provisional IRA*
CONVICTED:	*Yes. Sentenced to life without appeal*
MOTIVE:	*Rivalry between terrorists*
DIRECT CONSEQUENCES:	*Further entrenchment in Ulster*

"What would they want with an old man like me?" Lord Louis Mountbatten replied in early 1979 when he was asked if he was frightened of the IRA. For 35 years, he had come for his yearly vacations to the small fishing village of Mullaghmore, overlooking Donegal Bay on the northwest coast of Ireland.

He owned a turreted stone castle named Classibawn, an ancient punctuation jutting from the green hills behind the fishing docks, and, at the age of 79, with wars and diplomacy, statesmanship, and the rearing of part of the British royal family behind him, he looked forward to a benign old age in which he could spend more time in the Ireland he dearly loved.

He was a well-known figure in Mullaghmore, where he fished for shrimp in the shallows, and gave rides to younger village children on his 27-foot fishing vessel *Shadow V*.

Although in the past he had been guilty of some extreme cases of bad judgment, particularly in the partitioning of Pakistan and India when he was given the task of conducting the British pullout, he had mellowed in his later years into someone no one could hate enough to kill.

"I loathe all manifestations of extremism," he told *Time* magazine in 1978, "and I believe we should strive, above all else, for the dignity and human rights of mankind, regardless of race, color, and creed."

And yet, for all of this, Lord Louis Mountbatten was killed by a terrorist bomb, not because he was necessarily hated by the IRA terrorist who planted it, but because he happened to be in Ireland on the 10th anniversary of the dispatching of troops to that province, and happened to be caught in the crossfire of competition between two warring, prideful factions within the IRA.

Tall and regally erect, Lord Louis Mountbatten was the personification of the proper English gentleman. As French President Valéry Giscard d'Estaing eulogized at his funeral, "He personified British courage, dignity, and elegance."

Born at Frogmore House, in the grounds of Windsor Castle, on June 25, 1900, he was christened Louis Francis Albert Victor Nicholas Battenberg. The multiple names had multiple significances: His father was an Austrian-born aristocrat, Prince Louis of Battenberg; his mother was Princess Victoria, Queen Victoria's granddaughter. Legend has it that, at his christening, the future Lord Mountbatten managed to swipe Queen Victoria's eyeglasses off her nose, smashing them on the floor near his cradle.

At the age of 13, young Louis, or Dickie as he was and would be known to his family and friends, entered the Royal Naval College. It was natural, since his father was the first Sea Lord, in command of Britain's Royal Navy. One year later, in 1914, Prince Louis was forced, by Winston Churchill, Lord of the Admiralty, to resign. Anti-German hysteria had forced it, and young Dickie wept bitterly over his father's disgrace. It was an unfair humiliation, he felt, for he knew how deeply loyal his father was. If he had changed his name from Battenberg to Mountbatten before the war instead of during it, he might never have undergone the agony. But fate chose its own timing.

Young Dickie took part, as a 16-year-old midshipman, in the battle of Jutland during World War I. In 1922, he married Edwina Ashley, daughter of financier Sir Ernest Cassel. They led a suitably roaring life in the twenties, making the society columns, hobnobbing with international celebrities. Douglas Fairbanks and Mary Pickford lent them their Hollywood home for their honeymoon; Charles Chaplin entertained them; Cole Porter put Mountbatten into the lyrics of one of his songs

IN WORLD WAR II, Lord Mountbatten commanded a destroyer flotilla which plied the North Atlantic. His flagship, *HMS Kelly*, was hit twice by mines and torpedoes, once so badly that the British admiral heading operations signaled, "Abandon ship. I'm going to sink you."

Mountbatten signaled back, "Try it and I'll bloody well sink you," and brought the ship safely home.

The third attack on the *HMS Kelly* was fatal. She was sunk by German dive bombers off Crete, and Mountbatten spent four hours in the water before he was rescued. Churchill recognized his courage and command capabilities, and appointed him, first, Chief of Combined Operations, which planned the 1944 Allied invasion of Europe, and then Supreme Allied Commander for Southeast Asia. As such, he accepted the Japanese surrender in Singapore while the high command was capitulating to General Douglas MacArthur in Tokyo Bay.

After the war, he became the last viceroy of India, and negotiated the last year of withdrawal—a hasty departure that set up the explosive confrontational structure: Pakistan for the Muslims and India for the Hindus. It was a monumental blunder in an otherwise admirable career, and Churchill, for one, wouldn't speak to him for five years for his part in it.

Still, the royal family adored Lord Mountbatten and sought his council. Second cousin to Queen Elizabeth II and uncle to Prince Philip, he grew particularly close to Prince Charles, who described him as ". . . a person I admire almost more than anyone else."

GROWING OLDER, he wore his mantle of elder statesman with dignity but not necessarily humility. "I am the most conceited man I know," he confessed in his self-written description in *Who's Who*. Even that endeared him to his friends, who saw it as part of the package: a man of relaxed charm that overlayed tireless and sometimes ruthless energy. He could be, and sometimes was, imperious with subordinates.

In spite of this, as the years accumulated, he mellowed into enlightened liberalism. His keen political sense made "Uncle Dickie" as the royal family now called him, a valuable barometer whom they consulted often.

In 1965, Edwina, while doing charitable work in Borneo, died of a heart attack. A few months later, Winston Churchill died. According to his associates, the twin deaths were two cruel blows for Lord Mountbatten; he never did recover from Edwina's sudden departure. Still, he had much energy left. He retired from the ministry of defense, at which he had been working when his wife died, and spent his elderly years driving fast, exercising, fishing, riding for two hours a day when he was in the country. He looked forward to the one month a year when the renters of the castle at Mullaghmore vacated, and he moved in.

MONDAY, AUGUST 27, 1979 was a sunny day, and at 11:30 a.m., Lord Mountbatten, his daughter Lady Patricia Brabourne, her husband Lord Brabourne, their twin 14-year-old sons Timothy and Nicholas, 82-year-old Dowager Lady Brabourne, Lord Brabourne's mother, and 15-year-old boatboy Paul Maxwell boarded the *Shadow V* for a peaceful cruise up the coast of Donegal.

Local police kept a discreet watch on him and his 1,500-acre estate when he was in the area. He was, after all, a world-famous figure, and Mullaghmore was only 12 miles from Northern Ireland, near an area well known as a refuge for "Provos"—members of the Provisional IRA—fleeing across the border.

What the security forces failed to watch was his boat, the *Shadow V*. And sometime during the morning of August 27, Provo Thomas McMahon had sneaked aboard the *Shadow V* and planted a radio-controlled bomb in it. McMahon was a loyal Provo, and that IRA group's council had decided, weeks ago, that they would embark on a series of multiple bombings on August 27, to assert their power within the IRA.

The Irish National Liberation Army, a splinter group, had, the previous March, assassinated British Tory Member of Parliament Airey Neave on the grounds of Parliament itself. It was a daring act which brought great publicity beyond Ireland to the I.N.L.A., and the Provos were set on bettering it with an act that would arrest the attention of the entire world.

Having set the bomb, McMahon stationed himself on a cliff that overlooked the harbor and the bay, and waited.

DAILY Mirror

Tuesday, August 28, 1979 8p

LORD LOUIS MOUNTBATTEN Captain of HMS Kelly, Admiral of the Fleet, Viceroy of India, hero of Burma..

Murdered by the IRA

PROVOS MASSACRE SOLDIERS—Back Page

Lord and Lady Mountbatten in 1948 in their official regalia as viceroy and vicereine of India.

Shortly before noon, the three cylinder engine of the *Shadow V* turned over smoothly, and the craft and its party made its slow and easy way up the sunlit coast.

They slowed and stopped, 10 minutes after their departure, to inspect the lobster pots that Lord Mountbatten had set that week. Suddenly, a roar and a lightning flash lifted the boat momentarily above the surface of the water, then splintered it into hundreds of pieces. All seven aboard were hurled into the water.

Stunned for only a moment, nearby fishermen turned their boats toward the disaster site. They arrived in minutes, and began to fish bodies and survivors from the oily, blood-red water. Lord Mountbatten's grandson Nicholas and the Ulster boatboy Paul Maxwell were dead, floating face down in the water. Lord Mountbatten was still alive, though both of his legs had been nearly torn off by the blast. Fishermen dragged him into their boat, and he died within minutes.

The others were badly injured. By the time the fishing boats reached the wharf at Mullaghmore, two Belfast doctors on holiday had set up a makeshift aid station. Old doors were used for stretchers and brooms were pressed into duty as splints. Ambulances arrived and took the wounded to Sligo General Hospital. Doctors worked through the night to save the Dowager Lady Brabourne, but she died the next morning.

There was a stunned silence in Ulster. But it only lasted for a few hours. Later that afternoon, the calm was shattered by another bomb blast. This one was placed in a hay wagon just inside the Ulster border, between Narrow Water, an estuary of Carlingford Lough, and a golf course. The detonation flung a three-ton army truck across the road, killing six of the British paratroopers in it.

The survivors radioed for help, and a contingent of the Queen's Own Highlanders commanded by Lieutenant Colonel David Blair arrived immediately by helicopter.

It was a planned, multiple ambush. No sooner had the helicopter landed and dispatched its troops than another bomb went off in a nearby gatehouse, killing Colonel Blair and eleven of his men and wounding several others. The stunned soldiers opened fire on two men who had stopped innocently to witness the carnage. One was killed, the other was wounded. More British soldiers died that afternoon than in any one single incident since they had come to Ulster.

And it wasn't over yet. The next day, a bomb went off near a bandstand in the Grand Palace in Brussels. The British military band that was to give a concert to celebrate the Belgian capital's millenium was delayed by a traffic jam, so the time bomb caused no fatalities. Still, four band members and twelve spectators were injured.

Meanwhile, the Provos lost no time in taking credit. "The IRA claim responsibility for the execution of Lord Louis Mountbatten," the statement read. "This operation is one of the discriminate ways we can bring to the attention of the English people the continuing occupation of our country." Later, they would add that they were determined to "tear out their sentimental imperialist hearts."

THE WORLD reacted in outrage. India declared a week of mourning. U.S. President Jimmy Carter announced that he was "profoundly shocked and saddened" by the death of "a leader of monumental ability." Pope John Paul II called the murder "an insult to human dignity" and canceled plans for a trip later that month to Ulster.

British and Irish reaction was less restrained. The headline in London's read simply THESE EVIL BASTARDS. In Belfast, a Catholic was shot dead by two Protestant gunmen. A contingent of Belfast soccer fans who had followed their team into the Republic of Ireland rioted, leaving more than one hundred people injured.

Prime Minister Margaret Thatcher, trying to prevent a further escalation of violence, took a risky trip to Belfast, where she mingled with shoppers, urging a united stand against terrorism. She found sympathy among Protestants and shouted threats from Catholics. "Go to hell, Britain, Ireland must be free!" shouted one woman who was set upon by Protestants, who were finally dragged off her by police. "We have disgraced ourselves again," said a local official in the northwest of Eire the day after the massacre.

The bodies of Lord Mountbatten, his grandson and the Dowager Lady Brabourne were flown to Broadlands, Mountbatten's Hampshire estate, where they would lie in state prior to a state funeral in Westminster Abbey.

Meanwhile, back in Ireland, plans for a trial were going forward. Three hours after the murder, an Irish policeman at a road block stopped a car containing two plainly nervous men. The two, a 24-year-old farmer named Francis McGirl, who was driving, and his passenger Thomas McMahon were arrested on suspicion of being members of the IRA.

Only McMahon was, and investigators found traces of nitroglycerine on his clothing. His boots contained sand from the slipway at Mullaghmore where the *Shadow V* had been berthed, and flakes of green paint on them matched the paint on the boat's hull. In the trial, McGirl was acquitted. McMahon was convicted of the assassination and sentenced to life imprisonment with no appeal.

THE MURDER of Lord Mountbatten had, it was learned in the trial, been the result of a feud between two rival IRA factions, a public horror designed to increase the public relations image of one of them. It resulted in a stiffening of Protestant resolve against any political resolution whatsoever. The conflict, which has, to date, resulted in 3,000 deaths and 41,000 injuries, moved a notch closer to outright civil war.

And it was all so illogical. A man who had distinguished himself thoroughly, and was as dedicated as any man toward understanding rather than conflict, fell victim to nothing more than internecine rivalry between two splinter groups anxious for publicity. "I do not mind death," Lord Mountbatten had said, a few months earlier, on a BBC-TV program, "as long as it is a reasonably peaceful and satisfying sort of death." His was neither.

ANWAR AL-SADAT

POSITION:	*President of Egypt*
DATE:	*October 6, 1981*
PLACE:	*Nasr City, near Cairo, Egypt*
HOW:	*Gunshot, grenade fragments*
WHO:	*Muslim fundamentalist conspirators*
CONVICTED:	*Five executed, 17 imprisoned*
MOTIVE:	*To install a Muslim religious government*
DIRECT CONSEQUENCE:	*Stronger ties between Egypt and the West*

FREQUENTLY, the sheer and terrible horror that accompanies assassinations produces precisely the opposite effect the assassins wish to achieve. This was the case in the brutal and highly public murder of President Anwar al-Sadat of Egypt on October 6, 1981. The killing was designed to pave the way for Muslim fundamentalists to seize control of Egypt, as they had in Iran. But worldwide revulsion led to further strengthening of the ties between Egypt and the West.

SADAT was born in the Nile Delta of Egypt on December 25, 1918. From early childhood, he was fascinated by the military; thus, it was ironic that he should die as a result of his insistence upon attending a military parade.

In 1938, he graduated from the Cairo Royal Military Academy. During World War II, he was active in the movement to liberate Egypt from the longtime rule of Great Britain, and in 1942 he was arrested by the British on charges of being a spy for Germany. Imprisoned in Cairo, he escaped shortly after, and remained a fugitive until the end of the war.

In 1945, he was again arrested and charged with complicity in a failed attempt to assassinate Egypt's prime minister, Nahas Pasha. Once more, he escaped, and surfaced again five years later as a member of Gamal Abdel Nasser's "Free Officers." His star rose dramatically when he took part in the overthrow of Egypt's monarchy in 1952. King Farouk was replaced by General Neguib, under whom the Egyptian Republic was proclaimed, and Nasser, as minister of the interior, shaped the Egyptian Revolution, breaking up former estates, forming Egypt's industrial base, and setting Egypt up as the major force in the Pan-Arab socialist movement.

WHEN NASSER ascended to the prime ministry in April of 1954, and the presidency seven months later, he took Sadat with him. Sadat became minister of state from 1955 to 1956, during the time when Nasser's move to nationalize the Suez Canal precipitated an international crisis. Israel invaded the Sinai region of Egypt on October 29, 1956, while an Anglo-French force occupied the canal zone in "police action" to recover it for the Suez Canal Company. Eventually the Suez Crisis was solved through intervention of the United Nations and America on the side of Egypt.

As Egypt's prestige continued to climb with the founding of the United Arab Republic, Sadat ascended to the chairmanship of the National Assembly, where he was also Speaker. The early 1960s were, however, tense days for Egypt. Syria withdrew from the United Arab Republic, Egypt allowed guerrilla attacks by Palestinians to originate in Cairo, and this climaxed in the Six-Day War, in which Israel inflicted a major defeat upon Egypt. By this time, Sadat had become vice president, a position he held twice, first from 1964 to 1966, and then from 1969 to President Nasser's death from a heart attack on September 28, 1970.

Nasser had resigned after the country's defeat in the Six-Day War, but reassumed the presidency 24 hours later, after massive demonstrations in practically every major city in the country. He devoted his remaining time in office to strengthening the ties between the United States and Egypt, and in keeping Palestinians in check.

WHEN SADAT took over as president, in October of 1970, he failed to ignite either the imagination of his countrymen or the fierce loyalty they had given Nasser, despite the fact that he accomplished nearly as much for Egypt as his predecessor.

Los Angeles Times

Circulation: 1,036,522 Daily / 1,290,194 Sunday | Wednesday, October 7, 1981 | CC†/124 pages/Copyright 1981, Los Angeles Times/Daily 25¢

Sadat Assassinated at Military Parade

Vice President Says Egypt Will Abide by All Treaties

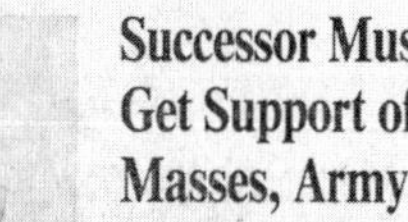

Associated Press

Anwar Sadat, center, with Vice President Hosni Mubarak, left, and Defense Minister Abdel Halim Abu Ghazala just before the shooting. Abu Ghazala was wounded but Mubarak apparently was unhurt and flew from scene in the same helicopter that took Sadat to a hospital.

He Moves to Assume Real Authority

By NORMAN KEMPSTER, *Times Staff Writer*

CAIRO—President Anwar Sadat was assassinated Tuesday by a band of assailants in army uniforms who fired automatic rifles into the reviewing stand where he was watching a parade of Egyptian military might.

Vice President Hosni Mubarak, in a dramatic television appearance seven hours after the attack, announced the president's death.

Seven other people were also reported killed in the assault. Twenty-seven people, including the Egyptian chief of staff, Abdrab Nabi Hafez, and three U.S. military officers were injured. None of the Americans were seriously hurt.

Mubarak announced that the speaker of the Egyptian People's Assembly, Sufi Abu Taleb, will serve as interim president. Officials later announced that Parliament will meet today to appoint a permanent successor to Sadat—almost certainly Mobarak himself.

The officials said a plebiscite to confirm Parliament's choice will be held Monday, although the constitution allows a two-month wait.

No Changes in Cabinet

Mubarak also told the nation that there will be no changes in the Cabinet and that Egypt will abide by all treaties and agreements that Sadat made during his 11-year presidency. Presumably, that includes the peace treaty with Israel.

The 52-year-old Mubarak, former commander of the Egyptian air force, is considered almost certain to be elected the next president. Vice president since April, 1975, Mubarak was apparently being groomed by Sadat to be his eventual successor.

At least three groups claimed responsibility for the killing in calls to newspapers in Beirut.

Egyptian sources speculated that the attackers—who numbered at least five—were either Muslim fundamentalists or followers of exiled Lt. Gen. Saad Eddin Shazli, a former Egyptian chief of staff who broke with Sadat in 1978 over the Camp David accords that led to the peace treaty with Israel.

Related stories and pictures, Pages 4, 5, 6, 7, 8, 11, 12, 16, 17.

The attack on Sadat and his party was swift and shocking, occurring toward the end of what had been a spectacular military parade. Nobody was paying much attention to the slow-moving shiny Russian trucks hauling behind them new South Korean artillery pieces on display for the first time. All eyes were turned upward toward the Mirage jets swooping only feet above the reviewing stand.

Suddenly one of the trucks came to an abrupt halt right in front of the reviewing stand where Sadat and the entire Egyptian military and political hierarchy were seated watching the parade marking Egypt's initial victory in 1973 over the Israelis along the Suez Canal.

Earlier in the review, one motor-

Please see SADAT, Page 16

Research Grows

Senility—a Ray of Hope for Afflicted

By HARRY NELSON, *Times Medical Writer*

Under the microscope the tiny nerve cells removed from the patient's brain resemble twisted bits of yarn. Interspersed among these tangled neurons, dense white clusters that resemble disordered piles of trash dot the slide.

Together these "tangles and placques," as they are called, are among the most concrete—and puzzling—features of a vaguely understood condition that affects as many as 500,000 Americans and kills 100,000 a year.

The condition is called Alzheimer's disease after its discoverer, a German physician named Alois Alzheimer. It is also known as presenile dementia, and it rapidly is becoming the hottest research area in aging.

There are more than 50 causes of senility, a feebleness of the mind that affects an estimated 3 to 4 million people. They range from poor nutrition to plugged cerebral arteries.

Most Relentless Cause

Senility that is attributable to many of these causes is reversible. But for victims of Alzheimer's, who account for 50% to 60% of all elderly people with severe mental impairment and half of all persons over 65 in nursing homes, there is no specific treatment.

It is the most relentless and devastating of all causes of senility, according to scientists at the National Institute on Aging.

But there has been a growing interest in Alzheimer's disease within the last few years, and some researchers believe the outlook will not always be as bleak. They believe that recent discoveries may lead them to a better understanding of the disease as well as a specific treatment.

A consistent finding in Alzheimer patients is that they have a deficiency of a brain enzyme that is essential for the manufacture of a specific message transmitter in the brain.

Difficulty in Reasoning

This transmitter, called acetylcholine, is required for memory formation. Memory impairment leading to difficulty in reasoning, thinking and making judgments is a hallmark of Alzheimer's disease.

The consistent lack of acetylcholine—as much as 90% below normal—is the first biochemical abnormality that has been identified for this disease.

For the first time, researchers have a concrete finding upon which to launch further investigations. The finding has led to several studies using different approaches in an attempt to arrest the memory deterioration by making the transmitter more available to the neurons.

One approach has been to use a drug that acts by making the transmitter that is available in the brain

Please see SENILITY, Page 28

Associated Press

Confused scene on reviewing stand after the attack. Right, behind chair, is one of the victims.

Successor Must Get Support of Masses, Army

By DON A. SCHANCHE, *Times Staff Writer*

Hosni Mubarak, the stocky, bull-necked air marshal handpicked by Anwar Sadat as his vice president, has inherited the leadership of Egypt by assassins' bullets, but he faces two potentially serious obstacles as he moves to consolidate his hold: his relationships with the masses and with the military.

He will need the support of both groups to deal with Egypt's long-standing economic problems and its more recent religious strife.

The first and perhaps most critical obstacle is his own lack of recognition among the Egyptian people.

During his six years at Sadat's right hand, Mubarak, 52, never established a personal political constituency among the nation's 43 million citizens. In the early years after his elevation from chief of the Egyptian armed forces to the vice presidency, Mubarak withdrew deep into Sadat's shadow. He was hardly seen by the people except on ceremonial occasions.

Seen as Political Lightweight

His largely innocuous appearances showed an amiable man who, because of his silence, was widely believed to be a political lightweight. Egyptians took to calling him "the laughing cow" after the trademark of the popular cheese, which is sold thoughout Egypt.

However, beginning with the 1978 Camp David agreements on a Middle East peace plan, Mubarak performed wide-ranging and important missions for Sadat, and in

Please see SUCCESSOR, Page 18

Slaying Casts a Cloud Over Mideast

Death of Sadat May Force Reassessment of U.S. Policy

By OSWALD JOHNSTON, *Times Staff Writer*

WASHINGTON—The assassination of Egyptian President Anwar Sadat casts an ominous shadow over the future of the Middle East and may call into question the basic premises of U.S. policy toward the region.

Despite early indications from Cairo that the expected transition of power to Vice President Hosni Mubarak will be smooth and that Egypt will carry out the terms of its peace treaty with Israel, the very foundations of the peace process begun three years ago at Camp David are now in doubt.

"A disaster, there is no way the outlook could not be gloomy," said a former Carter Administration official who took part in the Camp David conference. He spoke as early broadcast reports of Sadat's death filtered in from Cairo.

"There is a question," said Dan Pattir, a former aide to Israeli Prime Minister Menachem Begin, who also participated at Camp David. "Most Israelis trusted Sadat. But Israel now must decide if Egypt will remain committed to Camp David as Sadat was."

Arab Pressure Anticipated

Harold H. Saunders, the assistant secretary of state for the Middle East in the Carter Administration, said Tuesday that he anticipates Arab pressure on Mubarak's government to abrogate the treaty with Israel, even though he believes Sadat's policies will be continued at least for the time being.

Camp David, Saunders said, needs to be supplemented by a new U.S. blueprint for peace. And with Sadat's death, "It is all the more true that it's necessary" to bring Saudi Arabia, Jordan and Syria into a process that had dwindled into an increasingly barren dialogue between Sadat and Begin, he said.

In Washington, senior government officials and their spokesmen expressed shock, dismay and qualified their hopes for the future. But inevitably there were troubling echoes of past reversals in the sudden death of the man on whom Washington through four presidencies has relied for stability in the volatile Arab world.

Only last week, in a grim reminder of the fall of Iran's Shah Mohammed Reza Pahlavi, President Reagan declared a U.S. commitment to preserve political stability in Saudi Arabia, a pillar of the Administration's proposed "strategic consensus" against external threats to the Middle East.

Now Sadat, the all but indispensable leader of Egypt, the other Arab pillar of Reagan's policy, has suddenly fallen.

"If anything, the Saudis are more important now to the United States than before," one American specialist said. "It shows how thin U.S. policy is in the region, how many changes can come with the death of one man."

Please see POLICY, Page 17

Curb Officially Declares Candidacy for Governor

By RICHARD BERGHOLZ, *Times Political Writer*

Pledging to preserve "the traditional concepts of home, family and productive work," Lt. Gov. Mike Curb formally declared his candidacy for governor Tuesday.

The 36-year-old Republican portrayed himself as a businessman, "not a career government employee," and noted that "at some point in time, I intend to return to the private sector and I'll have to live under some of the decisions I have helped make."

Curb's experience during the last three years has been in the lieutenant governor's post, which has virtually no power and plays virtually no role in governmental policies.

It was when Democratic Gov. Edmund G. Brown Jr. was out of state that Curb was allowed to function as acting governor. And with a few notable exceptions, he generally worked closely with Brown's staff when he was Brown's stand-in.

It cost Curb a reported $120,000 to make his candidacy announcement. He did it in paid television commercials from Eureka to San Diego—but not in San Francisco or Oakland.

The half-hour program consisted about equally of a mini-documentary of Curb's political and business career, including his work in the record industry, and of exposition of his general view of state government, complete with a couple of charts.

The videotaped presentation came as Curb carefully avoided any

Please see CURB, Page 25

The Weather

National Weather Service forecast: Low clouds late night and early morning hours with mostly sunny afternoons today and Thursday. Highs today in the upper 70s and Thursday in the mid 70s; lows in the low 60s. High Tuesday, 86; low, 60. High Oct. 6 last year, 83; low, 65. Record high Oct. 6, 102 in 1955; record low 48 in 1898.

Complete weather details and smog forecast in Part II, Page 2.

INDEX

End to IRA Hunger Strike Brings British Concessions

By WILLIAM TUOHY, *Times Staff Writer*

BELFAST, Northern Ireland—The British government Tuesday unveiled a new program of prison reforms in Northern Ireland in an obvious reaction to the end of Irish nationalists' hunger strikes at the Maze prison last Saturday.

But the Conservative government of Prime Minister Margaret Thatcher stopped short of giving the convicted guerrillas the virtual political-prisoner status that they had demanded, and the British announcement stressed that the reforms will apply to all prisoners, not just the nationalists.

Under the new regulations, prisoners will be allowed to wear their own clothes at all times, they will be allowed greater freedom of association in recreation areas, and more time will be devoted to vocational training and use of educational facilities during work periods.

And those nationalist prisoners who—by joining protests at the Maze—have lost accrued time off their sentences for good behavior could regain up to half the lost time by conforming to prison rules for three months. That could mean quick release for 150 male inmates at the Maze and 20 women at Armagh prison. Normal procedures in Northern Ireland call for a 50% reduction of sentences for good behavior.

The announced changes were relayed to the inmates at the Maze, but there was no immediate reaction from the Irish Republican

Please see ULSTER, Page 30

Perhaps it was his military bearing, his love of pomp and circumstance. Ironically, Sadat *did* capture the rest of the world, who regarded him as the foremost power in the Middle East and its chief and fundamental hope for peace.

To ensure his safety, the United States contributed nearly 25 million dollars toward Sadat's security. Beginning in 1974, the U.S. secret service trained Egyptian security men in skills ranging from evasive driving to crowd control. The CIA supplied electronic equipment designed to protect messages from his bodyguards from interception; President Nixon supplied the president with a two-million-dollar Sikorsky CH-53E armored helicopter, and President Jimmy Carter provided him with AWACS protection against Libyan fighters.

But perhaps it was Sadat's own belief that no one in his military would ever rise against him—he often told his security guards, during military drills, "Please go away—I am with my children"—or perhaps it was the often-stated axiom that there is no defense against a dedicated terrorist that brought about his death by assassination.

CERTAINLY, his actions in office created enemies without and within. Almost from the very beginning, he set about moving Egypt further from the Soviet Union and closer to the United States. His friendship with the Shah of Iran gained him lifelong adversaries in that country. In October, 1973, he launched a lightning attack upon Israel again, this time across the Suez Canal. This, the beginning of the Yom Kippur War, endeared him to his fellow Arabs.

But then, in 1977, he enraged these followers by accepting an invitation from Israeli prime minister Menachem Begin to speak before the Knesset in Israel. This marked the beginning of several years of negotiations which culminated in the Camp David Accord, so named because the historic Israeli-Egyptian Peace Treaty, shepherded by U.S. President Jimmy Carter, took place at Camp David, the presidential retreat in Maryland.

Now Sadat's Arab enemies erupted in full fury. No matter that Sadat had managed to gain more land for Arabs from Israel by negotiation than Arabs had won by force for generations. The Nobel Peace Prize he won for his monumental achievement was a badge of treason to Arab nationalists in Egypt, Libya, Syria, Iraq, Lebanon, and a hundred other locations in the Middle East.

TENSION and concern for his safety rose as precipitously as his world fame. And perhaps he himself had set the stage for the final breaching of that safety, when, in the 1970s, during the first months of his presidency, he granted amnesty and freedom to the members of the fanatic Islamic organization *Al Taqfir wal Hijra*, who had been jailed by his predecessor, Gamal Abdel Nasser. This, the bloodiest and most dedicated organization of Islamic terrorists, became not only his unremitting foe, but the trainers of the assassins who would eventually murder him.

Al Taqfir wal Hijra, with approximately 4,000 members in Egypt and another 10,000 outside of the country, was described with chilling accuracy by Professor Saad Eddin Ibrahim of the American University at Cairo as being composed of ". . . hard-core members [who are] walking time bomb[s]—waiting to go off," and a U.S. State Department official described them to *Newsweek* magazine as ". . . a Moral Majority with AK-47s."

This group, enraged at Sadat's ties with the West, had a brief but bloody history, dating from its founding by its spiritual father, Sayyed Kotb, a Muslim firebrand who was executed in 1965 after botching an assassination attempt against Nasser. His and his followers' avowed aims were to spill the blood of all heretics who did not return to Islam, and to atone for the sins of decadent Egypt by violent acts.

Their presence and dedication were no secret in 1981, and Begin, in a visit to Alexandria in August, warned Sadat against over-complacency. The President countered that a purge would anger human rights advocates in the U.S. Congress, and he needed their support.

Still, the atmosphere was turning uglier by the day. Fundamentalists were brazenly pillorying the president in village mosques; death threats forced Sadat to cancel a planned stopover in Vienna after his summer visit to America. Shortly after Begin's departure in August, Egyptian intelligence uncovered a plot to assassinate Sadat and his wife Jihan in their Alexandria summer palace. Vice president Hosni Mubarak and interior minister Nabawi Ismail warned him that a coup d'état was in the making, and a purge was a necessity.

Sadat reluctantly agreed, and, in September, he ordered his security forces to round up and jail 1,600 dissenters, from government officials to cell leaders. The only government arm that remained untouched was the military. Sadat simply could not conceive that his faithful military could harbor traitors or potential assassins. And that is precisely where the assassination plot was centered, in the person of a first lieutenant named Khaled Ahmed Shawkyal Islambouli.

OCTOBER 6 was Anwar Sadat's favorite holiday. It was the eighth anniversary of his foray across the Suez Canal, the attack that began the Yom Kippur War. According to some, he looked forward eagerly to the huge military review that was to take place in the middle of the day. According to others, he was tired, confessed his fatigue to vice president Mubarak, and added that he wished he didn't have to attend the ceremony.

Sadat was impenetrable. He possessed the poker face of a world-class diplomat—which he was—and he rarely revealed either inner turmoil or weakness. Still, his vice president was a trusted confidant, and the reported story may be true.

He dressed in his field marshal's gold-braided blue uniform crossed by a green sash and topped by a multitude of medals. His plan was to attend the ceremonies, then drive to the family home at the Nile delta village of Mit Abu el Kom and visit the grave of his brother Atif, who had been a pilot, killed in the first hours of the October War.

He collected his eight bodyguards, boarded his black Cadillac limousine, open at the top, and made his first stop of the day, at the grave of Gamal Abdel Nasser, in Heliopolis. He prayed at the graveside, then returned to his limousine. Along the way, he was joined by Mubarak and his defense minister, General Abdel Halim Abu Ghazala. They left the wide boulevards of Cairo for the modern and anonymous suburb of Nasr City, and along the way, Sadat made one more stop, to place a wreath on the pyramid-shaped tomb of the Unknown Soldier.

By 10 a.m., his party arrived at the reviewing stand, occupied by 1,000 guests—military advisers, ambassadors, diplomats, and a battalion of journalists—to signal the beginning of the two-hour grand display of military and air power.

Above him, in the glass enclosure at the top of the massive brick and concrete stand, Sadat's elegant and regal 48-year-old wife Jihan sat with the grandchildren. It was the first military parade the children had ever witnessed, and they were intrigued and excited.

Once the president had taken his seat at the center of the first row of the elevated stands, separated from the review field by a five-foot-high concrete wall, the exercises began, with readings from the Koran. Following this, defense minister Abu Ghazala rose and delivered a long speech extolling the Egyptian military and its commander-in-chief. By 11:30, the first military units began to roll by.

THE DAY before, first lieutenant Khaled Ahmed al-Islambouli had given his three-man gun crew a leave of absence. He told parade officials that the crew had fallen sick, and three soldiers from another army unit would ride in their places. The following day, as they entered the heavily guarded, cordoned-off staging area, he elaborately and publicly "searched" the three new men for concealed weapons or forbidden ammunition.

They were actually well armed, with hand grenades and enough ammunition to assassinate a president and terrorize a reviewing stand. They boarded the back of the heavy truck, and Islambouli settled into the seat next to his regular driver.

The parade began with mortars firing miniature parachutes containing tiny portraits of Sadat and Egyptian flags. Fireworks exploded overhead, in preparation for the entrance of jets, screaming overhead in tight formations. The camel corps bounced by. It was a splendid display, and Sadat alternated between puffing contentedly on his pipe, bending over closer to Abu Ghazala to hear the defense minister's explanations of the equipment rolling by or roaring overhead, and training his binoculars on the stunt-flying jets.

At approximately 12:30, the contingent of 72 Soviet-made Zil-151 flatbed trucks hove into view. They were scarcely the most impressive and interesting vehicles in the parade, and to liven up the moment, a passel of French-made, Mirage 5-E fighters swooped low over the crowd, painting the sky with red, blue, orange, green, and gray smoke.

The crowd and Sadat concentrated on the jets. Hardly anyone noticed that one of the trucks in the second echelon had pulled off to the side and stopped, just opposite President Sadat. Islambouli had pulled a hand grenade from under his tunic and ordered the driver to stop. The startled driver hesitated, and Islambouli reached over and yanked the handbrake.

Sadat, Carter, and Begin in Washington at the signing of the Israeli-Egyptian peace treaty.

NOW EVENTS accelerated. Islambouli slipped from the truck's seat and approached the reviewing stand. Sadat and Mubarak, thinking he had come to pay his respects, rose to greet him. But instead of saluting, the lieutenant pulled the pin on his hand grenade and lobbed it directly at President Sadat. Simultaneously, the three ersatz soldiers stood up on the back of the truck, their automatic weapons blazing.

Pandemonium erupted. The first grenade landed at Abu Ghazala's feet, but did not explode. Islambouli reached into his pocket, withdrew another grenade, pulled the pin and threw it. It struck major general Abdrab Nabi Hafez squarely in the face, but it too didn't explode. He pulled a third one, and it exploded at the front of the reviewing stand. Islambouli dashed back to the truck and grabbed his automatic rifle. The three men leaped from the back of the truck and advanced with the lieutenant toward the stands, firing steadily. They encountered no resistance from the score of security guards protecting not only Egyptian officials but the international corps of diplomats in the stands.

Bullets began to strike home. Hundreds of dignitaries and journalists overturned chairs and each other as they stampeded for the exits. But the gunmen were concentrating on the front rows. They fired ceaselessly, emptying the clips in their guns. Two charged directly at the podium, one ran to the left, another to the right, firing into the dais from the sides.

Sadat had already been struck, many times and mortally, but those around him tried to shield him, forcing him to the floor of the stand, shielding him with their bodies and overturned chairs. "I felt the bullets flying all around me," said Abu Ghazala later. "I could feel the heat of them."

Sadat's personal bodyguards finally came to life, some 45 seconds after the attack began. The gunmen, their guns empty, now turned and fled to the truck. Security guards followed them, firing. One assassin was killed. The other three were wounded and captured.

IN THE reviewing stand, Sadat lay helpless, bleeding profusely from the mouth. Ten other members of the reviewing party were also either killed or fatally wounded and 28 were injured. Abu Ghazala and Mubarak were struck, but far less seriously, and Abu Ghazala immediately began to take charge of the situation, issuing orders to the young, red-bereted soldiers who now entered the reviewing stand, helping the wounded, clearing the tangle of overturned chairs. He radioed a nearby military facility to send a helicopter. It arrived three minutes later, just as Jihan pushed past the finally alert security guards and joined her husband, strapped to a stretcher, in the helicopter.

Mubarak, suffering only a cut hand, was taken by presidential Volvo to Maadi military hospital, where already Sadat was being rushed to a fourth-floor operating room in the hospital's heart and chest surgery unit. There, a team of 11 doctors worked furiously, despite Sadat's lack of pulse and reflexes.

The team of doctors removed clotted blood from his larynx, inserted an air tube in his throat, administered artificial respiration and a massive blood transfusion. They opened the left side of his chest and inserted a tube to remove air and blood, and tried to stimulate his heart into beating again by open chest massage and electric shock.

Sadat and Yasser Arafat, leader of the Palestinian Liberation Organization, exchange a diplomatic greeting. Arafat regarded Sadat's assassination as a positive step toward undoing the Israeli-Egyptian peace treaty.

Nothing would—or could—revive the President. Although the official time of his death was given as 2:40 p.m., two hours after the attack, he was actually dead on arrival at the hospital, from, according to the official report, ". . . heavy nervous shock with internal chest hemorrhaging and laceration of the left lung and the main blood vessels at the base of the left lung." He had been raked by five bullets and several pieces of shrapnel. The assassins had accomplished their task.

One of the attending doctors descended to the first floor, where Jihan Sadat waited. "Only God can live forever," he told her, quoting the Koran.

It would be hours before the news would reach either the people of Egypt or the outside world. And then, the reaction would be swift and definite. The West reacted in shock; the enclaves of fundamentalist Muslims in the Middle East conducted grisly celebrations. In Libya, crowds danced in the streets, waving flags and shouting approval. "We shake the hand that pulled the trigger," said one fedayeen commander, and the P.L.O. leader Yasser Arafat declared, "What we are witnessing is the beginning of the failure of the Camp David agreement with the fall of one of its symbols."

When Nasser died, millions had taken to the streets of Egypt in clothing-rending grief; the death of Sadat produced no such demonstrations, partly because he never commanded the emotional loyalty that his predecessor enjoyed; partly because, along with the declaration of a 40-day period of mourning, the Egyptian government also decreed a year-long state of emergency, which prohibited public gatherings and marches. When the funeral procession began, police fired shots in the air to disperse a crowd of 2,000 who assembled merely to attend the funeral.

The body of Sadat was flown by helicopter from the hospital mosque to a sports stadium in Nasr

City, then carried on a horse-drawn caisson for the final 800 yards to the very reviewing stand in which he had been murdered. There, in the row where he sat to receive the assassins' bullets, his family received dignitaries from all over the world. French president François Mitterand was there; so was Britain's Prince Charles and Israel's Manachem Begin. President Ronald Reagan did not attend, for security reasons (he was still recovering from an attempt on his life), but he sent a huge delegation which included an uneasy alliance of former presidents Nixon, Ford, and Carter, defense secretary Casper Weinberger, U.N. ambassador Jeane Kirkpatrick, and Henry Kissinger.

It was massive symbolism. Even as Sadat's body was being lowered into a grave recently dug before the tomb of the Unknown Soldier, the newly installed president Mubarak was affirming his determination to continue the policies of Sadat and the Camp David Accord.

MINDFUL of the imminent threat of a coup d'état with the determination to establish an Iran-style Islamic fundamentalist regime, security forces moved swiftly, rounding up every Islamic fundamentalist in sight: 356 members of *Al Taqfir wal Hijra* were arrested, among them sheik Omar Abdul Rahman, who would, after his acquittal in Egypt and subsequent resettlement in the United States, be implicated in the 1993 bombing of New York's World Trade Center.

Twenty-four men were put on trial in a military court on November 21, 1981. Five, including Islambouli, were sentenced to death. Seventeen others received prison sentences ranging from hard labor for life to five years. Two others, including sheik Rahman, were acquitted for lack of evidence. At dawn, on April 15, 1982, the five assassins were executed, the two military men by firing squad, the three civilians by hanging.

The public trial and conviction of the assassins and the tight security enforced by the Mubarak regime foiled the *Jihad*, the holy war of the Islamic fundamentalists, and cemented Egypt's strong ties to the West.

To this day, periodic uprisings occur, and are as swiftly put down. The truce, as all truces in the Middle East, is an uneasy one. But the coup that was to accompany the assassination of Anwar al-Sadat failed, as did its religious mission.

BENIGNO AQUINO

POSITION:	*Political opponent of Ferdinand Marcos*
DATE:	*August 21, 1983*
PLACE:	*Manila, Philippines*
HOW:	*Gunshot*
WHO:	*Conspirators reaching back to President Marcos*
CONVICTED:	*16 sentenced to life imprisonment*
MOTIVE:	*To protect the power of the Marcos family*
DIRECT CONSEQUENCE:	*Defeat and exile of Ferdinand Marcos*

BENIGNO AQUINO Jr., like Caesar and John F. Kennedy, was warned by those closest to him not to appear in public in an unfriendly location. Leaving the safety of his new home in America and returning to the Philippines would, in all probability, be a fatal choice, he was told. And yet, like Caesar and Kennedy, facing fate and almost certain martyrdom, feeling that destiny was more important than safety, Benigno Aquino climbed aboard an airplane on August 20, 1983, and, surmounting a series of obstacles that were arrayed to prevent him from reaching that place at that time, walked into his own death.

His enemy was a vain and foolish man, Ferdinand Marcos, who entertained his own visions of immortality. Safely surrounded by his loyal military, insulated from the people from whom he had stolen billions, and catered to by Western powers that were willing to tolerate his despotism, so long as he prevented the Philippines from becoming communist and allowed their military bases to remain in his country, Marcos felt he could accomplish anything with impunity, even public assassination. What he did not realize was that a living Benigno Aquino was a danger; a martyred Benigno Aquino was a force that could—and would—drive him disgraced from power.

BENIGNO AQUINO was born on November 27, 1932, the scion of a prominent family in the province of Tarlac, in the Philippines. He began his professional life as a journalist, but soon became involved in politics, and was elected, at the age of 22, mayor of Concepcion. In 1959, he became vice governor of Tarlac Province, and, two years later, governor. In 1966, he was elected secretary-general of the Liberal Party, and the following year he became the only member of that party to be elected to the senate. His rise was meteoric and astonishing; he was the Philippines' youngest mayor, youngest governor and youngest senator; and, as he continued to hold his senate seat with increasing distinction and popularity, it became a foregone conclusion, that, at age 40, he would succeed Fernando Marcos as president. Marcos would conclude his second term in office then, and, under the Philippine constitution, he would have to step down.

BUT MARCOS had no plans to give over his power. On September 23, 1972, he declared martial law, and, as supreme commander, assumed a position he could hold for life, if he wished. Prompted, some said, by his wife Imelda, who seemed to have already crowned herself queen, Marcos embarked upon a purge of his political enemies.

The first of these enemies to be jailed was Benigno Aquino, who had already gained the reputation of "the boy wonder from Tarlac." He was accused of murder, rape, illegal possession of firearms, and subversion. Convicted on all counts, he was summarily sentenced to death.

But Marcos didn't execute his rival immediately. For seven and a half years, he kept Aquino in solitary confinement, and during that time, they carried on a lively correspondence. The two men had been fraternity brothers at the University of the Philippines. Marcos regarded the younger man with some awe. "I envy you," he had said to him once, before he had trumped up the charges to imprison and discredit him. "You have earned your presence in history. I'm still fighting for mine."

By all accounts, there was a love–hate relationship between the two men. "Four times Marcos asked me, 'Brother, what would you do if I released you tomorrow?'" Aquino told a *Time* magazine reporter on his last flight to Manila. "I said, 'I don't know, because you keep me in the dark. I have not received any newspapers in five years. If people are happy, I'll just go home to my province and retire there, but if they are unhappy, then you can bet I'll be mounting a soap box. So if you think you've done well, release me. If not, don't release me because it would only exacerbate the situation.'"

Over and over again, Marcos tried to talk Aquino into pledging that he would not oppose him if he set him free, and over and over again Aquino refused to extend the assurance. In fact, in the election of 1978, he very nearly defeated, through write-in ballots, Imelda Marcos for a seat in the National Assembly.

THEN, AQUINO developed heart trouble. The Carter administration asked the Marcos regime to allow the imprisoned senator to come to America for surgery, and Marcos agreed with alacrity. It seemed a perfect solution. Out of the country, Aquino would soon be out of the minds of the Philippine people. So, Aquino was freed, and he and his family moved to Boston, Massachusetts, where he had heart surgery and took up research fellowships at Harvard and M.I.T.

The Aquinos stayed in the United States for three years, while conditions in the Philippines worsened, and the Carter administration, dedicated to preserving human rights, was replaced by the Reagan administration, dedicated to containing Communism. A symbiotic relationship developed between Manila and Washington, while more and more civil rights for the Philippine people diminished, and the bank accounts of Ferdinand and Imelda Marcos increased.

Marcos himself was growing old and ill. A kidney ailment and lupus erythematosus had been diagnosed, and his wife Imelda was widely believed to be making plans to succeed her husband, should he become too ill to continue in office.

Martial Law was lifted in 1981, and Marcos was reelected in an election widely believed to be fraudulent. In America, Benigno Aquino became restless. Not only was there a dangerous alliance forming between the Marcos and Reagan administrations (Vice President George Bush had visited Manila in 1981, nine years after Marcos had suspended democratic rule, and told Marcos, "We love your adherence to democratic principle . . ."), but reports of widespread oppression, corruption, and discontent reached him regularly. The left was gaining strength, Aquino felt that with a parliamentary election nearing, the only chance the moderates would have to gain power would be with him there to lead them. "I feel that if I go home and turn myself bodily over to Mr. Marcos, it will be the best proof of my sincerity—that here I am not really out to overthrow him," Aquino said. "On the contrary, I put my life completely at his mercy." In the spring of 1983, he openly discussed his plans to return to Manila.

Imelda Marcos came to New York to talk him out of it. "Ninoy," she is reported to have told him, "there are people loyal to us who cannot be controlled." It was a clear and chilling warning that Aquino either ignored, failed to hear, or regarded as a challenge.

THE PHILIPPINE consulate in New York refused to issue passports to Aquino and his family. A spate of public statements erupted from the United States. and the Philippines. Aquino asserted his rights as a Philippine citizen to return to his homeland. Marcos restated the charges against Aquino and intimated that he could not guarantee his safety once he landed.

Friends in the Philippines urged Aquino not to make the trip. "I'm committed to return," he told one of them. "If fate falls that I should be killed, so be it."

He announced that he would be landing in Manila on August 7, 1983, aboard Japan Air Lines. The Philippine government countered by asserting that it would revoke the landing rights of any JAL flight that contained undocumented passengers. JAL returned Aquino's ticket.

He decided to fly to the Philippines by a roundabout route, through China. On August 14, he left, accompanied by a corps of supporters and journalists. For a week, he wandered through several Asian capitals. The last leg of his journey took him to Taiwan, where he boarded a China Airlines Boeing 767. The name he gave was "Bonifacio"—ironically, a 19th-century Filipino martyr. One of the female journalists in the party posed as his companion. The rest of the accompanying party pretended indifference and ignorance of his identity until the flight was airborne.

It seemed like an effective ruse, but on the ground in Manila, everyone seemed to know the exact time of Benigno Aquino's arrival. Manila was

Can the Redskins make it to the Super Bowl again?
NFL Profile '83 examines their prospects: Section E

The Washington Times

MONDAY, AUGUST 22, 1983 ★ WASHINGTON, D.C. PHONE: 636-3000 SUBSCRIBER SERVICE: 636-3333 **25 cents**

Marcos foe slain on return home

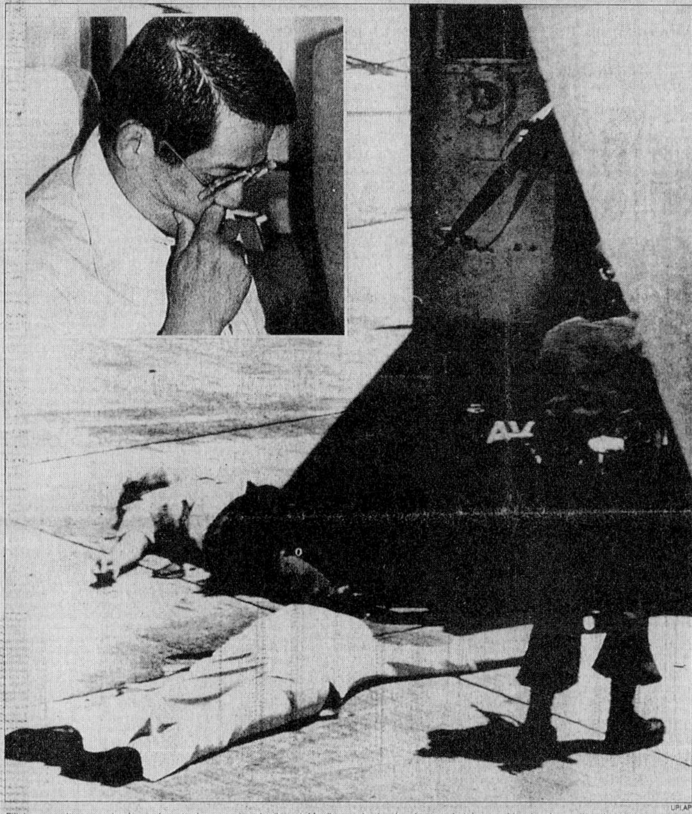

Filipino security men stand guard yesterday over two bodies at Manila International Airport. Body in foreground that of opposition leader Benigno S. Aquino Jr., who was shot down on his return home; the other is the assassin's. Moments before his jetliner landed, Aquino was photographed praying (inset). UPI, AP

Aquino, his assassin shot down in Manila

MANILA (UPI) — Opposition leader Benigno S. Aquino Jr., defying President Ferdinand Marcos by returning from self-exile in the United States, was shot to death yesterday by an assassin who was then killed in a barrage of military gunfire.

Aquino — Marcos' main political rival and a symbol of opposition to his 18-year rule — was killed seconds after stepping off the plane wearing a bulletproof vest and escorted by three soldiers.

His assailant had penetrated a tight security net by disguising himself as an airport maintenance man, the government said.

A burst of gunfire left Aquino, 50, and the assassin sprawled on the tarmac at the Manila International Airport.

"Assassination is part of public service," Aquino had told a reporter while flying to Manila. "I cannot be petrified by inaction or fear of assassination and therefore stay in a corner."

The government said the unidentified assassin penetrated an off-limits section, where the plane pulled up, and shot Aquino in the back of the head at close range with a .357-caliber pistol.

"He (Aquino) was about to board a . . . van, but suddenly a man darted out and the security was caught flatfooted," said the Manila police chief, Maj. Gen. Prospero Olivas. "When they heard the shots, they noticed the man then. They fired at him and then took the senator to the hospital."

Olivas said Aquino was declared dead on arrival at an army hospital. Doctors confirmed he was killed with a single shot.

Slain Philippines opposition leader Benigno S. Aquino Jr. seemed destined someday for the presidency. Page 7A.

see SLAIN, *page 12A*

Reagan, Filipino exiles voice outrage at killing

From combined dispatches

President Reagan led the chorus of voices expressing outrage at the murder yesterday in Manila of Filipino opposition leader Benigno S. Aquino Jr.

But the president said he has no intention of changing his plans to visit the Philippines on his 14-day trip to the Far East in November.

In a statement made public at Santa Barbara, the White House said: "The murder of Sen. Benigno S. Aquino Jr. in Manila on Aug. 21 is a cowardly and despicable act which the U.S. government condemns in the strongest possible terms.

"The U.S. government trusts that the government of the Philippines will swiftly and vigorously track down the perpertrators of this political assassination, bring them to justice and punish them to the fullest extent of the law."

Leaders of the Filipino opposition movement in the United States reacted with shock, anger and prayers to the slaying of Aquino, the man they hoped would replace Ferdinand Marcos as president of the Philippines.

Many of them said they believed Marcos was responsible for the murder.

Sergio Osmeno III, grandson of former Philippine President Osmeno, called the assassination in Manila "the most disgusting thing I've ever seen.

"This is the normal modus operandi when Marcos wants to get rid of people," Osmeno said from his home in Los Angeles. "His entire career has been fraught with violence and assassination."

"It's a very big tragedy to democracy in the Philippines. I was very sorry to hear the news," said Gen. Alejo Santos, who lost to Marcos in the last Filipino presidential election in June 1981. Aquino was in self-imposed exile in the United States.

Alex Esclamado, publisher of the San Francisco-based Philippine News, a national weekly newspaper, said he had strongly advised Aquino not to return to his homeland because there were reports

see OUTRAGE, *page 12A*

How Cuban agents deliver arms to leftist guerrillas in El Salvador

Fidel Castro's attempts to export his brand of communist revolution throughout the Western Hemisphere and, indeed, anywhere he perceives an opportunity to de-stabilize governments and push their people toward the Soviet-Cuban block, are detailed in a five-part series beginning today by veteran Latin American correspondent Jay Mallin, who has just joined the staff of The Washington Times. Today, Mallin tells how Cuba sends arms to leftist guerrillas in El Salvador and outlines the structure and operations of Castro's intelligence-gathering and subversion-spreading organizations operating beyond Cuba's borders.

CASTRO'S SPIES

By Jay Mallin
WASHINGTON TIMES STAFF

Soon after dusk, a small Nicaraguan freighter pulls out of the port of Estero Padre Ramos on the northwest coast of Nicaragua. It carries a cargo of M-16 rifles, other weapons, ammunition and field equipment.

The vessel heads straight out to sea and into international waters. Forty or so miles from shore, it slows its speed. A light flickers nearby. Soon three speedboats pull up and are lashed alongside.

The weapons are loaded aboard the small craft, and they pull away, heading northwest to El Salvador's Bay of Jiquilisco, an isolated area of swamps, waterways and river tributaries.

The speedboats anchor, canoes pull up and the weapons are again transferred. The canoes now take the arms to depots hidden among the swamps. From there, they will be transported by pack animals, or in concealed compartments of vehicles, to the leftist guerrillas fighting in El Salvador.

The operation described is one of the ways that weapons have been and are being sent by Cuba to the Salvadoran guerrillas. There are other operations by sea, as well as by air and by land. Today, approxi-

see 5 SPY, *page 5A*

Paul Woodward Washington Times

3 unions accept new phone pact

By Marc Lerner
WASHINGTON TIMES STAFF

The leadership of three unions representing 675,000 striking telephone workers yesterday approved a tentative three-year agreement expected to put workers back on the job by early Thursday.

Glenn E. Watts, president of the Communications Workers of America, said the union's executive board approved the contract proposal by American Telephone & Telegraph Co. that will give CWA's 525,000 telephone workers an average 16.4 percent wage increase over three years.

see AT&T, *page 12A*

INDEX

Monday, August 22, 1983
Volume 2, Number 166, 5 Sections, 76 pages

Magazine

ACCENT ON TRAVEL
Also:
- Outdoor Life
- TV pullout
- Hobbies

A new twist for moonshining in Franklin County

By Danelle Morton
WASHINGTON TIMES STAFF

SNOW CREEK, Franklin County, Va. — Making whiskey is a time-honored tradition in this farming county, where a father passes the secret of his mash down to his son as a birthright.

But a new breed of moonshiner has come of age in these rolling hills and wooded glens: large-scale operators who manufacture liquor in addition to selling drugs and stolen goods.

"Time was when these violators had pride in their product," said V.K. Stoneman, agent in charge of the state Alcoholic Beverage Control division whose 16 counties hide the highest concentration of stills in the Commonwealth.

"A man was proud his name was associated with making a good drinking whiskey. But these new guys, well, they aren't the Mafia but you could compare them to it."

Stoneman's men earlier this month blew up a still in Franklin County that was typical of this new breed — eight 100-gallon tanks capable of producing 1,000 gallons of whiskey per still every five to seven days.

"I know what you think when you think of a moonshiner," Stoneman said. "You think of Snuffy Smith with his little copper-topped still who makes about 50 gallons a week. He just doesn't exist today."

The old-time moonshiner was middle-aged and poorly educated, using whiskey as his major source of support, Stoneman said. His modern-day counterpart may never even see his still. He puts up the money for the tanks, sugar, yeast and grain and pays his still workers $50 for each 1,000 gallon pot of whiskey to start the mash and jug the liquor.

Just as city folk may carry a quaint image of the moonshiner as

see STILLS, *page 12A*

decorated with yellow ribbons. More than 20,000 supporters, including his 75-year-old mother Aurora, gathered at the airport to greet him. So did government security forces, who cordoned off the airport, effectively keeping the Aquino supporters out of sight of any landing airplanes.

THE AIRPORT lobby was cleared and locked. The military had assumed control of AVESCOM, the aviation security command, and they waited along with a phalanx of soldiers armed with M-16s on the tarmac, as China Airlines Flight 811 entered its final approach.

Aboard the plane, Aquino, attired in a white safari suit, strolled to the washroom and donned a bullet-proof vest. "My chances of surviving this trip are 10%," he had told a *Newsweek* reporter aboard the flight, and now he was attempting to up that percentage.

The plane landed and taxied toward Gate 8. The long, portable receiving tunnel snaked out from the terminal to receive passengers. The plane slowed to a stop. Benigno Aquino waited calmly in seat 14C, in economy class. He was aware that armed forces chief of staff General Fabian Ver had publicly vowed to send him "back on the same plane he arrived on." And so, when three armed security men, one from the Philippine Constabulary and two from AVESCOM, boarded the plane from the passenger tunnel, he fully expected them to try to prevent him from debarking.

But they walked past the former senator, and only surrounded him when he stood up. Then, instead of forcing him back to his seat, they turned him toward the rear of the plane, where another exit door had been opened, and a steel staircase had been positioned. The rest of the entourage pressed close to Aquino, jockeying to see what was happening. But the security guards shoved them back. Aquino was smiling slightly and placidly as he was moved, within the triangle of the three security guards, to the open door and the staircase.

More uniformed men were waiting at the top of the staircase, and they closed in, further hiding Aquino from view. The journalists dashed to the windows to see what was happening. The door was shut behind him. Reporters rushed to it and tried to open it, but were pushed back by two security guards stationed at the door.

And then it happened. First, there was the sound of one gunshot, then a fusillade. The security guards inside the airplane slammed a television cameraman against the bulkhead, keeping him from filming through the plane's windows.

But those who managed to get to the first-class windows saw a grim scene. Aquino lay face-down on the tarmac. Blood was spurting from a huge hole in the back of his head. Near him, face down also, was another man, clad in the blue coveralls of an airport mechanic. Three AVESCOM men were standing over him, pumping shot after shot into his prone body. The guards who had taken Aquino from the plane were nowhere to be seen, but swarms of AVESCOM troopers crisscrossed the scene, firing their rifles in the air. Two of them gathered up Aquino's body and flung it into an AVESCOM van parked next to the metal staircase. The van sped off. It had all taken less than 30 seconds.

Now, the killing's effects began to spread, like the waves from a rock dropped in water. The government announced immediately that a lone gunman was responsible, and he had been shot on the spot by security forces. For days, that man, whom journalists had seen, face down on the tarmac, remained unidentified. The only clues, said government sources, were his signet ring, engraved with the initial "R," and the word "Rolly" embroidered on his underwear.

Then, rumors were leaked that the killer was Rolando (Rolly) Galman, an AWOL Manila-born police sergeant with a decidedly mean streak.

MEANWHILE, Benigno Aquino was displayed, gruesomely, in an open, glass covered coffin at the Aquino home in a Manila suburb. He had been embalmed, but no effort was made to disguise the bullet wound that horribly disfigured his face. During three days 30,000 mourners filed past the coffin, and when the funeral cortege wound slowly through the streets on its 10-hour trip from the Quezon City church of Santo Domingo to the Manila Memorial Park cemetery, over a million more accompanied it, shouting "Ninoy! Ninoy!" and "*Democrasya, Kalayaan, Himagsikan!* (Democracy, Freedom, Revolution)."

The funeral service had been, at the request of the Aquino family, small and quiet. Despite the Philippine foreign office's disapproval, officials from Japan, Canada, Australia, and the European Community attended, along with U.S. ambassador Michael Armacost. No one from the Marcos regime was there, and no high-level representative was sent from the United States, despite the fact that Oregon Senator Mark Hatfield was in the capital, and dined with Marcos that evening. Young Filipinos, banging pots and pans, gathered outside the presidential palace, shouting *"Laban* (fight)!" Marcos identified them as "local communists."

IT WAS obvious to the world and the people of the Philippines that a cover-up was occurring. The questions multiplied; How could this deranged police sergeant pierce the security net thrown around the airport? How did he know that Aquino would be descending the stairs at the rear of the plane, rather than exiting through the passenger tube? And most importantly, how could he have shot Aquino from the front, when the body lying in state clearly showed that the fatal bullet had entered from the *rear* of his head?

Finally, acceding to international pressure, Marcos convened an investigatory panel, which submitted its report 14 months later. The document was grim and revealing, suggesting indictments for 25 military personnel and one civilian. The 457-page narrative described businessman Hermilio Gosuico and Colonel Arturo Custodio had set Galman up. As for Aquino: he was, the report affirmed, shot from behind by the security guards escorting him from the airplane.

The planning of the operation, according to the panel, was done at the highest echelons of the military, commanded by Marcos's cousin, former personal chauffeur, closest confidant, and armed forces chief of staff General Fabian Ver. In close alliance was the entire AVESCOM, commanded by Brigadier General Luther Custodio.

MARCOS disavowed both knowledge and complicity. At first, he attempted to protect his cousin, General Ver, then announced that Ver and General Luther Custodio would be granted an "indefinite leave" while an investigation of military involvement in the assassination was conducted.

The trial began, and in its earliest stages, it was apparent that it would be rigged in favor of the defendants. Rebecca Quijano, a witness for the prosecution, who testified that she saw a military man shoot Aquino from behind was called a perjurer and mentally unstable by Marcos. The Philippine Supreme Court allowed the withholding of evidence by the military. On December 21, 1985, a three-judge court acquitted all 26 defendants, and Marcos immediately reinstated his generals.

An early election was called for February, 1986, and Benigno Aquino's widow Corazon announced that she would oppose Marcos, win, and put the president on trial for the murder of her husband.

It was apparently clear to all of the world except President Ronald Reagan and C.I.A. chief William Casey that the chain of command in the assassination of Aquino ended with Ferdinand Marcos. Both men continued to stubbornly support the Philippine president even after it became clear that the February election was blatantly stolen by Marcos. Members of the U.S. congress affirmed the ballot larceny, and television cameras recorded the bodies of murdered Aquino campaign workers.

"Stop bellyaching," Reverand Jerry Falwell of the Moral Majority chided members of Congress. "Filipinos get good benefits from the Marcos family." Citing the importance of Marcos's support of U.S. military bases in the Philippines and his staunch anticommunist stand, Reagan and Casey tried to shore up the dictator parading as president. But rapidly unfolding events in the Philippines—the surging public support for Corazon Aquino, the defection of parts of the Philippine military, the appearance of "People Power", which consisted of Philippine citizens willing to kneel in front of Marcos's tanks in order to protect pro-Aquino military units, and the daily emergence of evidence undeniably linking Marcos to the assassination, finally caused the Reagan administration to acknowledge reality in the Philippines.

DEPRIVED of U.S. support and facing a revolution, Ferdinand Marcos was deposed on February 25, 1986, and fled, with Imelda and General Fabian Ver, to exile in Hawaii. Mrs. Aquino ascended to the presidency of the Philippines.

The Philippine Supreme Court now overturned the acquittals of those charged in the assassination, and ordered a new trial. On September 28, 1990, General Luther Custodio and 15 other defendants were sentenced to life in prison.

The presidency of Corazon Aquino would not be an easy one. She would face a constitutional crisis, a military takeover, terrible economic and political problems, and eventually lose her popularity. But it would be through a democratic process, not through official terrorism and assassination.

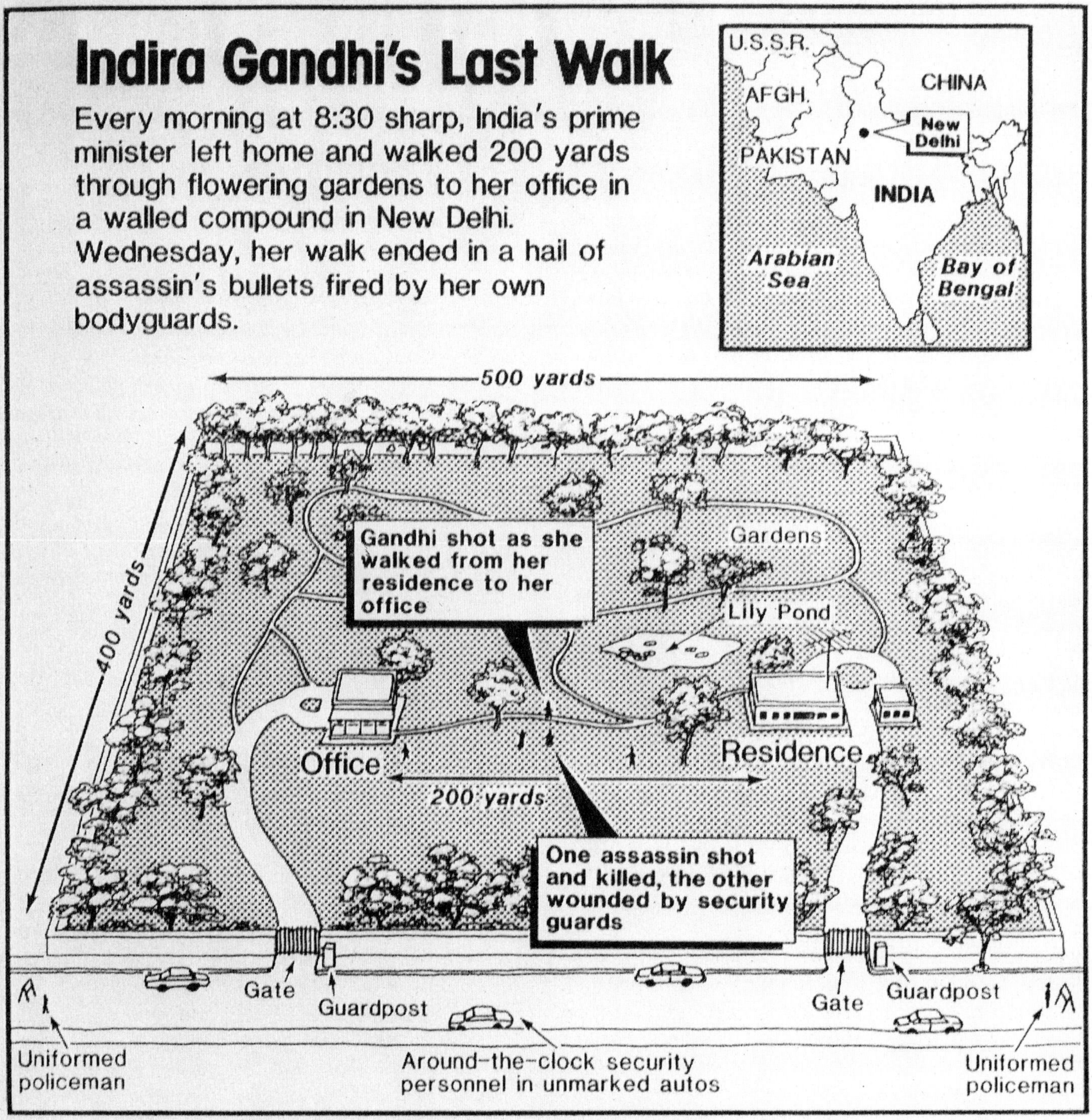

Indira Gandhi's Last Walk
Every morning at 8:30 sharp, India's prime minister left home and walked 200 yards through flowering gardens to her office in a walled compound in New Delhi. Wednesday, her walk ended in a hail of assassin's bullets fired by her own bodyguards.
U.S.S.R.
AFGH.
CHINA
New Delhi
PAKISTAN
INDIA
Arabian Sea
Bay of Bengal
500 yards
400 yards
Gardens
Gandhi shot as she walked from her residence to her office
Lily Pond
Office
Residence
200 yards
One assassin shot and killed, the other wounded by security guards
Gate
Guardpost
Gate
Guardpost
Uniformed policeman
Around-the-clock security personnel in unmarked autos
Uniformed policeman

LUP/WAP103134-10/31/84-NEW DELHI: Indian Prime Minister Indira Gandhi was assassinated 10/31 while walking from her residence to her office. She was killed by two Sikh members of her own security force. This UPI graphic illustrates the scene. UPI par/gude

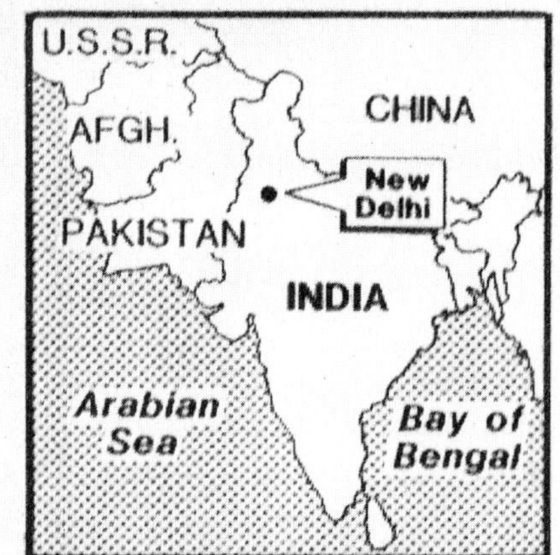

INDIRA AND RAJIV GANDHI

POSITIONS:	*Prime Ministers of India*
DATES:	*October 31, 1984; May 21, 1991*
PLACE:	*New Delhi, India;Sriperumbudur, India*
HOW:	*Gunshot; bomb*
WHO:	*Sikh militants; Tamil militants*
MOTIVE:	*Revenge*
CONVICTED:	*Satwant Singh; others died violently*
DIRECT CONSEQUENCE:	*End of Nehru-Gandhi "dynasty"*

THERE IS no country in the world whose image tends more toward the spiritual than India. Its mosques and temples are the signatures of both urban and rural landscapes. Mohandas Gandhi, the greatest spiritual leader of the 20th century and a man who gave force and strategy to civil rights movements around the world was both a product and a symbol of India. Its exportation of self-realization through meditation and spiritual practice has calmed governments, minds, and the terminally ill.

And yet, the very abundance and dedication of this subcontinent's many religious sects and ethnic entities have also contributed to the dark side of its image: that of a country riven with fervent, ethnically and religiously rooted violence. The intensity and worldly demands of its Muslims, Sikhs, Hindus, and other religious sects and its ethnic rivalries have brought about staggering clashes that have left ten of thousands dead in the five decades since India acquired its independence from Great Britain. And nowhere has this violence seemed more dramatic than in its three major assassinations: Mohandas Gandhi's death at the hands of a Hindu extremist in 1948, Indira Gandhi's death at the hands of her Sikh bodyguards in 1984, and her son Rajiv Gandhi's murder by a suicidal Sri Lankan fanatic in 1991.

BORN IN 1917 in Allahabad, India, educated at Swiss and English schools and at Somerville College, Oxford, where she became a member of the youth wing of the British Labor party, Indira Gandhi was the daughter of Jawaharlal Nehru, India's first prime minister. She joined the Indian Congress in 1939, and, like Mohandas Gandhi, spent time in prison during the threat of a Japanese invasion of India.

In 1942, she defied her family and married Feroze Gandhi, a Parsi (she was a Hindu). Gandhi, who was not related to the revered Mahatma, was a journalist who became a member of Parliament, fathered two sons, and died in 1960. Before that time, their marriage had foundered on the rocks of the demands of Indira's father, who insisted that his daughter take over the state duties that his wife, now dead, would have assumed.

In 1966, Lal Bahadur Shastri, Nehru's successor, abruptly died, and the Congress party, thinking Indira Gandhi would submit meekly to their directives, appointed her prime minister. Out of the shadow of her father, she became anything but meek. Like Mohandas Gandhi, she had a vision of a united India, and this she pursued with a single-minded force that swept away both dissent and opposition, often unceremoniously. In 1971, she called a general election a year ahead of schedule, and, campaigning on a slogan of *garibi hatao*—abolish poverty—she won the mandate of an enormous majority.

In December of that same year, India intervened in the East Pakistan-Pakistan secession conflict, and brought the war to an end and Bangladesh into being. It was a triumph for Mrs. Gandhi, not only as a military victory but as the first tangible affirmation of the possibility of peace between Pakistan and India.

MUCH of this image and triumph was swept away, however, in the scandal that erupted in 1975. A high court in Allahabad found that the election of 1971 had been riddled with fraud and malfeasance. Mrs. Gandhi should have stepped down, but by then, her dreams of a Nehru dynasty had begun to take root. She was already grooming her ambitious youngest son Sanjay to take her place.

Late City Edition

Registered No D-(c) 167

AIR SURCHARGE Udaipur, Jodhpur, Patna, Ranchi and beyond by rail: 5 paise
Kathmandu, Calcutta and beyond by airlift: 10 paise

THE HINDUSTAN TIMES

Vol LXI No 302 New Delhi Thursday November 1 1984 16 Pages Eighty Paise

INDIRA GANDHI SHOT DEAD

'Need for calm in hour of crisis'

Hindustan Times Correspondent

NEW DELHI, Oct. 31 — Prime Minister Rajiv Gandhi today called upon the nation to exercise calm and restraint in this hour of crisis and moment of profound grief.

Referring to incidents of violence in various parts of the country in his broadcast to the nation at midnight, he said, "nothing would hurt the soul of our beloved Indira Gandhi more than occurrence of violence in any part of the country."

"It was of utmost importance," he said, that "every step that we take is in the correct direction."

In a poignant reference to his mother who was brutally assassinated this morning, he said, "Indira Gandhi is no more. But her soul lives".

He sought the support and co-

Continued on back page col 1

The body of Indira Gandhi on a gun carriage outside the All-India Institute of Medical Sciences on Wednesday before being taken to 1, Safdarjung Road.—S. N. Sinha

World leaders condemn outrage

UNDATED, Oct 31 (AP, PTI, UNI)—Western and Third world leaders joined in condemning the assassination of Prime Minister Indira Gandhi today and mourned her as a courageous leader of India and the Non-Aligned Movement.

Tass called the shooting "villainous". China's Communist Government said it was "shocked".

Soviet President and party chief Konstantin Chernenko said "the name of Indira Gandhi will remain forever in the grateful memory of the Soviet people".

In a telegram to Mr Rajiv Gandhi, Mr Chernenko as general secretary of the Communist Party of the Soviet Union recalled that

Continued on page 4

Funeral fixed for Saturday; 12-day mourning

Attack near house by two security guards

Rajiv Gandhi sworn in PM

Hindustan Times Correspondent

NEW DELHI, Oct. 31–Prime Minister Indira Gandhi, who steered the nation for 15 daunting and often turbulent years to bring India on the threshold of greatness, was assassinated this morning on the lawns of her residence here by two of her security guards.

Both the assailants were shot at by the other security guards in the Prime Minister's house. One of them, sub-inspector Beant Singh, died on the spot while the other, constable Satwant Singh, is reported to be serious in hospital. Beant Singh had been on security duty at the Prime Minister's house for eight years.

A pall of gloom spread over the country as reports came that doctors at the All-India Institute of Medical Sciences were waging a desperate but losing battle to save Mrs Gandhi's life. The Prime Minister, who received 16 bullets from an automatic gun and a pistol at point-blank range around 9-15 a.m., passed away at 2-30 p.m.

Within hours of her passing away, Mr Rajiv Gandhi was sworn in by President Zail Singh as the new Prime Minister. The President advanced his schedule of a three-nation tour to return to the country on learning of the assassination attempt on Mrs Gandhi.

Mr Rajiv Gandhi also rushed back to the Capital from West Bengal. Finance Minister Pranab Mukherjee and Railway Minister Ghani Khan Chaudhury also were away in Calcutta and Home Minister P. V. Narasimha Rao was in Andhra Pradesh. They all flew back to the Capital, and Defence Minister S. B. Chavan was on his way back from Moscow.

Mrs Gandhi's body, draped in tricolour, was taken from the hospital to her residence at 1, Safdarjung Road at 9.30 p.m. The body on a gun carriage will lie in state at the Teen Murti House where her father Jawaharlal Nehru lived as Prime Minister. The funeral takes place on Saturday.

State mourning will be observed throughout the country for 12 days (upto Nov. 11), it was officially announced here tonight.

Central Government offices all over the country will remain closed tomorrow.

During the period of mourning, the national flag will be flown at half-mast throughout the country, and there will be no official entertainments.

A black-bordered extraordinary gazette notification was issued this evening announcing the sad demise of the Prime Minister. Signed by the Home Secretary, the gazette notification said the "Government of India announced with most profound regret the death of

End Of An Era—See Edit.

Shrimati Indira Gandhi, Prime Minister of India, at New Delhi, on 31st October, 1984."

Indira Priyadarshini Gandhi, who would have been 67 on Nov. 19, and who was described by Sarojini Naidu at her birth as a "new star on India's horizon", was resplendent in a saffron saree when the assassins struck. She was getting ready for a session with an Irish Television team led by the renowned British actor, Peter Ustinov. Mr Ustinov, who had accompanied Mrs Gandhi on her tour of Orisa from where she returned last night, told a news agency that the TV camera could take shots of the Prime Minister when she lay in a pool of blood.

Around 9 a.m., word was sent to her at the Safdarjung Road bungalow that the TV team was ready for filming. Mrs Gandhi came out and walked towards the lawns of the adjoining 1, Akbar Road bungalow forming part of the Prime Minister's house complex. Near the gate that led to the Akbar Road bungalow, the two assailants shot at her. There were no family members with the Prime Minister. As she slumped on the lawns, other security guards fired at the assailants.

Mr H. Y. Sharada Prasad, Information Adviser to the Prime Minister, who was waiting with the television team, told newsmen he heard the shots and ran towards the direction from where the sound came. The Akbar Road bungalow presented a direct view, and as he reached the spot he found the Prime Minister being attended to by the security staff.

Mrs Sonia Gandhi with some relatives rushed out of her house amidst a loud shriek. Behind Mrs Gandhi were her Special Assistant, Mr R. K. Dhawan, and Mr D. K. Bhatt, Assistant Commissioner of Police, Special Security Zone.

Mrs Gandhi was helped into an ambassador car and rushed to the All-India Institute of Medical Sciences at 9.30 p.m. Dr A. N. Safaya, Medical Superintendent of AIIMS, said that Mrs Gandhi was alive when she was brought to the emergency ward. A team of doctors headed by Prof Venugopal attended on her. The 16 bullets

Continued on back page col 2

Cremation near Shantivana

Hindustan Times Correspondent

NEW DELHI, Oct. 31 — The funeral of Mrs Indira Gandhi will take place on Saturday at 4-30 p.m.

This was announced here today by Mr H. Y. Sharada Prasad, Information Adviser to the Prime Minister. He said that her body will lie in state at Teen Murti House from tomorrow at 7 a.m. to enable the public to have a last glimpse of their beloved leader.

She will be cremated near Shanti Vana, which was the last resting place of her father late Jawaharlal Nehru and her younger son late Sanjay Gandhi.

He said that our embassies abroad have been informed and they expect large number of leaders of different countries to come here to attend the funeral.

UNI, PTI add:

One full brigade of the Indian Army consisting of 3,000 men and another 1,000 personnel from the Navy and the Air Force have been 'moved' to line up the route of Mrs Indira Gandhi's funeral from Teen Murti House to a place near Shantivana.

The Chiefs of Staff of the Army, Navy and Air Force will act as pall bearers. The general officer, commanding, of the Delhi area will lead the funeral march.

The Indian VIPs and foreign dignitaries will follow the gun carriage in which Mrs Gandhi's body draped in the national tricolour will be taken in procession.

Senior officers of the armed forces will maintain a continuous vigil over the body of late Prime Minister which will lie in State at Teen Murti House. The three chief of staffs will be the first to stand on vigil.

All Central Government offices throughout the country would be closed tomorrow and on Nov. 3, the day of the funeral.

Premonition of death

NEW DELHI, Oct. 31 (PTI) —Prime Minister Indira Gandhi seemed to have had a premonition about this morning's attempt on her life.

Addressing a mammoth public meeting to round off her [illegible] tour of Orissa, Mrs [illegible] in an emotional tone last night said that even if she died in the service of the nation, she would be proud of it. "Every drop of my blood, I am sure, will contribute to the growth of this nation and to make it strong and dynamic."

Members of her Party were surprised over Mrs Gandhi's statement. One of the members remarked to a correspondent travelling with her: "Where is the need for her to talk about blood?"

'Crime against humanity'

Hindustan Times Correspondent

NEW DELHI, Oct. 31 — President Zail Singh today appealed to the nation to demonstrate to the world that India's stability cannot be jeopardised by a handful of "sub-human assassins".

In a broadcast over All India Radio, he said, "the dastardly act of assassins which is not only heinous but a crime against humanity itself, has put the nation to test at an extremely critical juncture of our history."

Mr Zail Singh said the unity and integrity of the nation was being challenged. "Let our grief not cloud our good sense and maturity, both as individuals and a nation". A grief-stricken President said and prayed "God shall grant us the strength to meet the new challenges".

"Let us rally behind the ideals we have inherited from our forefathers."

Mr Zail Singh said "on this the saddest day of my life, I speak to you when I am totally overtaken by the dark cloud of cruel fate. Our beloved, Mrs Indira Gandhi is no longer with us. I have lost my

Continued on back page col 4

Army moves into riot-hit Delhi

Hindustan Times Correspondent

NEW DELHI, Oct. 31 — Three columns of the Border Security Force marched through the congested walled city areas late tonight as frenzied crowds rampaged and looted shops and houses, burnt down vehicles and beat up members of a particular community in the Capital following Mrs Gandhi's assassination. Army units also started moving into Capital tonight.

The Capital's streets were ablaze with a large number of scooters, cars, buses and trucks as the irate public vented its venom by setting them on fire. Though the police officially denied any casualty, unconfirmed reports said a few persons were killed and scores of others injured in the violence.

Units of the Central Reserve Police Force and the BSF were deployed after the local police found it impossible to control the mob. The riots which began in the South Delhi areas in the evening spread to more areas by late tonight.

With the situation showing no signs of abating, the Delhi Administration has requisitioned additional para-military forces. Till the time of going to Press, reports about arson and violence continued to pour in from all parts of the city.

A high-level meeting of Lt.-Governor P. G. Gavai with the Police Commissioner, the Chief Secretary and other top functionaries of the administration was held at the police headquarters tonight in which the situation was reviewed.

Despite promulgation of prohibitory orders throughout the Union Territory, youths wielding iron rods, lathis and other weapons took to the streets, blocked traffic, looted and burnt shops.

The public transport was paralysed and most taxis and autorickshaws went off the roads. Throngs forced to walk back added to the strength of the marauders who were disrupting traffic and indulging in violence, a scale on which the Capital had not witnessed before in recent memory.

In South Delhi, the mob fury was at its worst. A number of shops in the posh South Extension market were gutted and many houses were attacked by about 100 men. Vehicles were still smouldering and shops with their shutters broken open were seen being looted when this correspondent went around the city late tonight.

Earlier, people were taken out of buses and beaten up. Those who managed to escape were chased in lanes and bylanes. Police were hardly to be seen most of the time.

In Sadar Bazar, trucks and scooters were burnt in an uncontrolled mob frenzy. At the IIT crossing, violence continued unabated for a long time. Large crowds had gathered outside the Yusuf Sarai market checking the inmates of private vehicles. A number of scooters and motorbikes could be seen smouldering nearby.

At the Badarpur border, a number of trucks were set on fire and the hysterical mobs went unchecked attacking anything coming their way.

Fire-Brigade personnel were attacked at a number of places and prevented from reaching their destinations. Two firemen of the Mathura Road fire station and three of the Safdarjung fire station were injured. A spokesman of the Fire-Brigade said that most of their tenders were blocked at the Defence Colony flyover.

Maximum distress calls were received from South Extension Parts I and II, Defence Colony, Yusuf Sarai and Safdarjung. Incidents were also reported from Munirka, Maharani Bagh, Yamunagiri, Sadar Bazar, Panchkuin Road and many other areas.

In Vasant Vihar, a group of labourers belonging to one community were bashed up. They ran for shelter to nearby houses.

The heavily outnumbered police forces were powerless to cope with the situation. The mob, wrecking havoc everywhere, would retreat when the policemen advanced and return when they withdrew.

At the Prithviraj-South End Road crossing, however, police were able to intervene effectively. There, members of a community travelling in a DTC bus were being beaten up mercilessly. The po-

Continued on back page col 5

Solemn ceremony at Rashtrapati Bhavan

Hindustan Times Correspondent

NEW DELHI, Oct. 31 — Rajiv Gandhi, the 40-year-old pilot-turned-politician, was sworn in as Prime Minister by President Zail Singh at a brief and solemn ceremony at the Ashoka Hall of the Rashtrapati Bhavan.

Also sworn in was a small team of four Ministers, Mr Pranab Kumar Mukherjee, Mr P. V. Narasimha Rao, Mr P. Shiv Shanker and Mr Buta Singh, all Ministers in Mrs Gandhi's Cabinet.

Practically the entire Council of Ministers of the deceased Prime Minister, Mrs Indira Gandhi, several State Governors, members of Parliament, Chief Ministers, political personalities and officials attended the ceremony.

More Ministers would be sworn in later, it was officially announced later.

As soon as President Zail Singh arrived at Rashtrapati Bhavan, he was given a letter on behalf of the Congress-I Parliamentary Board conveying its choice of the new leader.

The Board members, Mr Pranab Mukherjee, Mr Narasimha Rao, Mr G. K. Moopanar, Mr Sitaram Kesari arrived together at the Rashtrapati Bhavan, 45 minutes before the President reached.

At the end of the ceremony, President Zail Singh came up to Mr Gandhi, hugged him and spoke to him with his right arm around the shoulders.

A calm and composed Mr Gandhi, his eyes blood-shot and his voice low, told newsmen he would like to "do some work first". He would like to meet the media only later.

"What is your immediate programme?"

"The immediate thing is to hold the first Cabinet meeting," he re-

Continued on page 7

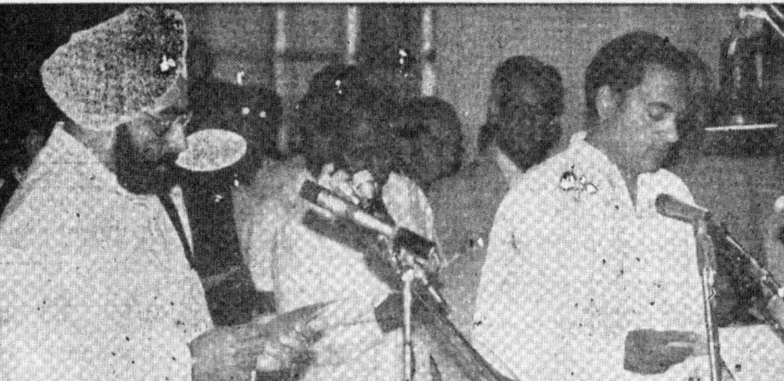

Mr Rajiv Gandhi being sworn in Prime Minister by President Zail Singh at Rashtrapati Bhavan on Wednesday.

Violence erupts in many States

Hindustan Times Correspondent

NEW DELHI, Oct. 31 — About 100 people were injured in violence across the country as news of Mrs Indira Gandhi's assassination spread today.

Curfew was imposed in Jabalpur, Jammu and Agartala as a precautionary measure following reports of tension and violence.

Police reinforcements were rushed to Kanpur where three places of worship and more than 20 business and residential premises were set afire.

Army was called out to help the civil authorities following sporadic violence in South Calcutta tonight.

Incidents of violence were reported from parts of Tripura, Bihar, Orissa, West Bengal, Uttar Pradesh, Jammu and Kashmir and Madhya Pradesh.

Mr Benoy Choudhury, West Bengal Minister for Land and Land Revenue, told reporters in Calcutta after a Cabinet meeting that one person belonging to a particular community was stabbed near the Commercial Tax offices at Beliaghata. He added that several other incidents took place in the city during the day involving the community.

Mr Choudhury said that eight buses were set on fire by miscreants during the day — of which five were gutted. When reporters pointed out that the public transport system had virtually collapsed since early afternoon putting commuters to great hardship he maintained that the police were taking steps to restore the system. He denied that Government buses and trams had been taken off the roads.

As darkness fell, Calcutta was virtually deserted. There were few traffic policemen around and fewer vehicles. Trams and buses had been withdrawn in early afternoon. Office-goers and others were seen walking home.

Suburban train services also came to a halt in both the Howrah and Sealdah sections of the Eastern and South-Eastern Railways, putting thousands of commuters to great hardship. Mr Choudhury said in the evening that efforts were be-

Continued on page 13

And so, instead of stepping aside, Mrs. Gandhi declared a national emergency, jailed thousands of her political opponents, suspended civil liberties, censored the press, and established, for all intents and purposes, a dictatorship. For two years, she ruled under these circumstances, and then, in 1977, called another general election, fully confident that she would be reelected.

Her excessive usurpation of power, however, was her undoing, and this, coupled with accusations of corruption and the institution of a program of coercive population control by her son Sanjay lost her the election by a huge majority. The Jananta party, under Morarji Desai and Charan Singh, abolished the state of emergency and attempted to rule.

Their three years of office were a dismal failure, and in 1980, Mrs. Gandhi ran again and was swept back into office. Once more, she governed from a position of strength, balancing the two superpowers—the U.S. and the U.S.S.R.—off against each other, ascending to the chairmanship of the 101-member group of non-aligned nations.

BUT AT home, all was anything but sanguine and safe. In 1980, the year Mrs Gandhi returned to power, Sanjay, the extrovert to his brother Rajiv, took up a plane he was unqualified to fly, attempted a stunt too close to the ground, and crashed to a fiery death. It was both a personal tragedy and the darkening of a dream for Mrs. Gandhi. Rajiv, a pilot for Air India, had no aspirations whatsoever for high public office. Sanjay's widow Maneka, however, did, and, never a fan of her mother-in-law, she formed an opposition political party. Her efforts failed, as did Rajiv's pleas to remain out of politics. In June, 1981, he was elected to his brother's vacant seat in Parliament and Sanjay's place on the executive committee of the party's youth wing.

Meanwhile, separatist movements began to gain strength within India, particularly in Assam, Tamil Nadum, and the Punjab, where the Sikh separatist movement was particularly demonstrative. Mrs. Gandhi attempted to co-opt moderate Sikh leadership, but her attempts failed.

Sikh extremists were in control, and they escalated their demands for Sikh statehood. Thousands of them occupied the Golden Temple at Amritsar, their holiest shrine and the symbol of their identity.

The standoff remained charged but stable; and then, Mrs. Gandhi made a puzzling and fatal move. She sent troops to Amritsar, to clean out the Golden Temple. Over 600 Sikhs were killed, including their radical leader, Sant Jarnail Singh Bhindranwale, and over a thousand more were wounded. She may have won the battle and the moment, but its repercussions would lead directly to her death.

If she had had as much a sense of history as she did of destiny, Indira Gandhi would never have attacked the Golden Temple of Amritsar. It had been the scene of the Indian Mutiny of 1857, a bloody scene that was the forerunner of the pivotal Amritsar Massacre of April 13, 1919, when brigadier general R.E.H. Dyer murdered 379 unarmed Indians and wounded 1,200 others. His move, seen from the perspective of history, was the final nail driven into the coffin of British rule in India, and Indira Gandhi's decision to send troops to Amritsar sealed her own personal fate.

Seething Sikh resentment turned homicidal. Sensing this, her advisers set about purging her security forces of Sikhs. She stopped them. "How can we claim to be secular?" she wrote to the director of India's central intelligence organization. And so, some of her personal guards, who were Sikhs, were allowed to remain at their posts. Two of them, Beant Singh and Satwant Singh, were in her inner circle, and stationed within her compound, at the head of the gravel path that led from her living quarters, through a garden full of lovely aromas and melodic birdsong, past a hedge, and to her offices.

ON TUESDAY, October 30, 1984, Indira Gandhi seemed to experience one of those revealing epiphanies practically every assassinated leader from Julius Caesar to Dr. Martin Luther King has undergone. Addressing a crowd in Bhubaneswar, Orissa's capital city, she said, "I am not interested in a long life. I am not afraid of these things. I don't mind if my life goes in the service of this nation. If I die today, every drop of my blood will invigorate the nation."

She had been involved in a series of television interviews with British actor Peter Ustinov, and at 9 o'clock in the morning on Wednesday, October 31, she left her living quarters and began the short trip on the gravel path to join Ustinov and his camera crew on the other side of the hedge, near her offices.

It was a beautiful autumn morning, and Mrs. Gandhi was in a buoyant mood. Her security guards walked behind her; ahead of her, at the entrance to the hedge, her two Sikh guards stood at attention. She had known one of them, Beant Singh, for 10 years; he was one of her favorite and most trusted guards, and she tented her hands in the traditional Indian manner, smiled, bowed slightly to both of them, and said "*Nameste*." Greetings, it meant, and she fully expected a returned pleasantry.

Instead, Beant Singh drew a .38 revolver, and, from a distance of no more than several feet, fired three shots into Mrs. Gandhi's abdomen. She crumpled to the walk, but her body had scarcely touched the gravel when Satwant Singh pulled the Sten automatic weapon from his shoulder and pumped its entire 30 rounds into the prostrate leader. At least seven bullets penetrated her abdomen, three her chest, and one her heart. She was dead.

The two calmly dropped their weapons as the horrified security detail rushed forward, guns drawn, and seized them. "I've done what I had to do. You do what you want to do," said Beant Singh, and he and his accomplice were surrounded and rushed to the guardhouse on the other side of the hedge.

As the security guards began to open the guardhouse door, Beant Singh suddenly lunged desperately for the sten gun of the guard nearest to him. The others opened fire and both Sikhs fell, riddled with bullets. Beant was killed instantly. Satwant was critically wounded, and told doctors that he was a member of a conspiracy that had set out to kill both Indira Gandhi and her son Rajiv.

Meanwhile, Rajiv's wife Sonia, hearing the shots, ran from her upstairs quarters to the scene. Guards and Mrs. Gandhi's assistant, R. K. Dhawan, carried Mrs. Gandhi's blood-soaked body to her white limousine. There, Sonia cradled the dead prime minister's head in her lap while the limousine sped to the All-India Institute of Medical Sciences hospital.

Still showing no life signs whatsoever, Mrs. Gandhi was taken to the eighth-floor operating room, where 12 doctors desperately tried to bring her back to life. They removed seven bullets, put her on an artificial respirator, gave her 88 bottles of blood. "They could not believe she was dead," a young doctor later told reporters. "They would not accept that she was gone." It would be 1:45 in the afternoon before the official announcement was made, and it would be another hour before Rajiv, returning from Calcutta on an airliner, was told that his mother was dead.

UNPRECEDENTED SECURITY guarded Rajiv as he joined his family; within 12 hours, the elders of the Congress I (I for Indira) party chose him as their leader, which automatically made him India's seventh prime minister. He was the third member of the Nehru family to assume that post.

Not long before the assassination, Rajiv was asked by Western journalists if he missed his life as a pilot. "I sometimes get into the cockpit all alone and close the door," he had answered, "Even if I cannot fly, at least I can temporarily shut myself off from the outside world."

That possibility had now abruptly and viciously been rendered untenable. As plans were made to cremate the body of Indira Gandhi on the banks of the Jamuna river, where Mohandas Gandhi, Jawaharlal Nehru and Shastri Gandhi had been given over to funeral pyres, India became silent, then erupted in renewed violence.

Sikh communities, both in the Punjab and overseas, reacted jubilantly to reports of the assassination, though Sikh priests in the Golden Temple expressed shock and "deep grief," and 24 hours after the murder, fires burned all over India, as Hindus gutted Sikh communities and neighborhoods. "I want to kill Sikhs. I want to see Sikh blood on the streets," shouted one weapon-brandishing Hindu to a Western television reporter; 94 Sikhs were stabbed or beaten to death in a New Delhi neighborhood; 56 were killed aboard trains running through the Punjab. By the end of the week, the nationwide death toll topped 1,000. By the time the violence of vengeance had spent itself, over 3,000 Sikhs would die.

Not only this. A few short days before the assassination, India paramilitary forces had arrested a Sikh hit team within the Punjab. The team's mission: to assassinate Mrs. Gandhi. In their possession were arms, ammunition, and passports supplied by the Pakistani intelligence service. Pakistan officially denied complicity, but in January, 1989, at the end of the four-year trial that convicted and executed Satwant Singh and a third Sikh, government clerk Kehar Singh, evidence emerged that linked not only Mrs. Gandhi's closest aide,

India's largest selling daily newspaper

ESTABLISHED 1838

Stay secure with the Leader

THE TIMES OF INDIA

VOL. CLIV NO. 122 BOMBAY: WEDNESDAY, MAY 22, 1991 Rs. 2.00 28 PAGES

RAJIV GANDHI ASSASSINATED

A Lethal Tragedy

Lethal tragedy has struck India for the third time since Independence. Rajiv Gandhi, like Mahatma Gandhi and Indira Gandhi before him, has fallen victim to forces which did not believe in what he, like them, stood for: a strong, united, democratic India. His assassins chose both their moment and their target well. The country had just completed the first phase of a general election. Another phase was about to start. The brief interval between the election days seemed ideal to deal the devastating blow. The assassins meant to send a clear signal to the country that the verdict of the people was not their concern; the democratic process itself came between them and whatever goal they sought to realize. There can be no doubt that the prevailing climate emboldened them to commit the dastardly deed. At no time since it won freedom has India been as polarised along antagonistic lines as it is today. Caste has been pitted against caste and religion against religion with relentless fury. It has appeared as if the nation had taken leave of its reason. Those who preached unity and harmony were suspect; those who spoke for stability and progress were dubbed as renegades; those who counselled patience, circumspection and harmony invited ridicule.

Rajiv Gandhi did precisely that. His vision of India contrasted sharply with what his political rivals had to offer. Where others sought to recast Indian nationalism in a narrow religious mould, he, on the contrary, championed the cause of a secular order: one where the state would respect all faiths, where no one would sense fear or insecurity on account of his or her religious appurtenance. Similarly, where others, in the name of social justice, unleashed the demons of casteism, he sought to strike a balance between the public good as a whole and the good of sections of our population which, on account of their birth, suffered deprivation and indignity. This middle path may not have elicited the prompt applause of a crowd which had been made to drink the heady wine of bigotry and hatred; it may have invited only sneers from an intelligentsia which draws sustenance from radical sloganeering; it may have lacked the attractiveness of slogans that exploit atavistic passion. All the same, Rajiv Gandhi stuck firmly to this path in the belief that the people of India possess the uncanny ability to eschew extremes, to pull the nation back from the brink of the precipice. In a sense he owed his office when he first became Prime Minister to this belief: despite the brief but terrible anti-Sikh riots following his mother's [illegible] its reflexes.

His is the need of the hour. At the time of writing these lines no one quite knows who is behind the murder of Rajiv Gandhi. It is imperative that rumours are given a short shrift. All political parties owe it to the nation to make common cause to ensure that no section of our people is made the target of vengeance. No effort should be spared to quell a flame the moment it is lit.

All of us recognise that this is no easy task. The country is virtually without a government. Secessionist and terrorist forces in three of our states are on a rampage. India's neighbourhood is not entirely congenial: certain elements hostile to this country are bound to feel that their hour has struck. There is therefore every reason for our political class, our social and religious organisations, our armed forces and our people as a whole to rally together to ensure that our nation does not lose its nerve. The election process must continue if only as a tribute to Rajiv Gandhi's commitment to the democratic order. In the next few hours the Congress will be called upon to elect another leader. It must choose, as it surely will, a person who embodies the values that Rajiv Gandhi cherished: freedom and dignity for the individual and strength and progress for the nation. The most effective riposte to Rajiv Gandhi's assassins will indeed be this: that India strengthens its democratic institutions, reinforces its democratic temper, seeks to harmonise the diverse and even divergent interests of its people and steps into the next century with pride in her millenary culture and with hope in the well-being of all its citizens. It is in a moment of distress that a nation displays its virtues. This moment is now upon us. Our virtues of resilience, of grace under pressure, of courage under tragedy, of hope in the midst of gloom, of compassion in the face of evil must be summoned to enable us to move on, to conquer the forces that took Rajiv Gandhi away from us in the prime of his youth, to rededicate ourselves to the creation of an India free of ignorance, superstition, hatred and bigotry.

20 others dead in blast ★ Sonia, children are safe

By PUSHPA IYENGAR
The Times of India News Service

SRIPERUMPUDUR (near Madras), May 21.

THE former prime minister and Congress president, Mr Rajiv Gandhi, was killed at 10.20 p.m. today in a bomb blast that claimed at least 20 other lives.

Mr Gandhi, who was to address a campaign rally at this town, 40 km from Madras, was nearing the dais when the powerful blast occurred killing him instantly. The massive crowd that had collected for the meeting was stunned by the deafening explosion that caused a crater about a meter wide. A burst of fire crackers that was set off to greet Mr Gandhi on his arrival was completely lost in the blast.

Initial reports had put the number of deaths at five. Two securitymen and the DSP (Chengulpatt East) were among the dead. Among the seriously injured are the Sriperumpudur congress candidate, Mrs Maragatam Chandrasekhar, Mr Gandhi's press secretary, Mr Suman Dubey, and the Congress M.P., Ms Jayanti Natarajan.

Accompanying Mr Rajiv Gandhi's party in the press van, all that this correspondent could see was a cloud of smoke and flying fragments of bodies as the bomb went off. The blast set off a panic among the mammoth crowd, which began to run helter skelter, causing a near stampede. The area around the blast site was immediately cordoned off by the police and the injured were removed to the hospital.

PTI & UNI add:

Mr Gandhi was jostling with partymen and admirers at the venue when the explosion occurred. When police officials and party leaders, including Mr G. K. Moopanar, realised that the explosion had occurred, they found Mr Gandhi's body with his head severed.

On identifying Mr Gandhi's body, the Congressmen broke down even while they were in a state of tremendous shock.

Immediately after the explosion, people ran helter skelter. Chest-beating and wailing men shouted, "Rajiv enge, Rajiv enge" (where is Rajiv, where is Rajiv).

A PTI correspondent, barely 30 yards away from the explosion site, found Mr Gandhi's body lying his head smashed.

Several other bodies were lying nearby.

Dazed policemen were trying to bring about some semblance of order and control.

It took several minutes for the policemen to extricate Mr Gandhi's body from the pile of bodies at the spot.

Mr Gandhi's body has been brought to the government general hospital at Madras.

The Tamil Nadu police department, recovering from the shock of the explosion, has launched a full scale investigation and is combing for suspected militants.

The bomb was a remote controlled device, according to a first information report received by the police in Madras.

Police sources did not rule out the hand of Sri Lankan militant groups, especially the Liberation Tigers of Tamil Eelam.

The Prime Minister, Mr Chandra Shekhar, left Bhubaneshwar to return to New Delhi tonight, cutting short his election tour on hearing the news of the assassination of Mr Gandhi.

Nationwide alert

NEW DELHI, May 21: Police and para-military forces throughout the country were tonight put on full alert following the death of the Congress president, Mr Rajiv Gandhi, in a bomb explosion near Madras, reports PTI.

The cabinet secretary, Mr Naresh Chandra, held a high-level meeting with chiefs of security agencies, including the Intelligence Bureau, soon after receiving Mr Gandhi's death report.

The Delhi police has been put on extreme alert with police patrolling city streets.

Police personnel have fanned out into every nook and corner of the city to patrol sensitive areas.

Road-blocks have been set up at every three to five kms to check vehicles. People came out in the streets and were seen discussing the details of the assassination.

BHOPAL: The Madhya Pradesh police has also been placed on maximum alert.

The director-general of police, Mr R. P. Sharma, said that the district authorities in the state had been instructed to keep a close vigil over the situation.

CALCUTTA: The West Bengal government tonight put the entire state on alert, the chief secretary, Mr N. Krishnamurthy said.

JAIPUR: A red alert was sounded in Rajasthan too. The state chief minister, Mr Bhairon Singh Shekhawat, who received the news while he was on his way to Ajmer, cut short his journey and rushed back to Jaipur.

You said it

by Laxman

Stop acting silly! I have got to go and vote!

Shoot orders in Madras

The Times of India News Service

MADRAS, May 21: Sporadic violence broke out in the city and its ourskirts little after midnight in the wake of the killing of Mr Rajiv Gandhi. A bank at Ayanapuram was looted and passing vehicles were stoned by irate mobs.

Shoot-at-sight orders have been issued by the authorities and the state government has withdrawn all roadway buses with immediate effect.

Violence in Kerala

The Times of India News Service

THIRUVANANTHAPURAM, May 21: Sporadic violence erupted in this city immediately after the news of Mr Rajiv Gandhi's assassination was broken.

In some areas, street lights were broken. The police were caught napping. The chief minister, Mr E. K. Nayanar, and the opposition leader, Mr K. Karunakaran, were in Kasargod and Trichur respectively and were not available for comment.

Political leaders express grief

NEW DELHI, May 21.

In Nagpur, the senior Congress leader and former Union minister, Mr P. Narasimha Rao, was moved when told of the murder of Mr Rajiv Gandhi.

"It is unbelievable and very shocking. This is a big crisis before the nation. All of us should meet it very courageously," he said.

The politburo of the CPM has condemned the 'dastardly assassination' and said it was the handiwork of the enemies of the nation who were interested in destabilising the country.

It appealed to all patriotic forces to remain united. The politburo also conveyed its condolences to Mrs Sonia Gandhi , her daughter and son.

The senior Congress leader and former Union minister Mr Vasant Sathe, expressed shock over the assassination.

"It is a most shocking thing to happen, especially in this difficult time. It is a tremendous loss to democracy," he said.

Mr Sathe also hoped that the people would keep calm and rise to the occasion and maintain the unity and integrity of the country. "This is another martyrdom for the cause of India. This loss can never be made up," Mr Sathe said.

The Maharashtra chief minister, Mr Sharad Pawar, tonight described Mr Gandhi's assassination as "shocking beyond words," PTI reports from Pune.

The killing of Mr Gandhi had inflicted a cruel blow to India and its new generation, Mr Pawar told PTI.

Mr Pawar added the killing demonstrated the level of violence that had engulfed the country.

The Janata Dal spokesman, Mr S. Jaipal Reddy, condemned the "dastardly assassination" and termed it a "great blow to Indian democratic polity".

"Indian politics without Rajiv Gandhi is infinitely poorer," he said.

Mr Reddy said it was a tragedy beyond description. "Both words and ideas fail us in giving expression to our shock and sorrow," he said and added that this was an occasion when "all Indians should act with unity of purpose."

The deputy prime minister, Mr Devi Lal, who arrived in Ahmedabad this evening, said that the dastardly act must have been committed by a "misguided" person.

"We have lost Mr Gandhi at a time when the country most needed his services, Mr Lal said.

The Gujarat chief minister, Mr Chimanbhai Patel, who was campaigning in the Patan constituency, rushed back to Gandhinagar. He said that the crime was committed by Mr Gandhi's political opponents.

The DMK president and former Tamil Nadu chief minister, Mr M. Karunanidhi, expressed shock.

In a condolence message here, Mr Karunanidhi said no one could bear to see such a tragic end to Mr Gandhi who had carved out a niche for himself in Indian politics.

"On behalf of my party, I convey my deep condolences to the Congress movement and also to Mr Gandhi's family members" Mr Karunanidhi said.

Reacting to the killing in New Delhi, the Telugu Desam leader, Mr P. Upendra, expressed shock.

Condemning the "dastardly act", Mr Upendra said the nation had lost a "great leader."

In Thiruvananthapuram, the Kerala chief minister, Mr E. K. Nayanar, tonight expressed deep sorrow over Mr Gandhi's death.

Mr Nayanar, on hearing of Mr Gandhi's death, described it as 'most unfortunate'.

In a condolence message, he asked the people to remain calm and restrained.

The state government has declared a public holiday tomorrow.

The Maharashtra urban development minister, Mr Sushil Kumar Shinde, described the assassination of Mr Gandhi as the assassination of democracy.

In Calcutta, the president of the West Bengal Pradesh Congress Committee and former Punjab governor, Mr Siddhartha Sankar Ray, described the killing as "disastrous" and said that it was the lowest point in Indian history.

Reacting to the killing Mr Ray said that the enemies of the country had

(Continued on Page 15)

Narasimha Rao slated to lead

The Times of India News Service

NEW DELHI, May 21: Mr P.V. Narasimha Rao, who was counted by Mr Rajiv Gandhi as a dependable counsel, has been slated to lead the Congress party.

The Congress, at present, has very little choice, but to elect Mr Rao. After the election is over, the Congress may exercise its option to choose an appropriate leader to rescue the nation from the worst crisis it has faced since Independence.

Mr Gandhi's brave campaigning to restore the political process in this country may not be lost. For, his assassination might give the people, who were enthusiastically, if not ecstatically, responding to his campaign, the right determination to help mobilise nationalist forces to preserve the integrity of the nation. At this moment of despair, this could be an appropriate tribute to the memory of a young man who braved the most serious challenges and paid the ultimate price with his life.

From IA pilot to Prime Minister

NEW DELHI, May 21.

MR Rajiv Gandhi, who took over as prime minister of India in 1984 at the age of 40, was one of the youngest elected heads of government, reports PTI & UNI.

He became the country's seventh prime minister hours after the assassination of Mrs Indira Gandhi by her bodyguards on October 31 that year.

A former pilot in Indian Airlines, Mr Rajiv Gandhi, 47, was a late and reluctant political entrant. He was forced to join politics by his mother the then prime minister, after the death of her younger son and political heir, Mr Sanjay Gandhi, in an air crash in June, 1980.

This led to Mr Rajiv Gandhi's electoral battle in Amethi in a bye-election held in 1981 and his subsequent appointment as AICC general secretary.

The sympathy wave generated for the Congress after Mrs Gandhi's assassination helped the Congress to a thumping victory bagging 415 of the 452 seats in eighth Lok Sabha in the December '84 elections under Mr Gandhi's stewardship.

During his tenure, he signed the historic Punjab and Assam accords in 1985, the Indo-Sri Lanka peace accord in 1987 and sent an emergency task to the Maldives in 1988.

He also formalised bilateral trade treaties with Pakistan and China and thawed the ice in Sino-Indian relations with his Beijing visit in 1988.

Back home, Mr Gandhi introduced the Jawahar Razgar Yojna and Panchayati Raj Institution Bill for the upliftment of the poor in 1989.

He, however, lost power in 1989 elections fighting a united opposition led by the National Front, which projected the Bofors and other corruption related charges as a major campaign plank against Mr Gandhi.

Mr Rajiv Gandhi was born on August 20, 1944, in Bombay in the midst of World War II, the Indian freedom movement and the Quit India movement.

His grandfather, Jawaharlal Nehru, who was in jail at that time, described him as the 400 millionth and first Indian.

He spent his early childhood under the care of a Danish governess named Anna Ornsholt.

Rajiv was shy, well-behaved and courteous. He spoke little and in a low voice, but was considered by his

(Continued on Page 15)

Shock and disbelief at news in city

By A Staff Reporter

BOMBAY, May 21.

"MY God it's so horrifying. What is it going to do to the country," said a shocked Mr Murli Deora reacting to the news of Mr Rajiv Gandhi's assassination.

"I appeal to the people to maintain peace," he said." Only last week he was pushing away the police security cordon at the airport and now this has happened", he added.

Mr Deora while condemning the death of Mr Gandhi appealed to the Congress workers not to resort to violence and maintain peace in the city. He asked party candidates to suspend the election campaign for a day and pay homage to Mr Gandhi. There would be a prayer meeting at the BRCC headquarters tomorrow afternoon.

The BRCC is planning a Bombay bandh tomorrow and asked its party workers to observe it peacefully, according to BRCC sources.

Ms Chandan Patel, Feroze Gandhi's niece, was stunned and she only managed to say," I am in no position to talk". She got the news from this paper and did not believe it initially.

Ms Aloo Chibber, a former MLC and family friend of the Gandhis, broke into tears and was too shocked to say anything. With most ministers and candidates out campaigning, many did not know of the news and Mr B.A. Desai got to know after his son rushed to the meeting he was addressing. It was turned into a condolence meeting and a resolution was adopted expressing shock and condemning the assassination.

Mr Desai hoped the Congress would survive this dastardly act.

Mr Prem Kumar Sharma, the BJP-Sena candidate from South Bombay, said it was unfortunate for the country and it was a great loss to the Congress.

Mr Sudhir Joshi, the Shiv Sena leader, said it was a sad event and it should not have happened in Indian politics. "Mr Gandhi's death is a great loss to the nation", he added.

Mr Ram Naik, said it was shocking news, an assault on democracy. "This dastardly act should be condemned and citizens should maintain peace at any cost," he said.

Mr Madhu Mehta of the Hindustani Andolan, said "The Gods have been unkind to this country. This was the worst calamity that could have happened and our hearts go to Mrs Sonia Gandhi and her family," he said.

Meanwhile, the director general of police, Mr Vasant Saraf, said a meeting of top police officials had been called and a general alert had been sounded in the state. Additional police force had been deployed in the sensitive areas, he added.

Mr Madhav Gadkari, former editor of *Loksatta*, said it was a disaster and it was terrible that such a method should be used to express opposition to an individual's ideology.

Reactions continued to trickle in from politicians and the common person, many of whom kept telephoning the newspaper offices for comfirmation of the news.

Mrs Mrinal Gore, the state Janata Dal president, said the party strongly condemned the dastardly killing of Mr Gandhi. It is a matter of grave concern for the future of Indian democracy that there is a growing tendency to resort to violence instead of exchanging ideas as a means of political opposition," she said.

The Maharashtra governor, Mr C. Subramaniam, said, "This is a great national tragedy that in the land of Mahatma Gandhi political violence should overtake us. In the tragic death of Mr Gandhi India has lost a great national leader at a critical time. It is most unfortunate that when we are going through the democratic process, violence on a large scale should have erupted which is a negation of democracy."

Heinous crime, says RV

NEW DELHI, May 21 (PTI): The President, Mr R. Venkataraman, today condemned as a barbaric act the "heinous" assassination of the former Prime Minister, Mr Rajiv Gandhi, and said words cannot adequately express his grief.

Expressing his deep anguish at the death of Mr Gandhi, Mr Venkataraman said in a condolence message that a brave and a dedicated son of India has been felled by an act of a coward.

"This savage act should lead us all to resolve to fight the cult of violence in our public life," he said.

Mr Venkataraman appealed for maintaining utmost calm and to use the moment of grief to pray for peace in our motherland.

Rajendra Kumar Dhawan to the assassination, but pointed to an even larger conspiracy involving Pakistan.

Mrs. Gandhi herself had expressed fears that a Pakistan supplied with U.S. arms was a constant threat, and so Rajiv's first act as prime minister was to contact Pakistan's president Mohammed Zia ul-Haq, to calm relations between the two countries. Zia declared national mourning in Pakistan and announced a forthcoming diplomatic visit to New Delhi.

Faced with violence both within his country and close to it, Rajiv Gandhi entered a troubled world that was neither of his making nor to his taste, and many wondered if he was up to the task.

BORN IN 1944, a graduate of the Doon School in New Delhi and a student of mechanical engineering at Trinity College in Cambridge, he had never really aspired to anything more than his much-loved work as a commercial airline pilot.

He attempted to put his contemporary notions to work in India, modernizing the government, introducing Western innovations, pushing it, as he said, "toward the 21st century." His nickname became "computerji." And in this he succeeded, to a certain extent.

But terrible, violent events in India and a growing threat from Pakistan occupied most of his attention, and, although he dealt with each competently, he did it without engendering the fierce loyalty his mother seemed to draw from the country's populace. The events piled upon each other relentlessly.

Barely three months after he took office, the Union Carbide disaster occurred at Bhopal. In 1988, 1,567 Sikhs were killed in terrorist incidents in the Punjab. In 1989, the ethnic violence shifted when over 1,000 died in Hindu-Muslim riots in Bhagalpur, Bihar.

Meanwhile, Sonia, Rajiv's wife, constantly worried over her husband's safety. It was she who had cradled Indira Gandhi's head in her lap after that assassination, and she was haunted by the probability that it would all happen again.

But, with little distinction, Rajiv made it through to the end of his mother's term of office. Violent clashes continued to occur with Sikh separatists in Punjab, Kashmiri separatists in the predominantly Muslim state of Jammu and Kashmir, fundamentalist Hindus backed by the right-wing Bharatiya Janata party throughout all of India, and Tamil refugees from neighboring Sri Lanka who were blamed for election violence throughout the country.

One of the more marked failures of Rajiv's tenure in office, in fact, was the handling of the civil war in Sri Lanka. Although he and his mother had supported Sri Lankan separatists, in 1987 Rajiv Gandhi reversed this policy, made peace with Sri Lanka, and sent 50,000 Indian troops into this offshore country to help put down the Tamil rebellion. It was a quagmire, and troops remained there while Rajiv Gandhi lost the 1989 election to Vishwanath Prataz Singh.

SONIA breathed a sigh of relief, but it was shortlived. Rajiv had had a taste of power, and the vision of the Nehru dynasty must have figured in his decision to make a comeback in the elections of 1991. The country seemed to be rudderless. At least he could give it more leadership than it had.

In late October of 1990, the government of V. P. Singh had dispatched troops to a disputed Muslim mosque in Ayodhya. Hindu militants wanted to raze it and erect a temple, and the government protected it against attack. V. P. Singh staked his career on a secular India, but he failed to receive a vote of confidence in Parliament, and so resigned on March 7, 1991. Chandra Shekhar was appointed caretaker prime minister, and new elections were scheduled.

And Rajiv Gandhi roamed the country, campaigning for a return to office. V. K. Singh expressed an interest in returning to power, but Rajiv's most serious competitor was Lal Kishan Advani, of the Janata party.

The first round of balloting in May was marked by a wave of killings and vote rigging. The atmosphere was dangerous, but Rajiv Gandhi lightened his security forces. It was the presence of them, plus his bullet-proof vest, that had allowed V. K. Singh, his victorious opponent in 1989, to charge him with being out of touch with the people, retreating behind a phalanx of security guards.

In an effort to counteract this, then, Rajiv Gandhi entered the southern province of Tamil Nadu on the Sri Lanka border during the last week in May with hardly any security guards. It was a safe part of the country, he felt, one in which the Congress party was popular.

ON THE night of May 21, he entered the rural temple town of Sriperumbudur, 26 miles southwest of Madras. Ten thousand late-night revelers greeted him enthusiastically as he stepped from his limousine and made his way toward a temporary speakers' platform, bracketed by VIP and press enclosures.

The crowd closed around him; he stationed himself on a red carpet, and a queue of well-wishers pushed toward him.

Among them was a woman who appeared to be Tamil. She was about 35 years old, wore glasses and an odd sort of red wig. She handed Rajiv a garland, then bowed low, in a reverential, almost servile pose.

Underneath her clothing was a back brace containing three to five sticks of cyclotrimethylene-trinitramine—a plastic explosive which is usually used for demolition work. The explosive was surrounded by steel pellets, and at her waist, in front, was a detonation switch, which she now pressed.

She exploded. Her head was lobbed into the press compound. The blast split her back asunder and hit Rajiv full force, blowing away his face, ripping his torso apart.

In a 10-foot radius 17 other people were killed, and scores lay wounded and bleeding. It was the sort of suicide bombing that was closely associated with the Tamil Tigers, the most dedicated Sri Lankan separatists of all, who had been aided in their formation by Indira Gandhi and who felt most betrayed by her son's turnabout.

What Sonia Gandhi had most dreaded had come true. She flew, with her 19-year-old daughter Priyanka to Madras on an Indian air force plane to claim what was left of Rajiv's body. That night, Congress appointed her their candidate for Prime Minister, to replace her slain husband. The next day, she refused to accept the appointment. It was the last honor on earth she had wanted for her husband or herself.

And that night, India again erupted in violence, a situation that would continue and escalate to this day. A coalition government was formed with P. V. Narashimo Rao as India's ninth prime minister.

The hunt for the Tamil conspirators in the assassination plot would climax in late July, when Sri Lankan Tamil Sivarasan and six confederates, after a gunfight in which five policemen were killed, committed suicide in a house in Bangalore surrounded by government forces. In all, 22 Tamil militants would commit suicide during the police roundup. And the violence would continue, in all parts of India.

RAJIV GANDHI'S body had been consumed in a funeral pyre in the same revered location occupied by his mother and brother. It would be the end of the Nehru dynasty in an India that resembled a maelstrom of discontent and strife. At the funeral, Natwar Singh, a former deputy in Rajiv Gandhi's cabinet asked, "What has this country of Buddha and Mahatma Gandhi come to? We were an example to the world. Now we are a warning."

Bibliography

Jean-Paul Marat

Belloc, Hilaire: *The French Revolution,* London: Oxford University Press, 1911.
Bernier, Olivier: *Words of Fire, Deeds of Blood*, Boston: Little, Brown & Co., 1989.
Carlyle, Thomas: *The French Revolution*, New York: Random House (The Modern Library), 1934.
Donovan, Robert J.: *The Assassins*, New York: Harper & Brothers, 1952.
Ford, Franklin L.: *Political Murder: From Tyrannicide to Terrorism*, Cambridge, Mass. : Harvard University Press, 1985.
Gottschalk, Louis R.: *Jean-Paul Marat: A Study in Radicalism*, Chicago: University of Chicago Press, 1967.
Hibbert, Christopher: *The Days of the French Revolution*, New York: William Morrow & Co., 1980.
Kirkham, James F., et al.: *Assassination and Political Violence*, New York: Praeger Publishers, 1970.
Weiss, Peter: *The Persecution and Assassination of Jean-Paul Marat As Performed by the Inmates of the Asylum of Charenton Under the Direction of The Marquis de Sade*, New York: Atheneum, 1965.

Abraham Lincoln

Bishop, Jim: *The Day Lincoln Was Shot*, New York: Harper and Brothers, 1955.
Donovan, Robert J.: *The Assassins*, New York: Harper & Brothers, 1952.
Ford, Franklin L.: *Political Murder: From Tyrannicide to Terrorism*, Cambridge, Mass. : Harvard University Press, 1985.
Kingston, Jeremy and David Lambert: *Catastrophe and Crisis*, New York: Facts on File, 1977.
Kirkham, James F., et al.: *Assassination and Political Violence*, New York: Praeger Publishers, 1970.

James A. Garfield

Donovan, Robert J.: *The Assassins*, New York: Harper & Brothers, 1952.
Ford, Franklin L.: *Political Murder: From Tyrannicide to Terrorism*, Cambridge, Mass.: Harvard University Press, 1985.
Kirkham, James F., et al.: *Assassination and Political Violence*, New York: Praeger Publishers, 1970.

William McKinley

Donovan, Robert J.: *The Assassins*, New York: Harper & Brothers, 1952.
Ford, Franklin L.: *Political Murder: From Tyrannicide to Terrorism*, Cambridge, Mass.: Harvard University Press, 1985.
Kirkham, James F., et al.: *Assassination and Political Violence*, New York: Praeger Publishers, 1970.

Archduke Franz Ferdinand

Donovan, Robert J.: *The Assassins*, New York: Harper & Brothers, 1952.
Ford, Franklin L.: *Political Murder: From Tyrannicide to Terrorism*, Cambridge, Mass.: Harvard University Press, 1985.
Kingston, Jeremy and David Lambert: *Catastrophe and Crisis*, New York: Facts on File, 1977.
Kirkham, James F., et al.: *Assassination and Political Violence*, New York: Praeger Publishers, 1970.

Grigorii Rasputin

DeJonge, Alex: *The Life and Times of Grigorii Rasputin*, New York: Coward, McCann and Geoghegan, 1982.
Donovan, Robert J.: *The Assassins*, New York: Harper & Brothers, 1952.
Ford, Franklin L.: *Political Murder: From Tyrannicide to Terrorism*, Cambridge, Mass.: Harvard University Press, 1985.
Kirkham, James F., et al.: *Assassination and Political Violence*, New York: Praeger Publishers, 1970.

Csar Nicholas II

Crankshaw, Edward: *The Shadow of the Winter Palace*, New York: The Viking Press, 1976.
Donovan, Robert J.: *The Assassins*, New York: Harper & Brothers, 1952.
Ford, Franklin L.: *Political Murder: From Tyrannicide to Terrorism*, Cambridge, Mass.: Harvard University Press, 1985.
Kirkham, James F., et al.: *Assassination and Political Violence*, New York: Praeger Publishers, 1970.
Massie, Robert K.: *Nicholas and Alexandra*, New York: Atheneum, 1967.
Moorehead, Alan: *The Russian Revolution*, New York: Harper & Brothers, 1958.

Pancho Villa

Donovan, Robert J.: *The Assassins*, New York: Harper & Brothers, 1952.
Ford, Franklin L.: *Political Murder: From Tyrannicide to Terrorism*, Cambridge, Mass.: Harvard University Press, 1985.
Guzman, Martin Luis: *The Eagle and the Serpent (Pancho Villa)*, Garden City, N.Y.: Dolphin Books, 1965.
Kirkham, James F., et al.: *Assassination and Political Violence*, New York: Praeger Publishers, 1970.

Huey Long

Donovan, Robert J.: *The Assassins*, New York: Harper & Brothers, 1952.
Ford, Franklin L.: *Political Murder: From Tyrannicide to Terrorism*, Cambridge, Mass.: Harvard University Press, 1985.
Hair, William Ivy: *The Kingfish and His Realm: The Life and Times of Huey P. Long,* Baton Rouge, La.: Louisiana State University Books, 1991.
Kirkham, James F., et al.: *Assassination and Political Violence*, New York: Praeger Publishers, 1970.
Zinman, David: *The Day Huey Long Was Shot,* New York: Obolensky, 1963.

Leon Trotsky

Donovan, Robert J.: *The Assassins*, New York: Harper & Brothers, 1952.
Ford, Franklin L.: *Political Murder: From Tyrannicide to Terrorism*, Cambridge, Mass.: Harvard University Press, 1985.
Kirkham, James F., et al.: *Assassination and Political Violence*, New York: Praeger Publishers, 1970.
Payne, Robert: *The Life and Death of Lenin*, New York: Simon and Schuster, 1964.

Mohandas Gandhi

Donovan, Robert J.: *The Assassins*, New York: Harper & Brothers, 1952.
Ford, Franklin L.: *Political Murder: From Tyrannicide to Terrorism*, Cambridge, Mass.: Harvard University Press, 1985.
Kirkham, James F., et al.: *Assassination and Political Violence*, New York: Praeger Publishers, 1970.
Payne, Robert: *The Life and Death of Mahatma Gandhi,* London: The Bodley Head, 1969.

Anastasio Somoza

Cox, Jack: *Nicaragua Betrayed*, Boston: Western Islands, 1980.
Ford, Franklin L.: *Political Murder: From Tyrannicide to Terrorism*, Cambridge, Mass.: Harvard University Press, 1985
Kinser, Stephen, *Blood of Brothers: Life and War in Nicaragua*, New York: G.P. Putnam's Sons, 1991.
Kirkham, James F., et al.: *Assassination and Political Violence*, New York: Praeger Publishers, 1970.
Pastor, Robert A.: *Condemned to Repetition: The United States and Nicaragua*, Princeton, N. J.: Princeton University Press, 1987.

John F. Kennedy

Belin, David W.: *Final Disclosure: The Full Truth About the Assassination of President Kennedy,* New York: Scribner, 1988.

Buchanan, Thomas G.: *Who Killed Kennedy?* New York: Putnam, 1964.

Ford, Franklin L.: *Political Murder: From Tyrannicide to Terrorism*, Cambridge, Mass.: Harvard University Press, 1985.

Kingston, Jeremy and David Lambert: *Catastrophe and Crisis*, New York: Facts on File, 1977.

Lasky, Victor: *JFK: The Man & The Myth,* New York: MacMillan, 1963.

Manchester, William: *The Death of a President,* New York: Random House, 1967.

Scheir, David E.: *Contract on America: The Mafia Murder of President John F. Kennedy,* New York: Shapolsky Publishers, 1988.

Scott, Peter Dole, Paul L. Hoxh, Russell Stetler (eds.) *The Assassinations: Dallas and Beyond,* New York: Vintage Books, 1976.

Vankin, Jonathan: *Conspiracies, Cover-Ups and Crimes: From JFK to the CIA Terrorist Connection,* New York: Paragon House, 1992

Wilson, Colin and Donald Seaman: *The Encyclopedia of Modern Murder 1962-1982,*New York: G. P. Putnam, 1985.

Malcolm X

Cone, James H.: *Martin & Malcolm & America: A Dream or a Nightmare,* Maryknoll, N.Y.: Orbis Books, 1991.

Evanzz, Karl: *The Judas Factor: The Plot to Kill Malcolm X,* New York: Thunder's Mouth Press, 1992.

Ford, Franklin L.: *Political Murder: From Tyrannicide to Terrorism*, Cambridge, Mass.: Harvard University Press, 1985.

Friedly, Michael: *Malcolm X: The Assassination,* New York: Carroll & Graf/R. Gallen, 1992.

Malcolm X (with Alex Haley): *The Autobiography of Malcolm X,* New York: Ballantine Books, 1973.

Perry, Bruce: *Malcolm: The Life of a Man Who Changed Black America,* New York: Station Hill Press, 1990.

Wilson, Colin and Donald Seaman: *The Encyclopedia of Modern Murder 1962-1982,* New York: G. P. Putnam, 1985.

Martin Luther King

Cone, James H.: *Martin & Malcolm & America: A Dream or a Nightmare,* Maryknoll, N.Y.: Orbis Books, 1991.

Ford, Franklin L.: *Political Murder: From Tyrannicide to Terrorism*, Cambridge, Mass.: Harvard University Press, 1985

Lane, Mark: *Code Name "Zorro": The Murder of Martin Luther King Jr.,* Englewood Cliffs, N.J.: Prentice-Hall, 1977.

Scott, Peter Dole, Paul L. Hoxh, Russell Stetler (eds.) *The Assassinations: Dallas and Beyond,* New York: Vintage Books, 1976.

Wilson, Colin and Donald Seaman: *The Encyclopedia of Modern Murder 1962-1982,* New York: G. P. Putnam, 1985.

Robert J. Kennedy

Ford, Franklin L.: *Political Murder: From Tyrannicide to Terrorism*, Cambridge, Mass.: Harvard University Press, 1985.

Kaiser, Robert B.: *R.F.K. Must Die!,* New York: Dutton, 1970.

Scott, Peter Dole, Paul L. Hoxh, Russell Stetler (eds.) *The Assassinations: Dallas and Beyond,* New York: Vintage Books, 1976.

Wilson, Colin and Donald Seaman: *The Encyclopedia of Modern Murder 1962-1982,* New York: G. P. Putnam, 1985.

Lord Louis Mountbatten

Ford, Franklin L.: *Political Murder: From Tyrannicide to Terrorism*, Cambridge, Mass.: Harvard University Press, 1985.
Hough, Richard: *Mountbatten*, New York: Random House, 1981.
Wilson, Colin and Donald Seaman: *The Encyclopedia of Modern Murder 1962-1982,* New York: G. P. Putnam, 1985.

Anwar al-Sadat

Ford, Franklin L.: *Political Murder: From Tyrannicide to Terrorism*, Cambridge, Mass.: Harvard University Press, 1985.
Haykal, Muhammad Hasanayn: *Autumn of Fury: The Assassination Of Sadat,* New York: Random House, 1983
Wilson, Colin and Donald Seaman: *The Encyclopedia of Modern Murder 1962-1982,* New York: G. P. Putnam, 1985.

Benigno Aquino

Chua-Eoan, Howard: *Aquino*, New York: Chelsea House, 1988.
Ford, Franklin L.: *Political Murder: From Tyrannicide to Terrorism*, Cambridge, Mass.: Harvard University Press, 1985.

Indira and Rajiv Gandhi

Ali, Tariq: *An Indian Dynasty: The Story of the Nehru-Gandhi Families,* New York: G.P. Putnam,1985.
Ford, Franklin L.: *Political Murder: From Tyrannicide to Terrorism*, Cambridge, Mass.: Harvard University Press, 1985.
Gupte, Pranay: *Vengeance: India After the Assassination of Indira Gandhi,* New York: W. W. Norton, 1985.

Picture Credits

Key: **AP** Associated Press, London, UK, **BA** Bettmann Archive, New York, USA, **C** Colorific!, London, UK, **CP** Camera Press, London, UK, **DKC** David King Collection, London, UK, **FSP** Frank Spooner Pictures, London, UK, **HDC** Hulton Deutsch Collection, London, UK, **JFHNS** John Frost Historical Newspaper Service, Hertfordshire, UK, **M** Magnum Photos Limited, London, UK, **MEPL** Mary Evans Picture Library, London, UK, **PF** Popperfoto, Northampton, UK, **PNHP** Peter Newark's Historical Pictures, Bath, UK, **PNWA** Peter Newark's Western Americana, Bath, UK, **RF** Rex Features, London, UK, **TPS** Topham Picture Source, Kent, UK.

Page	Credit
8	BA
9	PF
11	MEPL
13	MEPL
14	PNHP
15	HDC
17	JFHNS
18	HDC
20	BA
21	PF
22	JFHNS
25	PNHP
26	HDC
28	BA
29	MEPL
31	JFHNS
32	HDC
34	MEPL
35	MEPL
37	JFHNS
38	HDC
40	PNHP
41	PF
43	HDC
44	HDC
46	CP
47	MEPL
49	JFHNS
50	HDC
52	HDC
54	BA
55	PF
57	HDC
58	PNWA
60	PNHP
61	HDC
63	JFHNS
64	BA
66	DKC
67	HDC
69	DKC
70	HDC
72	TPS
73	CP
74	British Library
76	M/Henri Cartier-Bresson
78	AP
79	HDC
80	JFHNS
83	PF
84	C
85	CP/F Bacharach
86	JFHNS
88	AP
90	HDC
92	BA
93	BA
95	JFHNS
98	BA
99	HDC
100	JFHNS
103	BA
104	BA
106	PF
107	CP
109	JFHNS
112	HDC
113	FSP
115	JFHNS
116	HDC
118	FSP
119	CP
120	JFHNS
123	RF
124	C
126	AP
127	TPS
129	JFHNS
132	PF
133	CP
134	JFHNS
137	JFHNS